EVIL in our Midst

a chilling glimpse of our most feared and frightening demons

DAVID E. JONES

SQUAREONE
PUBLISHERS

Cover Designer: Phaedra Mastrocola
In-House Editor: Carola Roseby
Typesetter: Gary A. Rosenberg

Square One Publishers
16 First Street
Garden City Park, New York 11040
www.squareonepublishers.com

Library of Congress Cataloging-in-Publication Data

Jones, David E., 1942–
    Evil in our midst : a chilling glimpse of our most feared and
frightening demons / David E. Jones.
        p. cm.
Includes bibliographical references and index.
    ISBN 0-7570-0009-6 (pbk.)
    1. Demonology. I. Title.
    BF1548 .J66 2002
    133.4'2'09—dc21

BF
1548
.J66
2002

2001005145

Printed in the United States of America

10 9 8 7 6 5 4 3 2 1

Contents

2. Demons of South America

6. Demons of the Pacific

For Nathan and Ian

Acknowledgments

I would like to thank Rudy Shur of Square One Publishers for trusting me with this project; and my wife, Jane M. Jones, for energy, support, and guidance. The final responsibility for this book is, of course, mine.

Pronunciation of Demon Names

Adro (ahd•roh)

Bolrizohol (boh•ree•zoh•hol)

Budu (boo•dew)

Chochoi (choh•choh•ee)

Ga-git (gah-get)

Genie (jee•nee)

Ghede (ged)

Hekura (hey•kuh•rah)

Huli Jing (hoo•lee ching)

Ialus (ee•ah•lus)

Kalengu (kah•ling•oo)

Kalona (kah•low•nah)

Karaisaba (ker•eye•sah•bah)

Kenaimas (ken•eye•mahs)

Kharisiri (kah•reh•see•ree)

Kikituk (kee•kee•tuck)

Kopuwai (koh•poo•wah•ee)

Kupe-dyeb (koo•pay-deb)

Kwifi Oto (kwif•ee oo•toh)

La Diablesse (lah dee•ahb•less)

La Llorona (lah yah•rown•ah)

La Malogra
(lah mahl•oh•grah)

Ligahoo (lee•gah•hoo)

Maereboe (mah•air•reh•bow)

Mai Tso (might so)

Mama Dlo (mah•mah dlow)

Mulukwausi
(moo•loo•kwah•oo•see)

Nia'gwai'he'gowa
(nai•gwah•hee•go•wah)

Nokondisi (noh•kon•dee•see)

Oni (oh•nee)

Oyasi (oo•yah•see)

Patupaiarehe
(pah•too•pah•ee•ah•reh•heh)

Pisatji (pee•saht•jee)

Rai Na'in (rye nah•een)

Rawa Tukump
(rh•wah too•kump)

Ruruhi-kerepo
(roo•roo•hee-keh•reh•poh)

Soucouyant (soo•koo•yant)

Tamboree (tahm•boor•ee)

Tavogivogi
   (tah•voh•gee•voo•gee)

Tege (teh•geh)

Tsi Sgili (see skil•ee)

Unkcegila (unk•she•gee•lah)

Wamu (wah•moo)

Wi-lu-gho-yuk
   (wee-loo-go-yuk)

Win (ween)

Windigo (win•dee•go)

Winti (win•tee)

Yacuruna (yah•ka•roo•nah)

Yamo (yah•moh)

Evil in
Our Midst

Introduction

R ecently, while waiting at the airport for a flight to California where I was scheduled to speak at an anthropology symposium, I came across the article "If You Liked the Movie . . ." by David Van Biema in *Time* magazine. Undoubtedly inspired by the re-release of the 1973 classic movie *The Exorcist*, the topic of the article was exorcism—an ancient religious practice of expelling evil spirits from a human host, which, not all that surprisingly, is still regularly performed today. In his article, Van Biema notes that in the early 1990s, New York's Cardinal John O'Conner appointed four exorcists to the archdiocese. Each year, this group of "demon fighters" investigates an average of 350 cases of possession and performs ten to fifteen exorcisms. Is this proof that demons are alive and well in the third millennium, some of them even walking the streets of New York City? As recently as 1999, the Vatican reviewed the Catholic Rite of Exorcism and made some modifications, one of which eliminated the physical description of Satan. This was an apt decision, since, as you will read, evil shrouds itself in many disguises—not just in the form of a horned, red-skinned monster with cloven hooves and pointed tail, wielding a pitchfork.

In many cultures, people know and vividly experience demons—collective images of ultimate evil. They know how evil incarnate looks and exactly what to expect from an encounter with one of these demons. Their most terrifying imaginings have been named and endowed with predictable, though horrifying, characteristics. These people often live in fear, expecting the worst on a moonlit night or a cold, rainy afternoon. . . .

What is the most terrifying being you can imagine? Perhaps you'll come across it in the pages to follow. But make no mistake. This is not a book of fairy tales. Nor is this book about bogeymen—the imaginary creatures that have terrorized children throughout the ages. This book explores the evil in our midst as it can be found in a myriad of cultures—past and present. The accounts you'll find here present images of ultimate evil that are often very real to the adults and elders of a particular society.

Demons seem to evolve along with the communities in which they are found and rarely cross cultural boundaries. A poor, white Alabama farmer would probably never encounter Ghede of Haiti while plowing his field, nor would a Mongol sheepherder be tempted by the powers of Nia' gwai'he'gowa—the Bear Monster of the Seneca. Demons seem to fit the perceived realities of those who nurture them, and they shift as external forces change the social reality in which they exist.

When considering that demons are found in every culture and in every age, many interesting questions arise: Why do people create these monsters, breathe perpetual life into them, and transmit them to the next generation? Why do people seem to need the threat of demons in their lives? Why don't demons go out of style? Perhaps after you've read the series of vignettes in this book, along with the related cultural background, you can draw your own conclusions, or maybe you already have some of your own ideas. As you read, consider these possibilities: demons are triumphs of the religious imagination; demons are reflections of the nature of mental illness in a particular society; demons represent the collected spiritual insight into the negative traits and tendencies that lead to social or psychological chaos; demons are a rationale for deviant or criminal behavior; demons are a reflection of some alternate reality; or demons are totally, indisputably real and are waiting just around the corner for their next victim. . . .

You'll notice that this book does not focus on the demonic beliefs among adherents of Judaism, Christianity, or Islam, since such lore is rampant in Western books, television, and movies. Rather, described in these pages are the more esoteric religious ideas of subarctic Inuits, Melanesians, tribes of the Amazonian Rainforest, and more. Each vignette details the usually gruesome, unfortunate outcome of an encounter with a particular demon. Informational background follows each story to give you some knowledge of the culture that, in many cases, perpetuates the belief in its demons. What you are about to read is neither ancient mythology nor mere folklore. It is a portal into the contemporary reality of living in a world of demons.

1. Demons of North America

Kalona

FROM THE CHEROKEE OF NORTH CAROLINA, TENNESSEE, & OKLAHOMA

"**P**lease don't leave me alone," the elderly Cherokee woman pleaded with her daughter as she and her husband, James, prepared to drive to Maryville for groceries. "I hear them out there," Betty Bright Wing added in a faint, trembling whisper. "They are all around now. . . ." She grabbed her daughter's shirtsleeve. "If you leave, they will come for me."

Mimi tried to be patient with the old woman, but her patience was wearing thin. Her mother had been going on for hours trying to convince her that something terrible was going to happen. She made little sense, and Mimi worried that her mother's mind was going. "Now, Mama, take one of your pills and get some rest. You know that doctor said you got the blood pressure. Calm down."

"No! Can't you hear them?" Betty cried. She quieted for a moment to listen, and then added with even more desperation, "Why are you leaving me? Why won't you believe me?"

Mimi gently pried her mother's hand from her arm. "Mama, we got to go," she said with finality, but then added with a little more compassion, "Do you want me to help you out of your wheelchair into bed before we go?" The old woman turned away from her. "Now, Mama, don't start pouting."

"You just go away and leave if that's what you want, if that's all you think of your mother," Betty said in an old, worn-out voice.

As Mimi and James walked to their pickup truck in the bright afternoon sun, James asked, "What's the old lady talking about?"

"Some old-time nonsense," Mimi answered. "I can't understand some of those old Cherokee words she's using, but it sounds like she's afraid of something she calls a *raven mocker,* or *it sounds like a raven.* I don't know. Something like that."

James thought for a moment. "Well, I have heard some strange birds around the place lately . . . crows maybe, or something that sounds like crows."

Mimi looked at him from the corner of her eye. "Now don't you get started . . ."

James hopped into the truck. "I'm just saying . . ."

"Saying what?" Mimi snapped as she slammed the door.

"Nothing." James said, turning the key in the ignition.

"Hey, Jimmy—" Mimi squeezed his arm. "I'm sorry for snapping. Caring for Mama is getting me down lately. I need a rest."

"Well, she hasn't got much time left," he reminded her.

"I know," Mimi said softly.

Back at the house, Betty listened to the silence surrounding her. With shaking fingers, she turned up her hearing aid. Nothing. Where were the crickets she usually heard chirping outside? And what about the songbirds? Then suddenly, a dry, cackling *Caw! Caw!* emerged from the woods beyond the garden outside the kitchen window. Betty gasped, and her heart thudded heavily.

She wheeled her chair into the bedroom and locked the door. "I got to calm down," she told herself as she maneuvered her chair to the window and looked out.

The scratchy *Caw! Caw!* sounded again, but closer this time. Wings fluttered nearby, and a large black bird crashed against her window. Startled, she pushed her chair back with such force that it tipped her onto the floor. She crawled to her bed but lacked the strength to pull herself up. Throughout the afternoon, she lay helpless, listening to the growing chorus of caws, announcing the gathering of the *Kalona*—the Raven Mockers. The phone in the kitchen rang several times, but Betty knew that she could never reach it to summon help, and she whimpered in frustration.

At a phone booth next to the filling station outside Maryville, Mimi hung up the receiver. "She must be asleep. Maybe she'll stay that way until we get home. That would be the best for her."

James rifled through his billfold. "I just hope getting this damn tire fixed ain't going to be too much."

As evening fell, Betty lay on her bedroom floor, watching the growing swarm of menacing black birds outside her window. She heard a deafening crash against the house, and a window shattered somewhere in the back. The caws were incessant now, and tears of fear swept down Betty's wrinkled cheeks. Then, another loud crash. It sounded like the front door had been battered down. Betty buried her face in her hands and wept, her frail body shaking. Footsteps echoed on the other side of the door, and her heart nearly stopped when a shiny black beak punched a fist-sized hole right through it. Again and again, the Raven Mocker hammered the old woman's door, ripping it to splinters with its murderous beak. Betty peeked through her fingers. A giant birdlike creature filled the doorway, fiery sparkles decorating its obsidian feathers. Its eyes were beads of black onyx. It cocked its head to the side and crossed to her, its talons *tick, tick, ticking* on the hardwood floor.

The Raven Mocker stuck its foot-long beak within inches of Betty's frightened face. Her lips quivered as if to beg for her life, but no words came. The old woman had never experienced such terror. Without her ribs to contain it, her heart surely would have leapt from her breast. With a flick of its head, the Raven Mocker picked her up by her dressing gown and flung her against the bedroom wall. The picture of a small blue bird she'd received for her eightieth birthday crashed to the floor, the glass shattering. Betty landed in a heap of old skin and bones. The Raven Mocker threw her again and again against the walls, but Betty was dead after the second time, nearly every bone in her fragile body broken.

The police report later concluded that a party or parties unknown had broken into the house with a pickax and had beaten Betty Bright Wing to death. Then, they had cut open her chest and removed her heart, lungs, and liver.

No one was ever arrested for Betty's murder. Her funeral drew only a small group of the old-timers, since most of her friends had passed away years before. The service was simple, part Christian and part Cherokee. Nothing was noteworthy except the swarms of large crowlike birds that wheeled high over the cemetery, cawing so loudly that at times it was difficult to hear the minister's prayers.

The word "Cherokee" is actually a corruption of *Tsalagi*—the name given to them by the Choctaw, a Native American group of central and southern Mississippi and southwest Alabama. In early times, the Cherokee referred to themselves as *Ani-Yunwiya*, meaning "the principle people," but they eventually adopted the Choctaw term. Though centered in eastern Tennessee and western North Carolina, the Cherokee are also found in eastern Kentucky and in parts of Alabama, Georgia, and South Carolina. Archaeologists say that they have been in that vicinity for several thousand years. In recent history, large Cherokee groups have occupied parts of eastern

Oklahoma because of their forced removal from their aboriginal homeland to Oklahoma in 1838, the infamous "Trail of Tears."

Traditionally, the Cherokee lived in scattered settlements, as extensive areas of flat land were difficult to find in the Smoky Mountains. Because they relied heavily on farming, the flat garden plot was absolutely essential to their way of life. People living on farms in close proximity formed a sense of community and often were given names indicating some local geographic feature—"People of the Twin Forks," "White Clay People," and so on. A large village might encompass 450 acres and support a population of 350 to 600 people.

The traditional Cherokee way of life persisted until the late 1920s, when a combination of factors—burgeoning population, expanding networks of roads, lack of enough land to support the population—led to an increasingly depressed standard of living. Tourism, particularly after World War II, saved the Cherokee economy. By 1950, over 2 million tourists a year were spending time in and around Cherokee, North Carolina. In 1985, over 9 million people visited the Great Smoky Mountains. The wealth brought by tourism has enabled the Cherokee to develop a variety of organizations, such as the Cherokee Historical Association, which strive to maintain, protect, and promulgate Cherokee culture.

The traditional spiritual beliefs of the Cherokee are complex. They acknowledge a supreme being, as well as various gods, spirits, cultural heroes, witches, shamans, monsters, giants, little people, and abstract spiritual power. The full weight of the complex social nature of Cherokee religion was expressed in a series of seasonal festivals, the most important of which was the Harvest Ceremony held in the fall after the maize had matured. During a four-day period, the Cherokee revitalized themselves, focusing on cleanliness, purification, and group harmony. The sacred fire in the council house was extinguished and re-ignited. Senior women in each house extinguished their hearths and brought fire from the new sacred fire to start new fires in their houses. The Cherokee, through this ritual, acted out a central belief that they were all children of the same God, people of the same fire.

The *Kalona,* or Raven Mockers, have been so named because, though not ravens, they mock the raven, or imitate its call. These creatures are so terrifying that even Cherokee witches fear them and will quickly leave the vicinity when these "birds" come calling. These demons are specters of the undead who must constantly renew their life force by drinking the blood or devouring the entrails of humans. Either male or female, they manifest as withered old people or large, frightening black birds. When they fly at night, they have been known to appear in human form with their arms outstretched like wings, which are outlined with flickering tongues of fire. The Kalona are drawn to those on the verge of death. They enjoy tormenting the dying and are known to toss them around to hasten their demise. When the victim is dead, the Raven Mockers feed.

Tsi Sgili

FROM THE CHEROKEE OF NORTH CAROLINA, TENNESSEE, & OKLAHOMA

Annie Old Man had worked as a maid and nanny for families around Franklin, North Carolina, for most of her life. It was an easy living and a good cover for her true identity: Annie was what the Cherokee of western Carolina called a *Tsi Sgili*—an Owl Witch. The powers of *Ane Li Sqi*, meaning "one who thinks," allow an Owl Witch to focus her psychic energy, at great distances, to kill or maim her victim with her thoughts. But Annie was growing old, and the winter cut more deeply into her bones each year. It was time for her to find a successor.

At the time these thoughts arose, Annie worked for a young white couple who taught at a local community college. Several years earlier, she had accepted the job for the chance to "care" for the couple's infant daughter, Elizabeth. Annie liked little children, both to play with and, occasionally, to eat.

Annie got along well with the family, and as the years passed she developed a deep bond with Elizabeth, or Butter as the child was nicknamed. The little girl followed Annie wherever she went and, to Annie's delight, called her "Grandma." One day, when Butter was three years old, Annie took the little girl on a picnic. She enjoyed watching the child splash in the stream that flowed through the park.

Butter collected rocks of different textures and shapes from the water's edge and brought them to Annie. She gathered wild daisies and presented them as a gift to the old woman. When she came to Annie with a turtle in her hands, Annie accepted the creature and said, "Watch closely, child." The Owl Witch tilted her head back and swallowed the turtle, whole. The young girl clapped her hands in delight and ran back to the stream. This time, she returned with a rock lizard.

"Again, Grandma, do it again," she said, and Annie complied, swallowing the wiggling lizard.

"Me, me," the little girl begged.

Annie spied a stink beetle sticking out from under the little girl's bare toes and snatched it up.

"Here, Butter, eat this," she said as she handed her the beetle. The child mimicked Annie, opening her mouth wide and swallowing the insect. Annie stared at the child and laughed at the wonderful thought of a little white Tsi Sgili. She had never imagined such a thing, but why not? She studied the face of the child who looked up at her so trustingly. "Yes," she thought, "why not?"

First, she had to teach the little girl to kill—and to enjoy it. As Annie had been taught when she was a child, she started small. Cornering a rat in the house one day, Annie called to Butter, "Come quick, my dear." Annie handed her a hammer. "Smash its head in," she said, and Butter obeyed. Annie hugged the child tightly and rewarded her with a plate of oatmeal cookies.

As Butter gobbled the cookies, Annie asked, "Do you like our games, dear?"

"Oh, yes, Grandma. They are more fun than anything," the child replied between bites.

"There is one rule," Annie warned. "You must tell no one, not even your parents, about our games or I will go away and show you no more."

"Please don't go away, Grandma. Please don't," Butter begged, and Annie knew that it would all work out.

When the seasons had come full circle, the little girl had graduated to cats and dogs. Each time Butter killed an animal, Annie rewarded her with one of her favorite treats. Soon, Butter was *asking* to kill something. She loved her "Grandma," and she had been slowly conditioned to enjoy the act. Annie knew that the next step would be major—killing humans. While waiting for an opportunity to teach her how, Annie continued to work with her on killing small creatures and eating lizards, bugs, and decaying carcasses.

Then, the opportunity to teach Butter to kill humans presented itself. Butter had come home from school terribly upset. "That Timmy Johnson said I was stinky. All the kids laughed at me. I hate him."

Annie drew the child to her. "How would you like to take care of Timmy Johnson, dear?"

"I sure would like to smash his head in," the pretty little girl said to Annie.

"I have an even better idea," said Annie. "You say he called you stinky?"

Butter nodded sourly.

"Well, then," said the Owl Witch with a slight smile, "why don't we make him stinky . . . to death."

Butter's eyes widened. She giggled and clapped her hands in delight.

After Butter's parents had gone to bed, Annie woke Butter and led her out back into the woods. Carrying a paper sack of dog feces she'd collected earlier that day, Annie motioned for the little girl to sit with her under an ancient hemlock.

"Take off your pajamas, dear," she instructed and handed Butter the paper bag. "Smear what's inside all over your body."

After years of training, the little girl did not question the request. She had learned that Annie had a reason for everything she asked her to do.

"I will help you this time so you can learn," said Annie. "We will use the power of Ane Li Sqi. Think of Timmy Johnson, dear. As strong as you can, picture that rotten boy in your mind."

Butter squinted and struggled to picture her enemy.

"Good, dear, very good. Now I will join my power with yours."

Suddenly, Butter felt that she was in the same room with Timmy Johnson, who was sleeping soundly in his bed.

"Touch his face quickly," whispered the old woman. "We must not linger."

Butter did as she was told, and Timmy's head was transformed into a pile of dog excrement.

The next day, Timmy Johnson was absent from school. Though the children were not told of his parents' horrible discovery that morning, word spread among the adults of the community that a child-killing monster was on the loose. They could not have known that a Tsi Sgili was in the making.

A few years later, when Butter menstruated for the first time, Annie knew the time was growing near. "There is one more thing that must be done before your powers are complete, but only when the moment is right," she told her.

That moment came a few weeks later when Butter's parents left her completely in Annie's care to attend an academic conference in Washington, D.C.

"My dear, it's time," the Owl Witch said the next morning. "The power we need comes from the mountains, and since the mountains can't come to us, we must go to them."

"But, Grandma, you are so old. Are you sure you can make a trip into the mountains?" Butter asked, worried for her aging teacher.

"At least one more time, my dear. At least one more time."

"Well, we better pack some food, Grandma," the girl said, heading to the cupboards, but her "grandmother" stopped her with, "No, dear. Food will not be necessary."

Moving slowly so that Annie could keep up, the two entered the mountains late in the evening. They carried neither food nor blankets. When Butter asked where they would spend the night, Annie replied, "On the ground."

For the next four days, they ate nothing. While the old woman walked up and down the stream collecting the materials for the last step in the initiation of the Owl Witch, Butter practiced Ane Li Sqi by moving small rocks with the power of her thoughts.

By the evening of the fourth day, both were starving and filthy, but Annie had what she needed—algae scraped from special rocks, phosphorescent wood extracted from a rotting stump, several assorted insects, and three hallucinogenic plants. She mixed them on a flat rock, explaining each step to Butter. Finally, she spat into the mixture and said, "Open your mouth, my dear."

As soon as Butter swallowed the concoction, her body shot into the air in flames. She flashed through the sky like a meteor and came to rest in front of Annie.

"Grandma! I am wonderful!" the girl exclaimed.

"Yes, my child, you are now Tsi Sgili, and soon I can rest."

Annie caressed Butter's filthy hair. With her touch, the pair turned into bats. "Going back will be easier than coming." The two headed for town, comfortable in their animal forms. When they reached home, they discovered that Butter's parents had returned prematurely from the conference. When two large bats flew through the open living room window, Butter's mother screamed, and her father ran to the den for his shotgun.

"Kill him! Kill him now!" ordered Annie.

Butter quickly formed her thoughts and shot a fiery hole into her father's back, killing him instantly. His burning body crashed into the wall, and the curtains went up in flames. Her mother fainted, and Annie leapt on the woman's body and slashed her throat open with ragged fingernails and began to suck the blood that oozed from the wound.

"Me too. Me too," moaned Butter, pushing Annie aside. But the fire spread quickly, driving the pair out the window.

As the bats rose into the sky, Butter asked, "Who were those people, Grandma?"

"Food," replied Annie Old Man. "Nothing but food."

Information about the culture and spiritual beliefs of the Cherokee can be found on page 7 under Kalona. Please refer to that section for some insight into their ways.

The word "Tsi Sgili" is the generic Cherokee term for both witch and owl. According to the Cherokee, witches are considered dead or non-persons. A person of any age or sex can become a witch, usually a person who lives far from society and is considered a malevolent supernatural force beyond social control. Dogs, owls, wolves, and lizards are the favored *familiars*, demonic animal assistants, of the Cherokee witch. Some say that a witch's stomach is filled with lizards that demand human flesh, and if the witch does not provide it, the lizards will devour the witch. Witches violate sacred spaces, and in modern times, they can be found perched on crosses set atop churches. They can soar through the sky, looking like balls of fire, or they can become as small as a fly to enter a building with locked doors and windows. Some use the power of *Ane Li Sqi*, which means "one who thinks," to make their murderous thoughts a reality. They are shape-shifters, ogres, cannibals, and vampires, and accounts of the horrors attributed to them continue today.

Budu

Born in Comanche County, Oklahoma, Tom Ten Killer had traveled far in his life, courtesy of the United States Navy. He had journeyed to distant places, not only geographically, but also in terms of what he wanted to accomplish. The spirit-killing life of American Indian poverty in southwest Oklahoma was not for him. He had learned a trade during his Navy hitch and was eager to return home and open an electronics repair shop. He wanted to be back around his relatives, but with a secure source of money rolling in. The service had accustomed him to eating three times a day.

While in the Navy, he had downplayed his Indian heritage. He neither spoke his native language nor talked of his early years in Oklahoma. Nothing about him reflected American Indian culture. Tom did not want to be reminded of his Comanche identity because he had become ashamed of it. It was the age of space travel, laser beams, and computers. How could he relate to old-timers sitting in a tepee beating on a rawhide drum and singing songs to the eagle?

Tom had been raised by his grandmother, a *shaman*—a traditional doctor of the Comanche—but he had communicated with her little during his service in the Navy. At first, his grandmother was saddened when Tom cut himself off from his roots, but gradually her sadness turned to anger. "He thinks he's too good for us," she would say. "I bet he is ashamed of us, his Comanche people."

Although he was once again living in Comanche County, Tom found no time to cater to his grandmother; he was too busy keeping his floundering repair shop afloat. He was having difficulty obtaining loans from the local banks since Indians were considered poor credit risks by most of the white bankers in southwestern Oklahoma.

When Tom's shop finally failed, he had nowhere to turn but his grandmother. He went to her, hat in hand, and she, a traditional Comanche, could not refuse a call for aid, especially from a kinsman—even a kinsman who had turned his back on her.

But after a week of living with his grandmother, Tom grew restless. The long walks he took during the day did not alleviate his agitation, and he started leaving the house at night as well. One evening, when he picked up his flashlight and announced that he was going for a walk, his grandmother strongly objected. "You don't want to go out there in the dark. Them old peoples are buried around these hills. There are Budu out there," the old woman warned him.

Tom knew that *Budu* was a loose translation for ghosts, and replied, "Oh, Grandma, there's no such thing as ghosts. That's for kids."

"Do you think I'm crazy? Is that it? Just some crazy old Indian lady?" his grandmother said, shaking a finger at him.

Tom didn't want to fight with her. "No, Grandma, I don't think you're crazy. I just think your ideas are old-fashioned."

"I don't care what you think. Just remember this: If you see a Budu, you must walk up to it and touch it before it has a chance to get you." She gestured as if she were touching an apparition. "Don't try to run away. Don't turn away no matter how awful it is. No matter what it might do. Do you hear me?"

"Sure, Grandma. I hear you fine," Tom said to appease her, and the door slammed shut behind him.

The night swallowed Tom as he walked down the dirt drive to the road and chuckled to himself. "Ghosts." He shook his head. "Sometimes these old folks seem like they're from another planet."

Crickets chirped a disciplined chorus along the barbed-wire fence that edged the old farm road. The hoot of an owl carried by a dry prairie breeze from some unknown place reached Tom's ears. He was enjoying the night sounds and the cool air, and he walked farther along, not even using his flashlight. Then, there was a new sound—a thump, from somewhere behind him. He stood still and listened to the night. Then again, *thump*. Tom turned and looked back down the road, shining his flashlight at the darkness.

"Who's there? Somebody out there?" There was no response. "That old woman's spook stories are getting to me," he laughed uneasily and started again on his way.

Thump. He stopped and searched the night in every direction. A storm front with mountainous thunderheads covered the moon.

"Maybe I should get back to the house before the storm hits," he thought to himself.

He picked up his pace. The thunder rolled, masking the sounds that he could feel through his feet. *Thump! Thump!*

Chills ran up and down his spine, goose bumps covered his skin, and the hair on his neck stood on end—he knew with a terrible certainty that someone, or something, was stalking him. He ran, faster, faster, but his pursuer kept pace and was, in fact, closing on him. The flashlight fell from his hand, but he didn't turn back to retrieve it. His grandmother's warning came to mind, and then he knew. "The Budu!" he hissed. His skin burned and his teeth chattered. A keen wail pierced the darkness, and the ground trembled with the heavy tread of the Budu.

Panting heavily, Tom reached the ridge about a hundred yards from his grandmother's house. He wiped cold beads of perspiration off his brow. The welcoming lights in the windows offered safety . . . if only he could make it there in time.

But there was no time. Tom swallowed a lump in his throat as something sharp pricked the back of his neck. Daring a glance over his shoulder, he found himself looking into the slimy, rotting face of an animated corpse. Long taloned fingers reached out and grabbed the left side of his face, puncturing tissue, muscle, and bone. Tom screamed in agony and tried to tear himself away from the monstrous beast. His knees buckled under him, and the only thing holding him up were the claws twisting his face. Within a few agonizing moments, Tom lost consciousness . . . forever.

The next morning, after only a short search, Tom's cousin found his body in a ditch by the road that led to their grandmother's house. His lifeless hands were clenched like claws and curled in front of his body; his face was oddly twisted to one side. The coroner's explanation was that an animal of some kind had somehow managed to rip Tom's facial muscles on the left side of his face from his cranium without piercing the skin. His grandmother had one thing to say when she was shown the body: "*Buduyai!*" The ghosts have done it.

They call themselves *Numunuu,* meaning "The People." The historical records call them *Comanche*—a word originally applied by the Utes of southern Colorado to the people they continually fought. In the 1700s, the Comanche left their homeland in the Great Basin, crossed the Rockies, and drifted south and east into present-day southwestern Oklahoma and northwestern Texas. They absorbed many of the life-ways shared by all buffalo-hunting Indians of the Great Plains. They lived in tepees; depended on horses for hunting, warfare, and travel; and organized into bands. At present, most Comanches live on 160-acre parcels, or portions thereof, which were granted to their ancestors on a per capita basis as a result of the Jerome Act in the early 1900s. They have a cultural center at Medicine Park, Oklahoma, and actively participate with their long-time allies, the Kiowa and Naisha Apache, in summer pow-wows, warrior society functions, and a wide variety of community- and church-related activities.

Like all Plains Indians, the traditional Comanche revere medicine bundles, honor shamans, and seek visions of supernatural beings through fasting and intense prayer in isolated places, called vision-questing. Vision-questing augments one's *Puha*, medicine or spirit, and thus extends life, intuition, and sensitivity, as well as powers to heal, bewitch, or control others. This, however, is unlikely to happen since the vision quest, as the Comanche understand the custom, is very dangerous because of interference by the *Budu*, loosely translated as "ghost."

The Budu look for weaknesses, an opening, or a mistake on the part of their human prey, and then they will attack. When a person dies, the Budu are there—waiting and watching. When one is alone in the night, the Budu will come, their heavy tread vibrating beneath the feet of the victim. An attack by the Budu results in a condition of unilateral facial paralysis, similar to that caused by Bell's palsy. This condition remains little understood. The characteristic "twisting" of one side of the face may last for only a few days or for the rest of the victim's life.

Ga-git

"**B**e careful on your way home tonight, my old friend," the elderly Nathan Bright Raven cautioned his dinner guest, Reverend Ambrose Hackett. "Lately, I have heard the Ga-git flying around out there just after dusk."

"Nonsense," huffed the Baptist missionary, dismissing the stories told by the Haida of a flying manlike beast that rips the hearts from the living bodies of its victims. "Nathan, it is the nineteenth century for goodness sake. We live today in a world of science. There is no scientific explanation for your *Ga-gits,* and more important, they are not mentioned in the Holy Bible. The Red Man must turn away from the demons of his heathen religion, or he will never progress from the shadows of paganism to reach true civilization."

Nathan Bright Raven had heard Ambrose's diatribes on the subject of rationality (meaning the ideas of white men), science, and the Christian religion before and simply smiled at him, understanding that Ambrose was just doing his job.

"Stuff and nonsense," the reverend emphasized under his breath, and he bid his friend good night. The reverend had taken several healthy strides toward his two-seater buggy when he noticed that his carriage horse, Baron, was not there. The traces and bit lying on the ground made it look as if the horse had simply dissolved, leaving all non-horse things behind.

"One of the local kids taking a joy ride, no doubt," he huffed in irritation, and tightened his jacket for the three-mile trek back to the rectory. As he walked along the dark lane through the hemlocks, he whistled the tune of "A Mighty Fortress Is Our God" to cheer himself.

Shortly, a soft whinnying up ahead caught his attention. He quickened his pace. "Come, Baron. Come on, boy," he called as he jogged toward the sound. But Reverend Hackett halted abruptly: There, on the side of the road, stood his horse and . . . *something*. He could not see clearly. The wind had picked up, and the trees cast faint, dancing shadows on the path. A deep, rumbling, continuous growl emanated from the *something*. It looked vaguely human, but instead of hands and feet, it had a pair of taloned paws, and instead of skin, a heavy black pelt covered the creature's body. Its beady eyes, which reminded Hackett of an owl's, rested upon the old reverend.

But the reverend didn't scream; instead, he laughed and said, "Oh, Nathan, you really had me there for a minute. Good joke, old friend." He shook his head, thinking that his Indian friend had dressed himself in one of the many dramatic costumes worn by the Haida in their elaborate rituals and ceremonies.

He moved toward the figure but hesitated when the growl increased in intensity. Baron pawed the ground restlessly. "Come on, Nathan, enough is enough," Hackett said, his voice shaking. Then, before his eyes, the Ga-git, in a flurry of motion, slashed the horse's throat open with its talons. The animal screamed and fell to its knees, blood soaking the ground.

The reverend gasped. *The Ga-git was real?* He tried to force his body to run, but everything was happening so very slowly. He felt as if he were stuck in a vat of thick syrup; every move took an eternity. The Ga-git, however, did not seem so constrained. It lifted the dying horse over its head and hurled it at the reverend. The gory carcass crashed to the ground and slid into the reverend, breaking both his legs and fracturing his spine.

Hackett's pain came in a torrent, but slipped away as shock lay its compassionate shroud over him. He couldn't move. He felt as if he were dreaming. The Ga-git, grumbling in some feral language, appeared and disappeared in the starlit shadows.

A revolting stench of filth, rot, spoiled meat, and dried blood poured from the creature. It casually lifted the dead horse off the reverend's crushed legs and tossed the beast of burden out of its way. Then, crouching next to the paralyzed reverend, it lifted him in an embrace. Overpowered by the repugnancy of the Ga-git, Hackett vomited, and the beast slipped one long talon into the reverend's open mouth, sliced out his tongue, and swallowed it. Thick blood gushed from the wounded man's mouth as the Ga-git again lifted the reverend in its obscene embrace and, this time, drank greedily from the flowing orifice until the reverend's body had turned quite cold.

In the following weeks, Nathan Bright Raven missed his old friend and their occasional evenings of conversation over dinner, but he had to admit that Reverend Ambrose Hackett had made a very nice after-dinner snack.

The traditional Haida of the Queen Charlotte Islands were a maritime culture focused on hunting and fresh- and salt-water fishing. They built commodious houses and large seagoing canoes from cedar planks and were one of the several tribes of the Northwest Coast Culture Area famous for their totem poles. Like their famous neighbors, the Tlingit, Nootka, and Kwakiutl, the Haida were much involved in trade and warfare. They made elaborate armor from bone and wooden slats and were so expert in fighting that they kept the early Russian explorers from taking control of their islands. Wealth, its acquisition and display, was a major theme of their culture. They possessed a custom called the *potlatch*, in which rich men would battle one another for the attainment of the highest prestige in their societies by giving their wealth away, and at times, even destroying it in a feverish demonstration of the quantities of riches they controlled.

A key feature in Haida religious belief is that everything and everyone is possessed by a spirit that, in turn, has a cadre of assistants. Through religious exercises, one could become aware of this spiritual dimension, first in oneself and then in others, and learn to control it in order to acquire greater powers, which would enhance one's ability to acquire wealth or to become a great artist or warrior. Haida shamans, using the power of vision-questing, were the most expert at this spiritual control and could use their power in a variety of ways, from healing to witching. The immense variety of Haida religious beliefs was acted out in highly theatrical rituals involving costumes with moving parts and houses designed to facilitate stage magic of the shaman's performances.

The Haida told of a terrible fate that sometimes befell fishermen whose canoes were wrecked at sea. Some of the fishermen who made it back to land, for reasons not understood, would wander deep into the forest and subsist on moss, roots, and berries instead of returning to their villages. They would go naked and eventually become little different from the wild animals. Gradually, these men would obtain the power to fly, perform superhuman feats of strength, and change their shapes at will. At this stage, they were considered Ga-git. Perhaps because these men had nearly once been drowning victims, the Ga-git had a fear of water.

These monsters were believed to hunt by night and hide in dank lairs during the day. The only defense the Haida had against them was to stay indoors at night and to avoid the farthest reaches of the surrounding forest. Still, the Ga-git sometimes came very close to villages to abduct and kill, and sometimes late at night, they entered houses and carried people off as they slept soundly under the Ga-git's spell. The Ga-git had one desire: to change others into Ga-git, so that they would experience the cursed life of the creatures. If the Ga-git breathed on their victim's face, the terrible change would occur within days.

Ga-gits were believed to possess inhuman strength. They could carry large whaling canoes, shake houses, and uproot trees. Their flying skills, however, were limited—most could fly only at face level, a couple of yards off the ground. Only a very strong Ga-git could fly over houses. Because of the creature's generally low flight patterns, it was advised that when under attack by a flying Ga-git, one should drop to the ground or run for the closest body of water.

Reverend Charles Harrison, who ministered to the Haida in the late 1800s, wrote that he witnessed a Ga-git scare in the village of Massett. The Indians were concerned about a roving Ga-git that could fly as high as a house. The warriors of the village ordered all women and children to stay indoors after nightfall while the men of the village, armed with shotguns and rifles, awaited the Ga-git's appearance from the roofs of their houses. Harrison writes, "Whilst they kept their vigil in the village, he [the Ga-git], however, amused himself elsewhere by carrying up from the beach a thirty-foot canoe to a hill about three hundred yards away, and there placed it on end against a house."

La Malogra

FROM HISPANIC NEW MEXICO

A beautifully tanned, golden-colored lamb fleece lay in the middle of State Road 419 and the old Santa Fe Turnpike. There was no reason for it to be there. The desert wind raked its fingers through the sagebrush at the side of the road and threw handfuls of sand in all directions, but around the golden-colored fleece, nothing moved. It was *La Malogra*—The Evil Hour—before whom even the Devil himself was wary. The golden-colored fleece was a vast hunger that could be satiated only by continued acts of the utmost evil.

In a bar about a hundred yards north of the intersection where the golden fleece waited, a fistfight was ending. There had been no contest. Ramon had beaten the stranger senseless. The stranger was older, lighter, shorter, and drunker, the kind of odds Ramon liked best. Because Ramon was such a bully, nobody liked him, and everyone feared him.

"Hey, idiot, get me a beer over here, " he ordered, slamming the bar with his fist. "Now!"

In his fright, the bartender almost bowed, caught himself, then hurried to satisfy Ramon's wishes. He put a mug of beer on the counter.

"Damn!" Ramon shouted, looking down at his shirt. "I'm covered with that little guy's blood. Damn! Damn!" He took a swig of his beer, the foam running down his chin, and turned away from the bar to kick the stranger, who was still on the floor, moaning quietly.

"Yeah, it's your blood, you asshole." He kicked the downed man again.

Ramon stripped off the bloody shirt, threw it on the man at his feet, and stumbled out of the bar. He staggered south on 419, arms crossed against his chest for warmth. Desert nights could be very cold. When he reached the old Santa Fe Turnpike, his attention was drawn to the fleece, its golden sheen vivid against the weathered asphalt.

"Well, look at what I found." Ramon inspected the fleece. "Damn. This must be Indian-made." He rubbed the finely tanned leather and draped it around his shoulders like a cape. But it wasn't quite big enough to offer much warmth. Then, an idea came to him. He fished around for his pocketknife and cut a hole in the middle of the fleece to make a poncho.

The golden-colored fleece, its body defiled and no longer perfect, slowly contracted.

Ramon pushed his head through the gash in the fleece, oriented himself, and stumbled in the direction of his trailer, a half-mile away. The fleece silently bore its pain and, by increments, drew itself together for healing.

Ramon didn't realize that the pelt was shrinking until, feeling overheated, he tried to remove the poncho. It felt tight around his throat. Finding that he couldn't enlarge the hole with his hands, he reached for his knife. But the fleece fluttered violently at the sound of the knife opening, and, startled, Ramon dropped it. The fleece tightened. Falling to his knees on the dark roadside, Ramon frantically searched the ground for his knife with one hand while pulling at the leather tightening around his neck with the other.

The hole grew smaller, and Ramon abandoned his search for the knife. He tried with both hands to stop the constricting pressure, but nothing he did helped. His head felt like it was about to explode. Then, the hole in the fleece shrunk to the point where he could no longer breathe, and before long, Ramon fell dead with bulging eyes staring into the sky.

But it didn't stop there. The fleece continued to contract, and an hour after Ramon died, his head was squeezed off his body as the fleece regained its wholeness.

A night-wandering wind carried the evil fleece to the clouds and, late the next day, released it. Fluttering like a giant leaf, the fleece tumbled down and came to rest in the backyard of the Santa Fe Children's Home.

"Oh, look at the pretty blanket!" squealed a smiling little girl in a bright yellow sundress. She picked up the golden-colored fleece and wrapped it around her shoulders.

The Spanish frontier penetrated North America during the sixteenth century through the explorations of men such as Juan de Oñate and Francisco Vásquez de Coronado. Over time, Spanish culture would mix and mingle with Indian, Anglo, and French influences, producing the Spanish-American and Mexican-American subcultures of the American Southwest. In particular, the Christianity of the Spanish, French, and Anglo explorers and traders would help mold the rich religious and folkloric heritage of the Aztecs and their neighbors.

Professor Aurelio M. Espinosa published the first scholarly work on Hispanic American folklore, "New Mexican Spanish Folklore," in the *Journal of American Folklore* in 1910. For the Hispanic New Mexicans he interviewed in the early 1900s, a figure called *La Malora*, meaning "The Evil One" and sometimes *La Malogra*, meaning "The Evil Hour," was more feared than the devil.

La Malogra is an evil spirit that wanders about in the darkness at crossroads and other places. Usually taking the form of a large lock of wool or the whole fleece of wool of a sheep, *un vellon de lana*, it terrorizes the unfortunate ones who wander alone at night. Sometimes it takes a human form, but this is rare; the New Mexicans say that when it has been seen in human form, it presages ill fate, death, or the like. When it appears on dark nights in the shape of a fleece of wool, it diminishes and increases in size in the very presence of the unfortunate one who sees it. It is also generally believed that a person who sees La Malogra, like the one who sees a ghost, remains forever senseless. When asked for detailed information about this myth, the New Mexicans gave the general reply, "*Es cosa mala.*" It is an evil thing.

Kikituk

FROM THE INUIT OF ALASKA

It was the first day of the four-day Messenger Feast. Inuit families from scattered and isolated villages across the south Alaskan wilderness gathered to socialize with friends, relatives, and neighbors. The young people played games and made tentative forays into courtship, while the adults renewed old friendships, relaxed, shared food, and discussed weighty matters related to resources, trade, and territorial disputes. Feasting and dancing continued all day and into the night. As was the custom, the village that hosted the annual gathering presented gifts to visitors, children being the favored recipients. The Inuit believed that children represented the return of ancient kinsmen; hence, they were respected, educated, honored, and loved. Carved and painted toys, sleds, boots, games, puzzles, and jewelry, often wrapped in fine buckskin, moved from hand to hand amid delighted smiles and many thank-yous.

Maupok had had a long day. He snuggled against his grandfather in the *kashgee*, the hunting house, a spacious earth lodge walled and roofed with logs, with a floor that was sunk three feet into the ground for additional insulation. The kashgee served as a community hall and as a meeting place for the hunters.

"Grandpa, look!" Maupok elbowed his grandfather sharply. "That man doesn't have an ear. He's funny looking, isn't he?"

"Hush, Maupok!" his grandfather whispered harshly. But it was too late; people had heard the rude remark. Fortunately, the old man knew how to respond to the boy's thoughtless comment. Aware that others were watching, he gruffly addressed his grandson. "It is impolite to mock people for any reason, Maupok. You know this. Your father and mother have taught you better manners. You are a big boy now and should not speak as a small child, without thinking or feeling for others. Did you ever wonder why Kaduk is missing an ear?"

Maupok's face burned with embarrassment. "No, Grandfather," he replied with downcast eyes.

"Kaduk is a great hunter. When he speaks in the kashgee, the men of this village listen closely. Kaduk is also very brave. He lost his ear killing a polar bear that had attacked an elder who lived alone on the edge of his village."

Maupok fought back tears of shame.

The grandfather tossed a stick onto the dying fire. "I have a teaching story about that, which I will tell you sometime."

"Hey, old man," someone called out, "is your story a good one? Is it about old times? Tell us all."

People drew their blankets closer to Maupok and his grandfather. It was chilly in the kashgee, and the visitors who were going to spend the night in the hunting house had brought pillows and blankets against the frigid night. During the time of the Messenger Feast, rules against women and children being in the kashgee were suspended in the atmosphere of informality, hospitality, and friendship that pervaded the feast. A good story was a perfect end to a night of celebration.

Maupok's grandfather said, "Since I have been asked, I will tell you a story about what happened in a village on the coast many years ago. This is a true story. I would not waste your time with stories for small children. Listen to me. I'll tell you what I saw, and what I later learned from people who had been there on that strange night. . . ."

It started simply enough—as simply as a story involving an evil spirit can be. It involved a young man named Tulak and an older man named Murba. Tulak didn't like Murba and often ridiculed him in front of the villagers for being short, fat, and bow-legged. But since Tulak was a coward as well as a tease, he would push Murba just enough to provoke him, and when Murba would react, Tulak would look to the people nearby and say, "Murba can't take a joke. I was just fooling around."

One day, as Murba entered the Hunting House to have his morning meal with the other men of the village, Tulak said loudly, for all to hear, "You're looking a little fat around the middle, old man. Maybe you should eat a little less today. You might have to chase down a wounded moose this afternoon, and with that blubber you're carrying, a moose could run circles around you."

Murba, who had in fact just returned from a successful hunt, only smiled at Tulak, and said, "The wind makes a noise, but there is really nothing there."

Tulak, with a wit too slow to respond in kind, just cried out, "Fatso!"

Murba said nothing. He looked at Tulak, shook his head, and left the hunting house without eating. After that night, Murba was not seen around the village for an entire month. His family said that he'd returned to his secret hunting ground in the northern barrens.

The day Murba returned, the village gathered around him for his story of the northern hunt. Murba looked as if he had been eating well. His greatly expanded stomach told the tale. But there was something else about Murba. It was hard to describe. His eyes looked different somehow, and he tilted his head every now and then as if listening to a voice that only he could hear.

"Where is Tulak?" Murba asked, looking around. "I need his help."

"You need Tulak's help?" one of the men asked with surprise. "You know he doesn't like you. He won't help you!"

Murba grinned crookedly with a glint in his eye. "I think he won't be able to resist this time." He rubbed his belly. "He will help me even if he doesn't know he is."

"I saw Tulak in the kashgee a little while ago," Murba's nephew told him, and Murba hurried to the hunting house.

When he saw Murba, Tulak's eyes widened and he laughed cruelly. "You are as fat as some old walrus . . . a very ugly, fat old walrus!"

With those words, Murba felt *it* move inside him. "Ah, good," he thought. "My friend is listening." Murba shed his parka and threw it to the ground. Extending his bloated stomach toward Tulak, he said, "Here is my wonderful stomach. Tell me more about how ugly and fat it is."

Tulak couldn't believe the opportunity Murba was giving him, and quickly took the bait. "That would be easy. Murba, old man, you've eaten so much that your stomach looks like a festering ball of pus about ready to pop and furthermore. . . ."

Murba grimaced as Tulak, who was thoroughly enjoying himself, continued to taunt the bulky, old hunter. Murba doubled over in pain and vigorously massaged his distended stomach. Finally, he straightened up. "That's enough," he said as he shrugged into his parka and went back outside, leaving Tulak alone once again in the hunting house.

Tulak was confused. "Enough?" he questioned the empty room. "But I was just getting started."

Once again, Murba disappeared for a month. His wife told all who asked that he was hunting to the south. On the day he returned, everyone who saw him was stunned by his appearance. Though all were too polite to say anything, Murba did indeed look very much like a pregnant walrus. His abdomen stuck out so far that he wobbled when he walked. His eyes bulged out as if there were a pressure building inside him, and his skin looked tight like the head of a drum.

After presenting gifts of meat and fur to his friends and family, he announced, "I invite you all to the hunting house tonight for more gifts. I have had a very successful hunt, and I want to share my good fortune with my friends."

The villagers gathered after the evening meal for Murba's *give away*—a custom in which outstanding hunters present portions of their hunt to members of the community. Even Tulak joined the others in the hunting house, but he remained in the back. Murba was acting strangely, and Tulak, perhaps feeling somewhat guilty about the way he had been treating him, thought it best to linger in the shadows.

Murba handed out bundles of caribou meat, wolverine pelts, and packets of dried fish, which were accepted with many thanks. Then, Murba addressed the gathering: "I have hunted far to the north, and I have hunted far to the south, but I did not hunt for food or fur. I hunted for wisdom and knowledge. I visited the *angakoqs* [shamans] of many tribes, and I learned of a . . ." he paused for a moment, and then continued, "a friend—a means to great power. I was taught by the shamans who live deep in the forest how to make this power my own."

"But you brought us furs and meat, Murba," interjected one of his friends. "How could you have done that if you were not hunting?"

"My friend did my hunting for me. I followed him closely and watched as it . . . he . . . hunted animals so that I could understand its . . . my friend's abilities . . . in order to better use it."

The crowd murmured and someone exclaimed, "What are you talking about, Murba? We don't understand you. Why do you sometimes call your friend *it?*"

"Well, I guess it's time to introduce my friend," Murba said as his eyes scanned the room. They rested on Tulak skulking in the back. "Tulak, I haven't given you anything yet. Please step forward."

Tulak hesitantly walked to the center of the hunting house, watching Murba intently.

"Well, aren't you going to insult me in front of everybody? Come on now, don't be shy. I'll give you a fine fox pelt if you call me 'fatso' or 'pregnant walrus' one more time. Come on, hurt my feelings!" He pulled his shirt off and exposed his obscenely bloated stomach. Some gasped. Some turned away. "Look, here it is. Say something mean, and I'll give you a present." Murba held out a top-grade white fox pelt.

Tulak felt very uncomfortable and, at first, couldn't find his voice. But he looked longingly at the fox pelt in Murba's arms and said, "You, Murba, are a fat, ugly old woman, so, of course, you need someone to do your hunting for you. You couldn't trap a mouse if you tried."

Murba clenched his teeth and doubled over. Friends rushed to him, but he brushed them aside. Straightening somewhat, he said, "Come on, one more time, Tulak." He tossed the fox pelt to the younger man.

Tulak ran a hand through the soft fur, cleared his throat, and uttered the most shocking insult he could imagine. "Murba must be a woman because only women can get their bellies as big as his."

Murba groaned. "Ah, yes, now my friend comes." His stomach rumbled and moved grotesquely. Suddenly, in a thick cloud of blood, Murba's lower abdomen tore open, and a fearsome creature with dark green scales leapt out. Shouts and shrieks erupted as the creature quickly traversed the area between the two men. While Murba's body seemed to repair itself instantly, the creature ripped into Tulak's body, his screams dying away as his skin and clothing were torn to shreds; the white fox pelt was soon drenched in blood.

Villagers cowered along the walls or bolted for the door. Those who chanced to look saw a *Kikituk,* a fierce reptilian creature, crouching amidst Tulak's gory remains. And before the Kikituk crouched Murba in a wide stance, chanting to the horrific monster that slithered on the blood-drenched floor: "My friend, my friend, come to me, come to me." Murba spread his arms wide in invitation and opened his mouth. To the wonderment of all, the creature leapt into Murba's mouth. And once again, his body swelled as it had before.

From that day on, not one person in Murba's village ever dared to say anything cruel to anyone again. How could they be sure that the person being insulted didn't have a Kikituk as a special friend?

When the old man finished, no one spoke. He had entranced them all with his story.

"Great story, Grandfather," Maupok finally said, breaking the silence, and others chimed in with "Good story, old man" and "Those old stories are always the best."

As the people gathered their blankets and pillows to return to their houses and the visitors prepared their pallets for the night, the grandfather spoke to Maupok. "Is there someone you need to speak to before we go?"

"Yes, Grandfather," Maupok replied respectfully. His grandfather moved toward the door and smiled to himself when the voice of his grandson reached his ears: "Kaduk, please accept my apology for commenting rudely about your ear."

"Don't worry about it, boy," the great hunter said as he slipped his hands under his parka and pretended to make his stomach grow. "But watch out the next time you insult me."

Maupok laughed—but not too loudly.

The Alaskan Inuit do not live on open ice, as one may think. Theirs is a world of forests, lakes, fjords, bays, and cascading streams and rivers. Instead of igloos, the traditional house of the Alaskan Inuit was a compound construction of log, earth, timber, and stone. Their villages were used as winter bases. In the summer months, they lived in crude tepees, while they took to the fields in search of game and fish. The center of village life was a large structure called a *kashgee*, a single room up to twenty-five feet across that served as a community center. Private rituals of male hunting groups were conducted there, as well as the boisterous social dances of the Messenger Feast and other celebrations. Today, wooden houses have replaced the traditional earth lodges of the Alaskan Inuit, but the Messenger Feast continues, as well as traditional hunting and fishing expeditions, where one may still see the old style tepees in use.

The religion of the Alaskan Inuit is centered on a strong belief in the power of charms and amulets, as well as on traditional songs, poems, chants, dances, and an immense variety of esoteric rituals. A key concept, without which it would be difficult to describe the range of Alaskan Inuit religious practices, is that of *inua*, meaning "owner; generic spirit." The inua concept is very subtle, but an important implication is that all animal species have a patron spirit that prohibits humans from needlessly abusing them. Alaskan Inuit hunters must perform numerous rituals and observe certain customs to maintain a good relationship with the inua of the game they must hunt to survive.

The souls of men and animals, both living and dead, abound in this culture. These souls can sometimes be dangerous, but not nearly as dangerous as *Tunerak*—demons with whom confrontation is lethal to all except powerful shamans. Alaskan Inuit recognize many demons—some giants, some dwarfs. Some, like the Kikituk, have the uncanny look, for the arctic, of a crocodile. Some are half-beings—a seal with a woman's head, a man with the hooves of a mountain goat, or a beaked child with wings—and some are unique to the individual who experiences them.

Wi-lu-gho-yuk

FROM THE INUIT OF ALASKA

The body of Wugum, a hunter from a coastal village to the north, was found floating in the icy waters of Norton Sound. The cause of death was obvious to those who fished him out—a ragged, fist-sized hole was centered where his heart used to be. The edges were too jagged to have resulted from a bullet wound. It looked like someone had stuck a knife into Wugum's chest, twisted it to enlarge the hole, and removed his heart.

The local police organized a search party to investigate the ice floes where the Inuit hunted. Only four men were needed. They were expert trackers, and more men would have disrupted the evidence they needed to see in the hard snow. The men came heavily armed, expecting to track down a murdering maniac. To find their way in the forbidding waters, they hired an Inuit guide named Muyaka. They showed the guide Wugum's mutilated body so that he would have some idea of what the search party was up against.

Muyaka made no comment upon seeing the body except to request that they delay the search until he could make a few purchases from the trader's store on Norton Sound. He returned a short time later with a small brown paper bag clutched in his mittened hands.

"What kind of piece are you carrying, old man?" the deputy asked.

Muyaka held up the paper bag, and the deputy raised his eyebrows.

"It is enough," Muyaka told him and gestured toward the canoes before the deputy could comment. "We must go now. The wind will change later."

The deputy shrugged, and they followed Muyaka to a peninsula on the northern edge of Norton Sound. Understanding the winds and currents of the area in which the murdered man had been found, the old guide had a rough idea of where the search should be centered. After a few hours of rowing, he signaled for the party to beach their canoes on an ice field that appeared to be solidly attached to the peninsula.

"We'll look around here first, " he said. "Watch the ground closely, my friends. There's . . ."

"Yeah, we know," interrupted the deputy. "We've made searches before."

"There may be more to it than that," Muyaka suggested quietly, but said nothing more.

By midday, the wind picked up and began blowing the light snow cover into a misty crystal haze.

"There's no one here," the deputy said. "We should think about turning back. The conditions are getting . . ." Suddenly, he trembled as if an electric shock had run through him. Then, he began dancing wildly, slapping at his legs and howling in pain. The three men watched, almost laughing at first, but their eyes widened in fear when they realized there was something terribly wrong. Meanwhile, Muyaka ran toward a large rock in the area where the ice field met the peninsula, and climbed atop it.

The deputy jumped up and down, grabbing at his chest, and screamed, "Help me!" before falling to the ice, where he lay motionless. One of the search party moved toward the fallen man and saw a small gray blur shoot from the deputy's parka and gnaw rapidly into the boot toe of another man who was walking toward him. He tried to call out a warning to his mate, but lost his voice as he watched the man go into the same crazed dance as the deputy.

Muyaka shouted to the men, "You must not move!" He knew that the creatures were drawn to the movement of their prey. But the wind muffled his warning. The second man fell to the ground. With wide eyes, the two remaining men watched as bright red blood seeped through their friends' parkas onto the ice. Then, one grabbed the other and motioned in the direction of the canoes. Together, they ran toward them.

From atop the rock, Muyaka yelled into the wind, "Stop! You must stop! Don't run!" One of the two stopped, but not because of Muyaka's warning. He twitched and began slapping his body as the others had, until he too hit the ice. The last man hesitated a moment, wanting to help his friend, but then thought better of it and turned to run. But whatever it was that he was trying to outrun easily caught up to him, and, in the same sequence as the others, the last man fell and lay motionless.

Muyaka watched the blood ooze from the men's bodies. Then, as he expected, he saw the little gray shape coming toward him, moving through the ice as if it were not really there. Luckily, Muyaka knew what it was.

"*Wi-lu-gho-yuk*," he called to the creature as he opened his paper bag. He pulled out a mousetrap and a small piece of hard cheese. "I thought it might be you," he said, and placed the baited trap down at the base of the rock upon which he stood.

A tiny mouselike creature popped through the ice just as Muyaka withdrew his hand. It stared up at the Inuit with its beady eyes and, with its nose twitching, sniffed the bait from a distance.

"Come on, get closer. Take a bite," Muyaka urged. "I'm getting cold."

The Wi-lu-gho-yuk tentatively stuck out its nose to sniff the cheese, moving closer and closer until *Snap!*—the trap slammed shut, breaking the creature's neck. Muyaka hopped down from the rock and kicked the little corpse into the frigid water. He crumpled the paper bag as he walked over to examine the bodies of the dead men. He noted the holes in the toes of their boots through which the Wi-lu-gho-yuk had entered. When he pulled open the men's parkas, he saw the gory gaps in their chests where their hearts used to be. What he didn't notice, however, was a faint, small gray shape quickly moving just below the surface of the ice, heading straight for him.

Information about the culture and spiritual beliefs of the Inuit of Alaska can be found on page 31 under Kikituk. Please refer to that section for some insight into their ways.

The Wi-lu-gho-yuk is a type of *Tunerak*—monstrous creatures that come in all shapes and sizes in the world of the Alaskan Inuit. In this case, it appeared as a seemingly harmless mouselike creature. Ordinary mortals cannot stand against the Tunerak. An encounter with one of these demons usually ends in death. Shamans, however, derive their powers to heal, divine the future, and bewitch from their ability to control creatures like the Wi-lu-gho-yuk.

La Llorona

FROM MEXICO

Newlyweds Frank and Judy Quinlin selected the sleepy little Mexican town of Barra De Navidad for their honeymoon. Friends who had visited Mexico the previous season told them of the beauty of the old Mexican village. Their friends' travel slides of the lovely bay, the Hemingway-esque thatched roofs, the beachfront bar, the jungle-cloaked mountains, and the fishermen casting nets from colorful dinghies in the sunset drove them to the travel agent. Sooner than they could have guessed possible, the hustle and bustle of the wedding was over, and Frank and Judy were alone in a simple but cozy room in the village's only hotel.

The next morning, they loaded their cameras before going down to breakfast. Their mutual love of photography had brought them together two years earlier in the Art and Method of Photography class in college. After coffee and sweet bread, the couple hit the streets where picture opportunities abounded. A traveling sidewalk magician in a grease-stained top hat and threadbare tuxedo performed for a handful of delighted children. Farmwomen pulled wooden carts loaded with flowers and melons to a market that sprung up on a corner across from the hotel.

"Hey! Mingo!" someone who was setting up the market called out, and a barefoot man with a revolver stuck in his belt waved.

Around noon, Frank and Judy found refuge from the glaring sun in the run-down garden of an adobe church, and ate the light lunch that the hotel chef had prepared for them. Frank took the last sip of water from a plastic bottle and surveyed the garden. It had been neglected for a long time; however, deep in the weed-choked shadows, a tangle of vines with several large white flowers caught his eye. Looking closer, he realized that they were moonflowers. The vines carried their delicate snowy blossoms throughout the garden and into the small adjoining cemetery, climbing up crosses and statues of angels, St. Francis, and the Blessed Virgin.

"You know, Judy, I think I'd like to come back here tonight. There's going to be a full moon, and I'd like to see if I can work with the flowers by moonlight."

"You're a regular photographer-poet, ain't ya?" she kidded.

"Well . . ."

"No," Judy said, "I think that's a good idea. I wanted to spend some time getting shots of the fishermen night-fishing in the bay. Shooting by moon- and firelight will make it an interesting challenge."

After a dinner of grilled kid, a hotel specialty, the honeymooners went their separate ways. In addition to his .35 mm Lica camera, Frank carried a tripod and a small bag of lenses and filters. When he arrived in the church garden, the conditions were perfect. The moon hung in the faint mist from the ocean and painted the ancient gravestones the color of pewter. The flowers absorbed the moonlight and softly glowed silver-white like tiny moons in the abandoned churchyard.

A cloud crossed the face of the moon. The radiant light effects turned turgid black and then returned as the cloud completed its passing.

"Better stop gawking at the show and get down to business," Frank said to himself, and he locked the tripod legs in place. His first shot was going to be of a moonflower-draped tombstone—a timed exposure to make the most of the moonlight. But when he put his eye to the viewfinder, he heard a woman quietly sobbing.

He looked up. "Is anybody there?"

Receiving no reply, he shrugged and returned to his camera. He was taking a last-minute look through the viewfinder when he saw, or thought he saw, a figure . . . a woman wrapped in mist. He looked up again. There was no one there. He pointed the remote trigger at the camera, and just before he pushed the TAKE button, the crying woman wailed.

Chills shot up Frank's back. He addressed the shadows in Spanish, *"Mostrarse el suyo yo hacer no como chivato y acechando por mi cuenta!"* Show yourself. I don't like people sneaking around and spying on me.

And before his disbelieving eyes, a figure formed from the moonlight—a tall, slender woman dressed in a flowing gown of white, also the color of her hair, skin, and eyes. She appeared distraught. Sparkling tears poured down her cheeks, and she paced back and forth, moaning in anguish.

"My babies. Where are my babies?" she cried.

Frank squinted into the shadow for a clear view of the woman, and said, "I don't know anything about your babies."

"I killed them, you know," the woman said, half moaning.

"You what?" blurted Frank.

"Yes. I threw them into an irrigation canal, stones tied around their tiny ankles . . . *Aiiieee!* . . . my babies," she wailed. "Where are my babies?"

Frank clapped his hands over his ears. Her cries were like ice picks against his eardrums.

"*Aiiieee!*" she wailed again.

Frank wanted to run from the garden to find a policeman, but forgot where he was going after taking just one step. His head buzzed. Against his will, he approached the woman in white and stood hypnotized before her eerily beautiful face.

"No, no, no," she said, "I didn't drown them. My poor babies . . . but I wish I had, because . . . do you want to know what I really did to my babies? Do you?"

Frank nodded his head dumbly.

"Listen, gringo. I cut them up into little pieces, cooked them up, and ate them," she said with a sneer. Then, her eyes darted to the left, and the white apparition wailed again, "*Aiiieee!* Where are my poor babies? Why can't I find them?"

The silvery woman floated closer to Frank. Her icy breath chilled his face. She smiled demurely and opened her cape to reveal, not a beautiful woman's body, but rather a skeleton, the light reflecting dully from its greasy bones. Frank's mind emptied. All that remained was the order whispered into his ear by the icy breath of the woman in white.

Frank packed his equipment and returned to the hotel, where he beat his new wife to death with his tripod. After all, what else could he do?

The Spanish presence in what is now New Mexico dates back to the sixteenth century, when conquistadors probed the area in search of the fabled cities of gold. The Spanish-American descendants of the conquistadors and the Mexican Americans still hold many traditional beliefs, folktales, festivals, and family activities in their ongoing adaptation to modern life in the United States.

In terms of mystical folk beliefs, one of the most widespread in Hispanic America concerns *La Llorona*—The Weeping Woman. Her presence was first described in Mexico City in the mid-1500s. It was said that on moonlit nights, one might see a woman dressed in white, wandering the streets wailing in deep anguish. She would disappear into the lake just before sunrise. Sometimes she cried for her lost children—children she had been accused of drowning in the Mexico City canals. It was said that if one were to encounter her, madness and death would inevitably follow.

Some claim that the prototype for La Llorona can be found in the old German legend of *Die Weisse Frau*—The White Lady—which dates back to 1486. However, sightings of a "white woman" have been reported in many areas. Take for instance the Banshees of Ireland, "white women" who announce impending death, as do the White Smoke Woman of New Guinea and the White Snow Maiden of Japan. A version from Santa Fe describes a forlorn young woman who wandered into the mountains grieving for her lost children. The locals say that one can hear her cries when the snow falls. In Santa Rosa, a boy claimed that he and a group of friends had chased a "white woman," and when they caught up with her, she reached out and touched the boy's head. The next morning, he had a lock of white hair in the spot where she had touched him.

Mai Tso

FROM THE NAVAHO OF NEW MEXICO AND ARIZONA

Billy Begay turned west off State Road 44 north of Naschitti as the sun set behind Bear Mountain. He was happy to be back home on the land of his mother's family, but he worried about the violent argument he had had with his brother-in-law earlier that morning. He was hitching up his trailer in front of his wife's house just west of Window Rock. . . .

"Where the hell are you going?" Jim Pinto demanded.

"Good morning, brother-in-law," Billy answered politely, and he checked the trailer hitch one more time. Jim had been verbally abusive and antagonistic ever since Billy had married his sister and the couple moved onto the land owned by her mother's clan. This was all shortly after another of Jim's sisters had mysteriously disappeared. Under the circumstances, Billy tried to be patient with him.

"I asked you where you are going! You're supposed to help move the old lady's sheep from the high pasture today. We got to get them ready for shearing," Jim said.

"I got to help my mother and her bunch," Billy replied. "They sent a message for me yesterday."

"The hell with them. You are married to my sister. You live on my family's land and in my family's house. We're Navaho, and that's the way of our people," Jim pressed.

"Look, Jim," said Billy, "my mother needs my help and . . ."

"And we need your help too," Jim interrupted, advancing on Billy. "Are you running out on our bunch after we have given you so much? My sister is your wife, you live on our land, you herd our . . ."

"Back off, Jim!" Billy said, gently pushing his brother-in-law out of his way.

"Don't you dare lay hands on me," Jim yelled into his face. "You'll be sorry you ever came around here. You're lazy and good for noth. . . "

"Shut the hell up!" Billy barked, losing his patience.

Jim stared hard at him and whispered, "You are a dead man."

"Go to hell!" Billy said as he jumped into his car and drove off in a cloud of dust.

The tense confrontation had faded by the time he pulled his small trailer into a grove of pines. He built a fire and prepared his camp, allowing the sounds of the night to soothe him. He cherished the howl of the coyote and the slapping of the bats' wings against the evening sky. The wind wafted fragrantly off the desert while the bats hunted in the last light of day. Then, the coyotes' ever-present howling stopped.

"Little brother coyote must have gone to bed early tonight," Billy thought. He chewed on some fried bread and finished the last of his coffee.

In the small trailer, he lit a kerosene lantern and settled back to read for a while. Soon, he dozed soundly while the lantern burned itself out. Hours later, Billy was awakened from a disturbing dream by something moving around outside the trailer.

"Who's there?" he called out. The noise stopped. He fumbled for his flashlight. "I got a gun in here!" he shouted. "Whoever you are, you better just move on and leave me alone!"

Then, the trailer rocked violently as if it had been hit by something very large. The flashlight fell from Billy's grip, and, once again, he was in the dark. His head turned this way and that in the directions of the muffled growls from outside the trailer; they seemed to be coming from everywhere all at once.

The trailer shook again, but this time a clawed handlike paw smashed through the thin trailer wall and ripped into his back, tearing his shirt and his skin. Billy felt warm blood dripping down his back, and he scrambled to the other side of the trailer. A feral stink permeated the air. Looking wildly around for an escape, Billy noticed the open hatch on the trailer roof and, despite the pain in his back, hoisted himself up and crawled out into the night air.

Below him, not quite discernible in the dark, several unidentifiable creatures smashed themselves into the trailer and clawed at the aluminum again and again. When the clouds moved off, exposing the moon, one of the awful beings spotted him. Billy could see the beast's eyes glowing in the moonlight and could clearly read its intention not only to attack him, but to devour him. The creature lunged at the trailer and scrambled up the side. Without hesitating, Billy jumped onto the roof of his car and practically did a somersault into the front seat. He fumbled with the keys in his right hand while he rolled up the window with his left. Just when he finally managed to get the key into the ignition, one of the slavering wolf-faced men smashed its grotesque head against the window. Billy stomped on the accelerator and turned the car onto the road; the trailer tilted to one side, and then righted itself.

Billy sneaked a peak in the rearview mirror—the wolflike monsters pursued him. Fortunately, the distance between the creatures and the car grew. Then, Billy heard a pounding—*his heart?*—no, it was above him. One of the creatures was on the roof! Suddenly, a long, furry arm reached through the passenger-side window, clawing blindly at the air. Billy remembered the tire iron under the driver's seat and groped for it with one hand. His fingers closed around it and he pulled it out. He smashed the hairy claw until it was bleeding. The creature withdrew its mangled hand, and with his peripheral vision, Billy saw a blur pass across the window and heard a thump. The injured beast had fallen from the car. Billy let out the breath he didn't realize he'd been holding.

But his relief was short-lived. Although Billy was going sixty-five miles an hour, a naked man with a wolf pelt hanging around his neck managed to run alongside the car, howling and waving a bloodied fist. Then, it seemed, the "wolf man" disappeared. Billy pushed the car to seventy-five and drove for a few minutes before something in the rearview mirror caught his attention. A giant wolf with glowing eyes, human facial features, and bared teeth sat in the back seat. Billy slammed on the brakes, and the car and trailer swerved off the road, rolled a few times, and slid to a stop a few hundred feet from the highway.

The following afternoon, the blood-drenched car and battered trailer were discovered by a Navaho police patrol. There was no sign of Billy Begay. He was presumed dead. *Eaten alive,* it was whispered.

A few days later, Jim attended Billy's memorial service with his newly widowed sister. His sister kissed and hugged the friends and relatives who came to bid their condolences, and shook the hands of acquaintances. But not Jim. He couldn't shake hands with any of the mourners: Thick bandages covered his right hand. "Hunting accident," he explained to all those who had asked, a strange smile playing across his face.

The Navaho, the most populous Indian tribe in the United States, have been farmers and herders in New Mexico and Arizona since shortly after their arrival in the Southwest in the early sixteenth century. They are world-renowned for their artistic enterprises, particularly in weaving and jewelry making. During World War II, it was the Navaho who provided the famous "code talkers," communication specialists speaking Navaho who befuddled the attempts by America's enemies to tap into the battle-field communications.

The Navaho are matrilineal people who trace their lineage through the female line. One belongs to the clan of the mother and lives on land that belongs to her clan. This sets up a tension between the demands of the husband's in-laws, since he is living on his wife's family's land, and the demands of his own mother and sisters. This tension is sometimes pointed to by anthropologists as one of the causes of the ongoing beliefs in Navaho society concerning the Mai Tso, discussed below.

Navaho religion shows the complex blending of ancient beliefs brought with them into the Southwest over 500 years ago from their ances-tral home in central Alaska, with the sophisticated cosmology and myth-ologies of the Pueblo Indians, who had been living in the Southwest a thousand years before the appearance of the Navaho. They perceive spirits in all things, as most ancient hunting people do, and at the same time conceive of the cosmos as an infinite serious of concentric "earth surfaces," a concept borrowed from the Pueblo peoples, as is their veneration of *Changing Woman,* their chief deity. The Navaho are terrified of ghosts, be-lieve in a vast number of sacred beings called "holy people," have created the most beautiful ritual poetry on the planet, and have carried the art of "dry painting," or "sand painting," to its highest level.

From the earliest times, the Navaho have told of the *Mai Tso,* meaning "human wolves" or "skin walkers." These are dreaded witches who pos-sess the power to devolve and make ancient animal powers of evil their own. The price of gaining these great powers, though, is the highest the Navaho can imagine: A man—Navaho witches are almost always men—must rape, kill, and eat his sister in the presence of a coven of "wolves" be-fore they allow him access to their mysteries. The "human wolves" use a variety of methods to attack their victims. They utter spells and brew magic potions. They use hair, clothing, or nail clippings to magically enter the bodies, minds, and spirits of their victims. They shoot corpse poison (pieces of human bone) into a victim's body. Sometimes they powder the bone and blow it into their victims' faces, forcing them to breathe it in. Witches are adept at the use of poisons and psychotropic plants in killing. Often, their attacks begin with a kind of psychological warfare. They might creep into sleeping quarters and leave behind dead animals or re-arrange the bedroom furniture while the victim sleeps—all messages that say, "I can get to you any time I wish." Often this psychological terrorism precedes the slow introduction of hallucinogens and poisons into the food or water of the victim to ensure a truly terrifying and agonizing death.

Windigo

FROM THE OJIBWA OF CANADA

Incoherent and bloody, the old hunter stumbled into his family's camp on the south shore of James Bay in Canada. For the first few days, his only word was "Windigo." That single word was enough for all to understand what had happened to him and his three hunting partners. When he recovered sufficiently to tell his story, his family gathered around.

"There were four of us at the start, my brother-in-law, Billy Golla; Ted Shears; me; and my wife's sister's boy, Andy. We hunted north along the Big Moose River up to the edge of the Barren Ground. Ted and Andy wanted to turn back because we were heading into territory unknown to our people and we had already had a good hunt. But my brother-in-law, Billy, and I convinced them to keep on going into the deep woods. We believed that there was a good chance we'd get some floundering caribou in the heavy snow.

"For three days we moved deeper into the forest, but we did not happen upon any caribou as we had expected. The temperature dropped, and the wind roared so loudly that it kept us awake at night. By the fourth day, we were going to turn back, but we realized we had lost our way.

"It was on the evening of that day when we first heard the bone-numbing screams. None of us had ever heard such a chilling sound, and we wondered what it could be. One of the boys thought it was a howling wolf, and the other thought it sounded like a person crying out in pain. The screams lasted for only a few minutes, but later that night, as we lay in the snow banks wrapped in our blankets, the screams started again—closer this time. They seemed to come from all around us. They went on all night.

"The next morning the snow was falling so hard that we could see only a few feet in front of us. We held onto one another's belts in an attempt to stay together. We trudged through the snow, not talking, hoping that we were heading in the right direction. Then, we stopped—all of us at once—to listen. A strange smell in the air warned us that something was wrong: Right there, in the middle of a blizzard, the air reeked of putrid meat. Close by on our left, we heard what sounded like bones splintering under pressure and the tearing of wet hide. We moved toward it. In a break in the storm, we saw *it*—a creature with big red eyes—feeding on a moose. It was huge, covered with lank, gray hair that had been horribly stained by blood. Its mouth was filled with large, jagged teeth that stuck out in all directions and was surrounded by bloody, shredded lips. It was the Windigo.

"Because I have lived a long time and have always listened to the wisdom of the elders, I knew exactly what to do. The others raised their rifles and shot at the creature, but I dropped mine and frantically began tearing wads of fur from the cuffs of my parka and stuffed the fur in my ears. Then I dove for cover.

"The Windigo opened its terrible mouth and from it came the heart-killing sound that paralyzes all who hear it. From the cover of a fallen tree, I watched with horror as the Windigo approached my hunting partners, who stood paralyzed, eyes wild with terror. With a fatal lunge, the Windigo bit my brother-in-law in half and swung the pieces through the air, splattering blood all over the white snow. As Billy's blood rained down on me, I tore my eyes away and ducked my head behind the tree trunk. Through the fur in my ears, I could still hear the Windigo hungrily tearing into the flesh of my brothers—the sounds of their bones splintering and their blood being lapped from the snow.

"I don't know how much time passed before the Windigo finally left. After what seemed like only moments and an eternity at the same time, I looked around—all that remained of my friends were a few shreds of bloody clothing and scattered remnants of what once had been their bodies."

At this, the old hunter paused for a moment and licked his lips, beads of sweat dripping from his forehead. When he spoke again it was as if from a trance. "Bloody meat was everywhere—lovely, dripping, bloody meat. As I looked around me, at the blood-covered snow, at my friends all gone now, I realized that it had been days since I'd eaten. . . ."

Slowly, the old hunter's family backed away.

Several thousand years ago, the ancestors of the Algonquin-speaking Cree and Ojibwa Indians migrated into central and eastern Canada to occupy an area between Lake Winnipeg and Labrador. The subarctic forests, where temperatures can drop to forty degrees below zero and famine is not an uncommon condition, proved a harsh challenge. Game was always scarce. This compelled the Indians to follow a nomadic existence—moving from place to place, hunting, fishing, and trapping—and precluded their building large villages in the manner of their relatives farther south. They lived in small family groups, always on the move, always hungry, and always on the lookout for the terrible *Windigo*—a supernatural monster of the deep subarctic forests.

Ojibwa spiritual beliefs are more organized and social than those of their neighbors—the Assiniboine, Kickapoo, Minominee, Sauk, and Fox. The primary religious organization is the *Mediwiwin*, the grand medicine society. Membership is achieved by having a vision of a supernatural being who grants one the power to heal, by paying heavy initiation fees, and by learning the complex ritual behaviors. Although *shamanism*—the practice of the medicine man/woman—exists among the Ojibwa, it is secondary to the Mediwiwin. Healing is at the heart of it all, and the Ojibwa believe that the entire group must be mustered to effect successful cures. Their rituals are so complex that they have had to evolve a type of notation system in which symbolic figures are etched on birchbark as a means of remembering elaborate procedure, songs, and prayers. Their religious notation system is the closest thing to writing found north of the high cultures of Mesoamerica—the Aztec, Maya, and Olmec.

Constructed from an Algonquin root that means both "evil spirit" and "cannibal," the word "Windigo" (sometimes Witiko, Wiitigo, Weendigo) points to an ice-hearted, cannibalistic giant who roams the forest, ravenous for human flesh. It is so addicted to its "meat" that when it can find none, it eats parts of its own body; and when it can no longer do that, it eats carrion, muck, rotten wood, and dead moss. Finally, when all else fails, the Windigo will eat its own family members, beginning with its youngest child.

The Windigo stands as tall as the tallest pine, and long, rank hair covers its entire body. Its heart is said to be made of ice; its odor, horrendous. Huge, jagged teeth jut from its mouth, and its large, blood-shot eyes protrude from its apelike face. The creature's feet are long and narrow, each with one toe and pointed heel. Blizzards always accompany the Windigo's wanderings. Many Windigo wander the frigid north woods, sometimes roaming in packs. Lurking in the deep shadows of the forest, a Windigo awaits its victims, which it paralyzes with its death-haunted scream.

Perhaps the most horrible aspect of the Windigo lies in its ability to possess humans and turn them into cannibals. Some people actually wish to become a Windigo to gain its great power, and will travel far into the forest, where they fast and offer their flesh to the monster in prayer. The forest beast will either devour the supplicants or adopt them. Once adopted, a person will feel his heart turn to ice. He will grow hair where none grew before, and slowly his compulsion to eat human flesh will become unstoppable. Converts never attain the height of the beast, but in all other ways the transformation is total. The possessed individuals will cry and moan and often chew off portions of their own lips and fingers as the monstrous hunger mounts. Involuntary possession by the Windigo, however, is more common.

Unkcegila

Long ago, before the Buffalo Nation had been brought to the earth's surface for humans to hunt, the Oglala of the Seven Council Fires wandered the northern plains in ignorance and poverty. In the world Above, gods and powerful spirits existed in supernatural splendor while spirits of evil lingered in the world Below. Both the Above and the Below ignored the hapless, primitive humans, only occasionally entering their lives—sometimes for good and sometimes for evil.

Only one man, Tanka-luta, understood the play of the Above and Below. He told his bandsmen that the truth had come to him in a dream. "The human beings are trapped between those of the Above and those of the Below. We have to make a choice. In my dream, the Old Man of the Above told me to offer sacrifice to the spirits of the Above, and they would aid the human beings in their struggles against the forces of the Below. The everlasting cold would be gone. The sun would shine. Food would be plentiful. We must all come to know that the spirits of the Below are evil."

Suddenly, Tanka-luta was sucked into a deep cavern miles underground. The huge vault glowed with phosphorescence emanating from fungi that grew thickly on the cavern walls.

A voice boomed and echoed, "Who are you to turn the humans against us? We of the Below are the root of all life. We receive the dead. We hold the waters. We anchor the trees and grass. For this we claim the right to prey upon the humans. Those Above are happy in their heights, in their light, tossing lightning, hail, and freezing rain at the humans. You have no right to turn the humans against us, to unbalance what the Creator has put into place. There is no room for you to take part in the play of the powers of the universe. You are less than vermin to the gods."

Tanka-luta cringed before the onslaught of *Unkcegila*, the Spirit of the Land. He raised his hands and cried out, "Tob-Tob, god of all, help me!"

With those words, Unkcegila took speech away from the feeble human. Tanka-luta's mouth moved and his thoughts struggled to find voice, but no sound came.

"You will be a stone forever. You will have no voice to spread your pitiful rebellion. You shall wait through eternity, stranded in the wilderness, a large boulder, until you offer me three humans as a sacrifice."

Tanka-luta shook his head in defiance. His mouth moved, though no sound came forth, and he thought, "You despicable spirit. You may do with me what you will, but I will never cause the death of fellow humans for your pleasure."

A thousand years passed. Tanka-luta existed all that time as a boulder in the Badlands. Perhaps it would not have been so terrible to be a rock, but Tanka-luta still had the thoughts and desires of a human. With time, madness came, and the ancient boulder had changed his mind. To escape the endless nothingness of his existence, he knew that he would sacrifice even his own mother to regain his life. But now that he was willing to kill to escape his curse, how could he ever expect three humans to come close enough to him so that he could make his sacrifice to Unkcegila. Several centuries earlier, a group of hunters had passed a half mile to the north, but regardless of how hard Tanka-luta tried to attract their attention, they passed right by him.

As he moaned to himself through the long, endless, lonely years, increasing snowfall in the mountains to the north formed a small stream a few hundred feet away from where he sat. In time, the stream became a river. Tanka-luta saw many humans paddle past in canoes, but none of them ever came close enough. By this time, he understood that the humans would have to come in contact with him before he could act against them. This was one of those realizations that simply come with time, a commodity that Tanka-luta had in abundance.

The river twisted and turned and finally formed a deep hole close by. Some Oglala boys, hunting along the river, found the swimming hole, and soon many humans came to the area. He couldn't understand them as they laughed and talked, the Oglala tongue of his time and theirs being different. Finally, one afternoon he looked down upon three teenagers—two male, one female—partying by the swimming hole, and watched as one pulled some strange, shiny, cylindrical objects from a strapped canvas bag.

"Hey, Chino, what kind of colors you got?"

"I got some good spray paint here, partner. Red, yellow, and black," Chino answered. "What about you?"

"Purple and silver," replied Jimmy Little Feather.

The boys shook the cans and approached the boulder. If Tanka-luta could move, he would have been shaking with excitement.

"What are you gonna paint?" Alice asked. She was Chino's girlfriend.

"I'm gonna write 'Oglala Rules,'" Jimmy said proudly.

"Me, I'm going to do a big rattlesnake . . . maybe put some wings on it . . . maybe put it on a motorcycle or something," Chino said with just as much pride.

In amazement, Tanka-luta watched the Oglala graffiti artists and Alice walk right up to him. His skin, the surface of the large rock, tingled in anticipation.

Jimmy Little Feather gave his can one more shake and sprayed a big red O. When the red paint—fittingly the color of life's blood—connected Jimmy and Tanka-luta, the boulder trembled, and joy raced through his hardened body.

"Holy . . . !" yelped Jimmy jumping backward. "Must be an earthquake!"

"Roll forward," Tanka-luta thought in his heavy boulder thoughts, willing himself to move.

The two boys dropped their paint cans, and the trio ran for the swimming hole as the boulder shook loose from its ancient base and rumbled toward them.

"You and Alice run to the left. I'll go right. I think we can make it . . . it should go between us," Chino yelled. But the boulder heard Chino's plan and split in two—one side rolled toward Jimmy and Alice; the other, toward Chino.

"Cut uphill," Jimmy yelled. They did, and so did both halves of Tanka-luta. First, he rolled over Alice, crushing the girl as she screamed. Tanka-luka felt no pity, only relief. Then, he smashed the two boys to paste.

With his mission complete, the two pieces rolled into the swimming hole and sank. A heartbeat later, Tanka-luta appeared treading water in the middle of the pool. With a look of stunned wonder on his face, he touched his body and splashed water with his hands while humming an old song from his long-ago childhood. He swam ashore with strong, sure strokes and climbed up on a rock to dry in the warm sun.

Soon, however, night came and the temperature dropped. Tanka-luta looked for fire-making material but could find none in the barren dry plain that surrounded him.

"Better keep walking to stay warm," he said aloud.

About the middle of the night, Tanka-luta's feet touched warmth, and he was so surprised he jumped back. Reaching out with his hand, he felt along the ground until he again touched the warm, smooth rock. The wide, flat path made of stone stretched to the horizon. Tanka-luta was exhausted from the unbelievable events of the past day and curled up in the middle of Route 13, grateful for the warmth radiating off the road.

His guardian spirit sent him a vision a short time after he fell asleep. Elements of the vision were revealed and he slowly awoke. A large gray dog was flying toward him, but it was not growling or baring its teeth. "It must be a spirit dog sent to guide me," he thought. At that instant, dazzling lights blinded Tanka-luta, and the bus from Indian Rock rounded the curve and smashed his body flat.

The Oglala are one of the seven subdivisions of those who speak Lakota, the Western Siouan dialect, the others being the Brule, Sihasapa, Minneconjou, Sans Arc, Hunkpapa, and Oohennonpa. In the mid-1700s, the Lakota emerged onto the northern Great Plains from their homeland at the headwaters of the Mississippi River to move closer to the horse trade that emanated from Santa Fe after the Pueblo Revolt of 1680. In time, they came to share a variety of cultural traits with the buffalo-hunting Indians of the High Plains.

The traditional Oglala believe that the universe is composed of a finite amount of energy; good and evil are thus two aspects of the same energy. The good aspects of energy are controlled by *Wakantanka;* the evil aspects, by *Wakan Sica.* Further, it is understood that Wakan Sica is subordinate to Wakantanka, and humans are subordinate to both. These energies can be visible or invisible. The invisible is to be feared. Individual religious life entails expanding the energy of Wakantanka in oneself through vision quests, prayer, dreams, and participation in religious ritual behavior, and attempting to defeat the effects of the Wakan Sica by empowering oneself with the good energy most potently manifested through Wakantanka. In such rituals, the use of the pipe and the burning of sage and sweet grass is common.

In the traditional Oglala pantheon of spirit beings exist dangerous ones such as *Unktehi*—Water Spirits; *Unkcegila*—Spirits of the Land; *Canoti*—Forest-Dwelling Spirits; and *Hohogica*—Spirits of the Lodge.

Win

FROM THE QUICHE OF MEXICO

"**Y**ou're fired!" shouted the sawmill owner to Luis Andrade when he stumbled into work late again.

"Hey, I was just . . ."

"No! I don't want to hear anything more from you. I gave you a chance, but you're just a lazy no-good loafer. You can't keep a job because . . ."

"Because of fools like you," interrupted the boy.

"Get the hell off my property, and don't show your face around here again."

"I got some pay coming," Luis argued.

"Not that I remember, kid," Señor Sommariba replied.

Luis's temper exploded, and he punched the old man in the face, knocking him down.

"Yeah, big shot. Big hero," Sommariba said, getting up. "Beating on an old man. The only thing you can do well is get into fights. Drink and fight. You lazy . . ."

Luis stalked out. He walked fast, kicking at loose stones, cursing under his breath. There had been a long line of stupid bosses. He had, in fact, about used up all the bosses in the town. This pig of a sawmill owner had been his last chance. But then, he stopped. It was something Sommariba had said. He was good at fighting. "Yes," he thought, "I am a good fighter." He had years of practice defending himself against his drunken stepfather. But how could his fighting skills help him? His village was too far from a town large enough for a recreation center program where he could perhaps find a trainer. There had to be some use for his fighting skills.

He was at his wits' end. He had no money and no job. Lost in brooding, he walked until he found himself by an old abandoned church, roof caved in, cemetery thick with weeds and overgrown hedges. It was called the Devil's Church by those who lived in the area because it had repeatedly burned down over the years. Finally, the villagers built their church on another location, and the fires stopped.

Luis leaned on the cemetery wall and stared into the dusk. Something pushed him from behind. He spun around, fists raised, to find an odd-looking man staring at him. Blood-shot eyes and starkly protruding canine teeth lent an animal-like look to the disheveled character. Some strange letters were tattooed at the base of his throat.

"Who are you?" Luis asked, stepping back.

"The answer to your problems, my son," came the reply.

Heat emanated from the man's body, and sulphur faintly tainted the air. "I don't know you," Luis countered. "How could you know anything about my problems?"

"Because I am your problem, lad," the man sneered in his face.

Luis pushed him. "Get back, you crazy, old . . ."

The man slapped Luis hard in the face, nearly knocking him off his feet.

"Come on, kid, I've got what you want if you can take it from me," he again provoked Luis.

The bosses who had humiliated him, his bullying stepfather, and his cruel stepbrothers all fused in the face of the stranger. His explosive attack surprised the man, who fell backward over a grave marker, and was momentarily stunned. Blind with anger, Luis ripped up a small tombstone bearing an engraved cross and raised it over his head. The man's eyes locked on the cross, and he mewed in fear. Sulphurous smoke steamed from his body. "You win, you win," he cried. "I give it to you. It is yours. Just let me go."

"What do you have to give me? I didn't ask for anything."

"I give you the powers of the Win."

Luis shuddered with delight. The powers of the *Win*—the transforming witch. "This is right," Luis thought. "I am now myself. Complete. I feel it in me now." He laughed hysterically. "Yes, I am the Win."

With a slight act of will, a little push of thought, he turned into a crow and lifted into the air above the cursed church ruin. He saw the stranger, a fiery red glow enveloping him, screaming and shaking his fist in rage. "I will find you, and we will fight again," he shrilled.

The Win crow flew to his stepfather's house where he found the hated old man passed out in the front yard. "This is too easy," Luis thought and changed into a large scorpion. As the drunkard mumbled and twitched in his restless sleep, the Win scorpion crawled up his pant leg and jabbed his stinger into the soft tissues of the groin. His stepfather awoke screaming. He leapt to his feet tearing at his trousers, but as the poison took effect, he lost control of his legs and fell. While the scorpion's poison coursed through the old man's body, Luis rematerialized in his human form.

"You," his stepfather moaned with this last breath.

"Let the punishment fit the crime," Luis said, and he turned away with satisfaction.

The next day was the sawmill owner's turn. Sommariba was preparing a log for the debarking machine when Luis magically appeared. He touched his former boss, and the man momentarily lost consciousness. When he came to, he was lashed to the log poised for the debarker.

"No! No! Please! Dear God! Don't," he wailed.

With a vengeful grin, Luis started the machine. Sommariba was shredded in a shower of blood and dumped out the other end looking like a bloody sausage. "Wonderful," Luis laughed. Next was Sommariba's wife, raped and killed by the Win as a giant boar. The mill owner's daughter, in turn, was eaten by a Win crocodile in her bedroom.

Luis burned the sawmill and scavenged all the metal he could find to sell to junk dealers. For the next three months, business owners in the village, all men for whom Luis had at one time worked, died horrible deaths. After each death, the deceased's business burned to the ground. Luis scavenged the remains and grew richer each time. Finally, he was the richest man in town, almost the only man in town. The others had packed up and left.

One day, a young priest rode into town on a mule. He had been sent by the local bishop to appraise the situation after the village priest had fled what he called the *Pueblo Diablo*, meaning the "Devil's Town," with a few surviving parishioners.

Luis decided that the priest would make a good meal and, as a jaguar, crept to his makeshift camp in the old town square. When the priest stepped out of his tent and saw the great cat, he knew that his only chance was to stay stock-still. He studied the jaguar that crouched, tail twitching, before him. The animal looked peculiar, even ugly. Its eyes were not balanced; one sat much lower than the other. Its nose was lumpy with running sores, and one of its ears was twisted and deformed.

The priest, having prepared for this event, removed a silver crucifix from his coat pocket, raised it before the cat, and chanted, "*Nema reve dna reve rof, yrolg eht dna . . .*" The jaguar flicked its tail nervously and kneaded the ground. " *. . . rewop eht, modgnik . . .*" the priest continued. The jaguar backed away, shaking its head to dislodge the searing pain that the priest's words caused. The priest raised his voice. "*Nevaeh ni si ti sa htrae no . . .*"

As the chant stripped the Win's powers, Luis rematerialized, groveling in the dirt. By the time the priest finished his strange prayer, Luis was dead.

The Quiche of Mexico value hard work and prudence in social behavior. They believe that one should never boast of one's accomplishments for fear of drawing the envy of others—a prime condition for becoming the target of evil magic. However, the Quiche also have the idea of the Win, a transforming witch—a being that is the polar opposite of the good Quiche citizen. The Win is considered the very image of loathsome evil.

Much of the religious life of the Quiche can be characterized as an ingenious mixture, or syncretism, of Roman Catholic and ancient Mexican Indian beliefs. They blend seamlessly into cults in which Catholic images of the saints are co-opted and mixed with those of the ancient gods. The demons of traditional Indian belief with shape-changing abilities become wed to Christian images of the devil.

A lazy, unethical man, frustrated by the strict economic morality of the Quiche and chafing under the restraints of peasant life, might select to risk his life to achieve the powers of the Win. The Quiche say that a man who sleeps in a cemetery for nine nights, praying to the devil the whole time, will on the ninth day be challenged to a fight to the death. If the devil wins, the challenger will be dead in seven days. But if the challenger wins, the devil will grant him the power of the Win. Wins may be killed in their animal forms, not with a gun or knife, but with the bare hands. The challenger must lay his hands around the neck of the creature before he can attack with his supernatural powers. Wins can be recognized as witches in their animal forms if the animal host acts peculiarly, is particularly ugly, or has unusually luminous eyes. The only way to defend yourself against the Win? The priest in the story knew: Chant "The Lord's Prayer". . . backwards.

Nia'gwai'he'gowa

FROM THE SENECA OF NEW YORK

Nangan ran along the stream bank. Next, he would cut up a steep slope that led to a ridge behind the village. He made this run every morning at the suggestion of his mother's brother, who encouraged him to build up his stamina and leg strength so that he could become a good warrior when he came of age. Though his family was poor, they were of the warrior class. The resulting opportunity to go to war meant that Nangan could build his family's wealth through the capturing of slaves and furs from his family's enemies, while at the same time weakening them. He ran, therefore, for himself, for his family, and for the good of the Seneca. He was proud—perhaps too proud—that his disciplined regimen had in time made him the fastest runner in his village.

That morning, as he pounded along the stream bank, a scrawny old man called to him from the shade of a hemlock. "Young man! Young man!" he man called out. "Stop and speak with me."

Nangan, taught his entire life to revere his elders, dutifully stopped. "What is it, Grandfather?" he asked.

"You run very well, boy. I've been watching you for a couple of weeks," replied the elder.

"Well, thank you. I have worked very hard to become this fast, and now I'm the best. Nobody can catch me," he said, puffing with pride.

"Want to bet on that?" asked the old man.

Nangan laughed. "What? Do you think there is somebody faster than I am, Grandfather?"

"Yes. In fact, I think I am," the elder said.

"You must be crazy. You look like you can barely stand up, let alone run a race," sneered Nangan, forgetting his manners.

"Again, young man, what would you bet?" the elder persisted.

"I am poor and have nothing to bet," Nangan replied, wishing that he did have something of worth to bet.

"Would you bet your life?" asked the old man.

Nangan laughed. "Bet my life? For what?

The old man said firmly, "If I win, your life is mine, and if you win, you will receive the powers of my life for one year."

"What do you mean?" Nangan asked, intrigued.

"Let me show you what you can win," answered the elder. The air shimmered around him, and before Nangan's eyes, the elder transformed himself into a tall warrior. Nangan looked up at him, guessing that he was nearly seven feet tall. He had never seen a larger or stronger warrior in his life. "Or what about this?" said the elder, and he transformed into a wizard with long white hair and eyes that glowed in his ancient face. "I know all things," said the wizard, "and I have powers to make all my wishes come true." Next, the wizard turned into a beautiful young woman and then into a panther and then into an owl.

Nangan's head spun. "Stop!" he cried. In his young life, he had never encountered such a being and didn't recognize the *Nia'gwai'he'gowa*—the Bear Monster—when he saw it.

The creature remanifested as the ancient elder. "Well, do we have a deal? You and I race, and if I win, your life is mine. If you win, you get one year's worth of my manifesting powers. You may make magic as a wizard or fly like an owl or stalk in the form of a panther."

Nangan thought for a few minutes. The old man's offer was very tempting, but he wanted to be smart about accepting it. "I agree," he said, "but only under these restrictions: You cannot race me in the form of a deer or wolf." These were the fastest animals that Nangan could think of. "And you cannot use your magical powers in any way to help you win the race."

"Agreed," said the old man. "We will meet here tomorrow morning and have our race." With that, the old man dissolved into the forest.

Nangan walked slowly back to the village. "I will talk with my father's father," he thought. "I have never dealt with magical beings before, and maybe he will be able to advise me."

Nangan's grandfather was well acquainted with his dilemma.

"Yes, I too agreed to race the Nia'gwai'he'gowa, not knowing at the time who he was. He made the same deal with me . . . my life if I lost and his manifesting powers if I won."

"Well, you're still here, so you must have beat him. Tell me how," Nangan urged.

"It was an accident," replied his grandfather. "Even though I was the swiftest runner in the village, and even though he ran as a decrepit old man, he still managed to pull in front of me. I saw my life being taken from me, but a short distance before the finish line, the old man stepped on a thorn with his right foot and fell down yowling in pain. I ran past him, winning the race."

"Did you win his manifesting powers, Grandfather?"

"I was warned by my grandfather not to take the old man's gift if I won, so I quickly declined his powers, and he disappeared. I never saw him again."

Nangan quietly digested his grandfather's story. He truly wanted the manifesting powers of the elder. By becoming people and animals with a variety of powers, he could raise himself and his family and bring glory to his household. "Grandfather, I have to do this," he said.

"If that is your decision, take this with you." So saying, his father's father removed a thong with a bear claw attached from around his neck. "This claw is from a bear that I killed as a young man. Keep it with you until the issue has been decided, but if you race and the old man manages to get by you, you must throw this amulet at his feet. It is your only chance because his one weakness is in the heel of his right foot."

Armed with this information and wearing his grandfather's bear claw, Nangan appeared the next morning for the race. The Bear Monster in the guise of the old man waited under the hemlock. "So glad to see you," he said.

"Likewise," replied Nangan coolly.

They quickly decided that the race would cover the course that Nangan ran every day. The old man hobbled over to the starting line next to Nangan. "When the next crow calls, the race will begin," suggested the elder. Nangan agreed. The two men stood motionless beside each other, waiting. The minutes went by. Songbirds flitted through the tree branches, and a blue jay squawked from atop a maple. Then came the call of a crow, and the racers were off.

Nangan left the old man behind within seconds, but soon footsteps approached. Glancing back, he saw the elder running backwards and quickly closing the gap.

"You can't use your powers," Nangan called out. "You promised."

"I agreed not to use my powers running forward in the manner of the deer or wolf. You said nothing about running backwards. You really must pay attention to what you agree to."

With these words the old man passed Nangan. Thinking quickly, Nangan tore the amulet from his neck and threw it under the elder's feet. The old man's right foot came down hard on the bear claw, and he tumbled to the ground, grabbing his foot and screeching in pain. Nangan ran past and crossed the finish line.

He sauntered back to the old man, who sat massaging his foot.

"What's the matter, old man? Did you step on something? You should have known better than to race with me. I'm younger than you, stronger than you . . ."

" . . . but not very bright," continued the elder.

"I'm bright enough to have won your manifesting powers, old man."

"Yes, you have won my powers. But no matter how strong or young or confident you are, if you are not smart, you will always come to ruin."

"I greatly appreciate your sage advice, old one," Nangan answered sarcastically, "but now I want what you promised."

"Oh, you shall have my powers, but again you missed something important when we decided the rules of our race."

"What is that, old man?"

"I said I would give you a year's worth of my manifesting powers, but you didn't ask when these powers would be yours—when they would start."

"Now, let them start now," said Nangan.

"All right," said the old man shaking his head, "You will receive a year's worth of my manifesting powers . . . now . . . and all at once."

Nangan opened his mouth to protest and heard a woman's voice come out. He had just looked down at a pair of breasts on his chest when he became an owl. As he flexed his wings, he became a wizard, then a puma, then a tree, and then a child. The manifestations came faster and faster until Nangan's true self was obliterated by the myriad of consciousnesses flowing through his awareness. In a few minutes, a year's worth of manifestations had been experienced by Nangan—or rather, experienced by the empty human shell that had once been Nangan. The Bear Monster licked his lips and led the empty boy into the forest.

In early times, the Seneca lived in villages with populations ranging from several hundred to several thousand, and pursued farming, hunting, trading, and warfare as major occupations. Their dwellings were called *long-houses*, buildings made of wood and sheets of bark. Today, most Seneca live south of Rochester, New York, while a smaller group can be found in

Oklahoma. In the 1990s, their combined population, including the Seneca-Cayuga, numbered about 10,000. They are members of the famous confederation of tribes known as the League of the Iroquois, along with the Cayuga, Onondaga, Mohawk, and Oneida. The Seneca are referred to by other members of the league as "Keepers of the Western Door."

A key concept in traditional Seneca religious belief is *orenda*—an invisible power that flows through all things and can be tapped through dreams and visions. In addition, the Seneca believe in various animal spirits, the Master of Life, and a variety of good and evil spirits. A core aspect of orenda belief is that a being with such power can transform itself into anything. Therefore, anything seen in nature may or may not be what it appears to be. Animals can manifest as humans and humans as animals. The traditional Seneca believe that everything is conscious and that all living things have souls. They believe in the power of dreams and the existence of monsters and wizards.

The *Fire Beast* is an ancient being that manifests as lightning or a shooting star. The appearance of such manifestations signals impending calamity. The *Whirlwind Spirit* controls powerful storms, while *Tawiskaro*, the second son of the daughter of *Sky Woman*, possesses a heart of ice and destroys by freezing. He created all vile serpents, animals, and insects; he is the one who comes as the winter. *Doonagaes*, the Horned Snake, monster-serpent of the deep pool, is a shape-shifter who seduces women and draws others to death by drowning. *Blue Lizard* lives in whirlpools and serves witches and wizards, while *Blue Otter* delights in poisoning springs and bringing sickness to the Seneca. The *Ghostly Legs* are demons composed of only a pair of legs with a head featuring glowing eyes located where the genitals on a normal man would be. *Big Breast*, a giant monster-woman, uses her breasts, which hang down like pillows, to suffocate her victims. The dried-up arm and hand known as *Oniata* flies around and kills by its touch. The most feared of the demonic beasts, however, is *Nia' gwai'he'gowa*, the Bear Monster. This demon delights in racing mortals and making them bet their lives on the outcome. Despite the numerous demonic beings—the above being merely a few examples—that stalk the traditional Seneca world, the Keepers of the Western Door survive today and, in fact, thrive.

Water Babies

FROM THE WASHO OF LAKE TAHOE

T he sign on the front door of the Stony Creek Curio Shop read GONE FISHING UNTIL FURTHER NOTICE—a fitting epitaph for Bink and Souther Fremont. After a few attempts, the two had managed to convince Jim Bucky, the previous owner of the curio shop, that it was time for him to sell out and leave town before "something terrible" happened to him. During these conversations, Bink would do his "crazy Vietnam veteran" routine, and Souther would toy with a loaded pistol. The founder of the Stony Creek Curio Shop agreed that it was time for a visit back East. And yes, Bink and Souther could sort of have the place until he returned. No papers were signed. It didn't matter. Jim Bucky was never coming back.

But today was a day for fishing, an enterprise dear to Bink and Souther's hearts. The men fished for meat, pure and simple. Using a forestry service map, they had located a medium-sized lake that had only recently been made accessible by a fire road.

"A lake that nobody fished before," exalted Bink. "We can't miss on this one."

The lake was magnificent, a fact lost to Bink and Souther as they tied large treble hooks to the light nylon rope. Souther sharpened the tips of each hook as well as the barbs, while Bink removed the kinks from the throw line. Soon the brothers moved apart on the bank to avoid snagging each other's lines as they spun their razor-sharp grappling hooks over their heads and tossed them far into the lake. They quickly hauled on the lines, hoping to snag a good-sized fish.

"Hey," yelled Souther, "I got something."

"How big, you reckon?" Bink dropped his grappling hook and ran to watch Souther land his fish.

A hard tug on Souther's line nearly yanked him into the lake. "Hey, help me out here," he yelled.

Together, the brothers fought the leviathan. Soon their combined strength won out, and the fight at the end of Souther's line lessened. They had won, but over what they didn't know. As they pulled in the dead weight, Souther said, "That don't feel like any fish I ever caught before." Bink agreed.

They saw the first outline of its body twenty feet from the bank. It was about two and a half to three feet long, a big fish for certain, but not one capable of putting up the fight that Bink and Souther had just experienced.

"My God," said Bink. "It's got hair."

Souther waded a few feet into the lake and picked the thing up. It looked like a human baby except that it was gray and clammy to the touch and seemed to be almost boneless. Its face looked human enough, but also fishlike, and its arms and legs were short and stubby. It had no fingernails or toenails.

"What in the hell?" blurted Bink.

"It's a freak of nature is what it is," said Souther. "Something got its genes messed up by those nuclear plants the government got hidden all over the place around here." He held the body up by its long hair and grinned. "I'm going to put this thing in a big old pickle jar full of alcohol and put it on the curio shelf at the shop."

"People will freak out and run from the place when they see that thing," Bink said, feeling sick to his stomach.

He was wrong. On the second day they displayed the thing, a curio dealer bought it for a hundred dollars. That night, Souther told Bink what they had to do: "The way I see it is that the best thing to do is use the old 'patoo.' Dynamite."

"What are you talking about?"

"The little freaks of nature. If there was one up there in that new opened lake, there must be more than one. That's the way it usually works. And what's the best way to get a bunch of fish . . . or whatever . . . quick? Use the old patoo."

Late that afternoon, they drove up to the lake with plans to do their work at dusk. Souther fixed three sticks of dynamite with waterproof fuses and tossed them one by one into the placid lake. The dynamite exploded six feet down as Souther had planned by the length of the fuses he cut. The surface of the lake buckled with a *whump*, and smoke and water blew into the sky. Soon, Bink and Souther saw the fruits of their effort. The freaks of nature floated to the surface—some dead, some stunned.

"There must be about fifteen of them little suckers," enthused Bink.

"Let's get them before they wake up and swim away," said Souther.

The brothers waded noisily into the lake and harvested their take into two burlap sacks. On their way back to their room behind the Stony Creek Curio Shop, they talked about how much money they would make from their freaks of nature.

"I figure we can get a couple thousand for this take," said Souther.

"And there's plenty more where they came from," laughed Bink.

Souther was right. The things sold quickly. Everything was running along fine until one afternoon when a Washo family pulled in to use the restroom and buy soft drinks. As the kids picked through the candy and the adults discussed how many drinks to buy, someone at the back of the store let out a piercing scream. An elderly woman in the group gestured to the freaks-of-nature display, shouting in her native language.

"What is she yelling about?" Bink asked the middle-aged man who was probably the old woman's son.

"She says you got the Water Babies in them jars. 'Very, very bad,' she says."

The Indians left their drinks on the counter and hurried out with the hysterical grandmother in tow.

"Well, what do you think of that?" Souther said smiling. "Now we know what we got." He slapped Bink on the back. "We got us some real Indian Water Babies. Quick, change the sign out front from 'Freaks of Nature' to 'Real Indian Water Babies.'"

A week later, their entire stock of dead Water Babies was sold to curio dealers, so Bink and Souther headed back to their secret lake for more. This time, however, when the dynamite exploded, only a few trout and a dozen or so chubs rose to the surface.

"What the hell," exclaimed Souther. "I know there's more here because I saw them last time."

They waded around, checking each fish to make sure they weren't overlooking a Water Baby.

Bink saw it first. "Hey, Souther. Real slow and easy . . . look to your left about a hundred feet up the bank."

Souther casually turned his head but snapped it back around. "It's one of them!" he shouted. "And it's alive!" He grabbed Bink by the arm. "Do you realize what we could get for one of them things alive?"

"How much?" asked Bink.

"I don't know . . . a lot." Souther ran toward the creature, who stood in the shallow water about three feet from the bank. He kept his eyes on it but he stumbled, and when he looked up, the creature was gone.

"Over here," Bink called out. "There's a bunch of them over here." He waded toward a group of the little creatures that seemed to be standing in shallow water, but he struck deep water quickly and had to swim. Dread gripped Souther. Bink wasn't a strong swimmer, and Souther could not swim at all. He noticed that the creatures were slowly drifting into deeper water, drawing Bink farther from the shore. "Oh, God! Bink! Get back here," he yelled.

"Souther . . . hurry . . . they're out here . . . come on, man." It was clear that he was tiring.

"Come back!" Souther shouted. "Get your ass back here!"

Bink couldn't hear him over the creatures' mournful mewing. In a blink, they dipped below the surface. Bink treaded water and tried to locate them.

"Souther, I can't see them anymore. Hey, what the . . ."

"Bink, what's the matter?"

"They're grabbing me. They're pulling me down. Souther, help me."

Souther froze with fear as his brother's screams quickly died.

He had failed to help his brother because he was afraid. His cowardice killed Bink. Souther wanted to die. Then he felt something soft and damp touch his hand. A Water Baby stood beside him, its hair floating in the air as if it were in deep water, its feet hovering several inches from the ground. Mewing in soft gentle tones, it led Souther into the lake.

The center of the Washo world is Lake Tahoe. Small groups live in the valleys east of the lake and in colonies in the California mountains to the west. Located in the western reaches of the Great Basin, this is one of the most inhospitable environments in native North America. In traditional times, the ancestors of the Washo possessed the cultural knowledge needed to collect seeds, nutritious roots, nuts, leaves, berries, and flowers. In addition, they made the most of the great number of gophers, antelopes, squirrels, jack rabbits, desert bighorn sheep, water fowl, pinion pine groves, and insects that lived in the Basin. To the east and west of Lake Tahoe are uplands and mountains where the Washo killed bear, mule deer, trout, and other lake and stream fish. However, because of their dependence on so many different food sources, they were forced to constantly move to coordinate their arrival with the peak production of their foods.

Washo traditional religion aimed to ensure the harvests of plant and animal products and to heal the afflicted. Certain favored individuals would experience doctor dreams in which a *wegaleyo*, or spirit, came to them and set them on the road of shamanism. Washo cosmology includes, in addition to the wegaleyo, a one-legged, one-eyed giant, the *Hanglwui-wui;* the *Ang,* a monstrous bird that carried off humans and terrorized the world in ancient times; mountain giants; and *Water Babies*—deadly water sprites. In his book *The Two Worlds of the Washo,* Professor James F. Downs writes of the Water Babies:

> All Washo today have heard the high mewing call of the Water Baby luring them toward some body of water at night. While many of the figures of Washo mythology have grown vague, their stories half forgotten and their place in Washo life reduced, the Water Baby has demonstrated an amazing vitality. Almost all the Washo are somewhat fearful of the consequences of the ignorance of white men in the matter of Water Babies.

In 1906, the Washo say that a white fisherman caught a Water Baby in Lake Tahoe and donated it to the San Francisco aquarium. The result of this atrocity, according to the Washo, was the great San Francisco earthquake. When the shock wave hit the aquarium, the large holding tanks tipped back and forth, causing the water to roll over the sides in waves. When the shaking of the earthquake had stopped, the Water Baby was gone.

2. Demons of South America

Kharisiri

R od Miller, a long-time Peace Corps volunteer and experienced hy-
draulic engineer, was assigned to the west-central highlands of Bolivia to assist in well-drilling operations in the area villages. He enjoyed
the people and the beautiful lakes and mountains of the high plateau. But,
because Rod was overweight, the high altitude posed significant problems
for him. His condition, however, was not a problem for Jorges Barron,
a wizened old Mestizo man who lived on the outskirts of the village of
Wirapampa. In fact, when he spied Rod waddling down the main street of
the small community, his mouth watered.

"All that fat. All that wonderful fat," Jorges muttered under his breath
as he wiped the saliva from his chin with a ragged handkerchief.

The old man lived in seclusion outside the town of Wirapampa because
the villagers suspected that he was a slaughterer, a blood-drinking fiend,
one they called a *Kharisiri*. They were right. In 1983 in Orinoca, a man accused of being a Kharisiri was hanged and his body dismembered and
burned. The people of Wirapampa, however, did not act against Jorges.
They feared the old man. Local lore held that he had lived over two hundred years and was impossible to kill. They were right again. But as long as
no one in Wirapampa died bearing the marks of an attack by a Kharisiri,
they were content to leave him alone on his lonely little farm. If he hunted
human prey in other places, the villagers considered that none of their business. The children of Wirapampa grew up learning to not go near Jorges
Barron, and the lesson was passed down from generation to generation.

No one in Wirapampa warned Rod Miller. He was a gringo, an out-
sider, and the villagers knew not only that he would disbelieve them but
also that revealing their belief in immortal vampire-monsters would make
them look like superstitious fools. They didn't really care what Rod might
think of them, but they did understand that he was a good source of rev-

enue: he bought food from their stores, rented a house, and used the local gas pump. Some of the old-timers watched him make his slow pace to the well site each day, his rolls of fat jiggling and his breathing labored. They knew that sooner or later, the temptation would prove too great for the Kharisiri. It was only a matter of time.

Late one afternoon, as Rod returned from the well-digging site, a stranger approached him. The sun was at the traveler's back, but Rod could still make out the form of a man wearing a monk's robe, which was cinched at the waist with a rope. A deep hood hid his face from view. As they drew abreast of each other, Rod bowed slightly and said, "Good evening, Father."

The stranger said nothing in return. His hands were crossed and hidden in his sleeves, and he carried an antique sword in a scabbard at his waist. Over his shoulder hung a pinkish-gray leather rope. Rod squinted as Jorges Barron pulled his hand from his deep sleeve and raised a tube fashioned from a human leg bone to his mouth. Rod's eyes widened as the figure blew a cloud of dried human remains in his plump face. His mind went blank as his massive body doubled over, and he hit the ground in an unconscious heap. Jorges knelt beside the fallen man. His lips curled back to reveal a set of needle-sharp teeth. He leaned over, sank his yellowed fangs into Rod's thigh, and sucked.

Rod awoke well after dark and struggled to stand. "Must be the altitude getting to me," he thought, figuring he had passed out. He had no memory of the meeting with the monk. Dusting himself off, he absent-mindedly scratched his thigh. He began to walk, but his hand returned to his thigh and he scratched again. The itch became so intense that Rod finally unbuckled his pants to take a look at the affected area. The light from a match revealed two small puncture wounds centered within an inflamed area about the size of his palm. "Damn Andean bugs," he muttered to himself as he set off toward Wirapampa.

The next morning as Rod dressed, he noticed that his clothing seemed looser. This pleased him. "Hmmm. All that walking back and forth to the site is paying off." He ate a hearty breakfast to reward himself and set off to work.

Jorges, having glutted on the gringo's fat, slept for three days. When he finally awakened, he was hungry again. That evening, as Rod walked back from the site, Jorges caught the fat man with a lasso of human flesh and dragged him into a thicket. The rope's inhuman powers held Rod immobile and unconscious as Jorges bent over his body and sucked at the rolls of fat on his back.

When Rod awoke, he found himself lying in a patch of brush. He credited his passing out to a rather severe case of vertigo caused by altitude sickness. As he returned to town, he scratched madly at the bug bites on his back.

The next morning, Rod punched another notch in his belt and rummaged in his suitcase for a tighter-fitting shirt. Although his weight loss pleased him, he was becoming increasingly concerned about his growing fatigue and the strange nightmares he'd been having. The symptoms of *soroche*, altitude sickness, seemed to explain what was happening to him.

Over the ensuing weeks, Rod's weight dropped so drastically that he had to have all his clothing altered by a seamstress. He had stopped being proud of his weight loss when he viewed in his mirror the droopy flaps of skin hanging from his limbs. He itched terribly from the growing number of inflamed bites all over his sickly body, and severe fatigue prohibited his working on the well-digging project outside of Wirapampa. His nightmares had become unbearable. He was afraid to go to sleep. Despite his efforts to remain awake, each night he dreamed that he was lying helplessly on the ground while the earth painfully sucked the life from his withering flesh.

Finally, the morning arrived when Rod could not lift himself out of his bed. He spent all day just lying there, moaning piteously. That evening, his next-door neighbor tapped at the door of his one-room house and gently pushed it open. Her dark eyes widened at the sight of the poor, decrepit gringo in the mussed-up bed. "Señor Miller," she said, "the priest you called from Chipaya has arrived."

"But I didn't call . . ."

The woman backed respectfully from the doorway, and a monk, his face hidden in the deep folds of his cowl, stepped into the room. When the nervous woman left, Jorges Barron removed a long knife from the folds of his robe and placed the tip against Rod's breast.

"Why?" he moaned.

"My son," Jorges murmured, applying pressure to the blade, "I bring you peace." Then he slid the knife into Rod's heart.

The villagers of the high Andes struggle to survive in a hostile natural environment. The altitude and cold make farming, as well as animal husbandry, difficult. Families must pull together, but because of the lack of resources, competition, jealousy, and violence often rend the fabric of village life. To further exacerbate the tensions, men must often leave their home villages for extended periods of time to seek employment in the cities of the lowlands.

As with people everywhere, the highlanders, in the face of adversity, turn to religion to seek solace and a sense of control. Christianity and ancient Incan beliefs often mix to form a unique religious life. The Incan creator god, *Viracocha,* is still foremost in the spiritual life of the villagers. The god's name can be translated as "Sea of Fat" or "Sea of Blood." Today, in rural areas of the Andes, all traditional religious ceremonies open with the slaughtering of an animal and the offering of its blood and fat to Viracocha.

A Kharisiri is described as a European or a *mestizo*—a person of mixed racial ancestry—who appears raggedly dressed, sometimes in the guise of a monk, and is often seen wearing a sword or a long knife and carrying a lariat made of human skin. He wanders the back roads, waiting at bends or bridges to attack lone travelers and suck the fat from their bodies. The word "Kharisiri" is derived from *kharina,* meaning "to cut something with a sharp instrument," and *lik'i,* meaning "tallow" or "animal fat." Among the rural peoples of the Andean plateau, it means "a slaughterer who specializes in extracting fat from the human body."

This concept has an ancient history. In 1571, the chronicler Cristobal de Molina wrote of the Indian belief that the Spanish had come to Peru in search of human fat. The Indians went into hiding, refusing to have contact with the Spanish. The power of the tale continues into modern times. In the 1950s, researchers working in the central region of Peru were told of the existence of blue-eyed gringos dressed in dark tunics, who carried long knives and blew powder into people's faces. And in 1980, the rumor spread that human fat was being exported to the United States to lubricate industrial machines, cars, airplanes, and computers. In September 1987, highland villagers said that the president of Peru had dispatched more than 5,000 slaughterers to collect human fat. These Kharisiri appeared as white men dressed in long green or black coats, armed with long knives, and carrying pistols and machine guns. The purpose of their diabolical fat-collecting forays . . . to pay off the national debt.

Kupe–dyeb

FROM THE APINAYE OF BRAZIL

Preto leaned against the wall at the station and carefully studied the gringos climbing off the rickety bus. An elderly couple did not interest him; they could provide nothing that he wanted. But the two young American men wearing expensive hiking boots and backpacks looked rather promising. He pulled his hat low and ran up to them.

"Hey, misters, let me carry your things. Very cheap. Very cheap," he said.

The two men gladly gave Preto the job. He was equally happy to heft their bags and discern through his touch what riches they might contain. His skilled fingers felt a camera case in one. As he guided the unsuspecting pair across the street to the little town of Bacaba's only hotel, he tried to guess where they kept their money.

"Let me check you in. You can wait in the cantina in the lobby," he said bowing deeply. "Get a cold beer. Relax and enjoy yourselves."

When Preto returned, he doffed his hat and asked, "Are you fine gentlemen here to hike and camp?" When they nodded, he added enthusiastically, "I am the most excellent guide around these parts, you know. I am Apinaye Indian. My family has lived here since the beginning of all time. I know every trail in these forests around here. I can take you to some good views, some pretty lakes. You'll like them very much. I promise."

Bill Stanton and Roger Marn were delighted with Preto. They had no idea how much practice this character had playing the dumb-but-charming Indian for naive tourists.

"Look, chief," Stanton said, "we aren't looking to bust our humps on some straight up-and-down mountain. We just want to do some light hiking, camping, sightseeing, take some pictures . . . like that. Nothing too heroic."

"Yeah, Bill and me aren't in the best of shape," added Marn before taking another swig of his beer.

"Oh, yes," said Preto, "I understand very much. I too have the sore muscles from time to time if I go too hard. But . . ." Preto pretended to ponder something, " I do know of an easy hike to the Serra dos Gavioes." Preto vaguely indicated the direction with a tilt of his head. "Just hills, but at the end of the hike is Bat Cave. Very few people have ever seen it. Only the old-time Indians around here know about it. It makes those North American caverns look like little holes that puppy dogs dig."

Stanton looked at Marn. "Well, should we go to the Bat Cave?"

"Let's do it," Marn replied.

"Most excellent," crowed Preto. "You two gentlemen get a good night's sleep, and I will be waiting out front for you tomorrow at dawn."

The next morning, Preto smiled as he expertly estimated the value of the men's brand-new hiking outfits. He knew the cost of all kinds of hiking and camping gear—everything from sunglasses to hiking boots to backpacks and sleeping bags. He didn't make a fortune at his work, but it was easy and paid enough to keep him happy.

The two men followed their guide along a well-worn path for the first two days, and as Preto had promised, the surrounding countryside was beautiful and the trail flat and open. Each night, Preto provided a wonderful campsite—one on the bank of a crystal stream, another on a little hill that offered a view of the distant Serra dos Gavioes.

"Tomorrow we will reach the last camp before Bat Cave," Preto informed his clients as he prepared them a light meal.

Late the next afternoon, Preto veered off the easy track onto a game trail. Bushes and thorn trees grew close to the meandering path, crowding the hikers as they pressed on.

"Hey, Pedro, this is getting way out of hand. When do we stop for the day?" Stanton asked, wiping beads of perspiration from his forehead with his bandanna.

"Oh, just a little bit more. Just a little bit, and we will be at our camp for the night," Preto promised.

Hours later, drenched in sweat with legs aching, Marn and Stanton cheered cynically when Preto finally announced, "We are here."

Marn looked around and sighed disgustedly. "This place looks like crap, Pedro. We're in the middle of a briar thicket."

"Yes," agreed Preto, "most unfortunate . . . but look up there." In the waning light, they saw a dark patch about halfway up the hill. "That is the mouth of Bat Cave."

With their destination in sight, Marn and Stanton stopped complaining and helped set up camp. They lingered around the campfire late into the night, enjoying the cool air and listening to the frogs and crickets, while bats flitted overheard.

The following morning, Preto hobbled over to them as they exited their tent. "You see, I have hurt my foot. But do not worry," he assured them, "I'll be okay in a day or two . . . it's just that I have a problem with this ankle every now and then. But you don't need me today. Go explore the cave up there while I rest. I can lead you gentlemen back to civilization in a day or two. No problem."

Marn and Stanton looked up to the mouth of the cave as they began to settle their packs on their shoulders. "It's only a few hundred yards up there," Preto told them. "If you leave your packs here, it'll make exploring the cave easier. If you need something, just come back here and get it. I'm not going anywhere with this foot hurting me the way it does, so I'll look after your equipment. Take a flashlight, a rope, and some water, and you'll be fine."

The hikers took their guide's advice and left the heavy packs behind. They were pleased to discover that the walk up to the cave proved as easy as Preto had promised.

"Man, feel that cool air blowing out of there," Marn said as they approached the cave mouth. It led into a wide gallery where multicolored stalactites dripped from the ceiling and glistening stalagmites rose from the floor.

"This is awesome!" exclaimed Stanton, his voice echoing into the darkness. He entered the second gallery with Marn close behind.

In the third cavern, the beams of their flashlights found a pool of water so clear that it was almost invisible. As Marn stooped to take a drink, he saw the reflection of the gallery ceiling in the sparkling pool. Water sputtered from his mouth. "My God, would you look at that," he whispered.

Stanton and Marn's eyes moved slowly and warily upward. The reflection in the pool was no illusion. Human bodies dangled from the ceiling by their legs—dozens of them in various stages of decay. Some of the fresher ones had deep gashes covering what was left of their lifeless bodies. Neither man spoke a word. Then, a rush of cool air on the backs of their necks drew their attention behind them. There, next to the pool, stood two large bats—bats the size of tall, bulky men.

"Holy shit," Stanton whispered, and one of the bats made a slight movement.

Within seconds, the hikers were on their feet. Marn broke for the cave mouth with Stanton close behind. The bats quickly swooped after them and easily lifted each into the air with sharp talons. The terrified men struggled to free themselves, but to no avail. They screamed for mercy, for God, for Pedro, and then found themselves in the glaring sun outside Bat Cave, dangling helplessly.

Preto had been waiting and watching. When the bats appeared with the frantic, screaming men in their grip, he raised his hands in salute to his kinsmen and set about rifling through Stanton's and Marn's belongings for items to sell at the Boa Vista market. He knew what would come next and thought nothing of it. He didn't have to watch to know that the bats would drop the men from several hundred feet above the rocks.

When Stanton hit the jagged rocks, he died instantly, but Marn, though many of his bones were broken, held on to life—but not for long. The bats lifted the men once again, rose into the air, and dropped them as before. Thoroughly dead, and now tenderized, Marn and Stanton were hung in the larder of the *Kupe-dyeb*—the bat-people.

Preto lived off the money he made from their belongings for about a month. Although Stanton's and Marn's families contacted the local police, nothing ever came of it. The police told the grieving relatives that there was no evidence of their ever having arrived in Bacaba. Preto was glad to have such cooperative kinsmen.

He was back at the bus station in Bacaba in time to watch a group of little boys in Scout uniforms disembark from the rickety bus with their scoutmaster. Smiling, Preto scanned the piles of equipment stacked beside the bus and ran up to the scoutmaster. "Hey, mister, let me carry your things. Very cheap. Very cheap."

The Apinaye live in the Amazon Rainforest, a world that abounds with rushing streams, verdant hills, and gallery forests. They live by small game hunting—mainly monkeys and tapirs—and by gardening, fishing, and gathering. Their villages are always built on high ground above streams and rivers to enable the Indians to have access to water and to be located strategically because of the ever-present danger of river-borne attack from their enemies.

Since the first outside contact was made with the Apinaye in the mid-seventeenth century, their population has been greatly reduced. Still, as late as the early twentieth century, they maintained their traditional tribal rituals. Warfare is mentioned in the earliest tales of Apinaye origin. These stories describe how the *Kupe-dyeb*, the bat-people—who are believed to have occupied the region in primordial times—united the four Apinaye villages for war against a hostile neighbor. The bat-people did this not out of love for the Apinaye, but because they wished for a war that would provide corpses to feed upon. If the Apinaye do not fight, the Kupe-dyeb will hunt them. This belief served to stimulate the warlike tendencies of the Apinaye. Better to kill others for the Kupe-dyeb than to have them hunt the Apinaye.

The Apinaye believe that all living things have a soul, which they call *me-galo*. The souls of the deceased, especially those of executed sorcerers, are potentially dangerous to the living. After living out their span of years as ghosts, these souls will die of pain on their right side and transform into stumps, animals, or termite mounds.

A crucial concern for the Apinaye is soul loss. Small children with undeveloped souls are particularly vulnerable. If an evil spirit steals the soul of a child, he or she will waste away and die. Souls can also be taken by evil shamans who enchant food, the soul of which acts on the victims from the inside. Enchanted wildcat meat cramps the hands or stomach, enchanted turtle meat slows down the victim, and enchanted deer meat speeds him or her up. Also, the Apinaye believe that a powerful evil shaman can bewitch an entire village by burying magically enchanted pieces of armadillo armor in the area.

Bat Mountain is in the Sierra of São Vicente, a vast range of dark, demon-haunted peaks and hidden valleys. The Apinaye say that the Kupe-dyeb live there today. You will know when you have found their lair by two features. The entrance to their cave is at the foot of a mountain, and above it is an aperture, a kind of large window that looks into the front galleries of the cave system. No Apinaye who has sought the lair of the Kupe-dyeb has ever returned.

Wamu

FROM THE BANIWA OF BRAZIL

Before suffering a paralyzing stroke, Benito Niwa had been headman of a Baniwa village located in Brazil close to the Venezuelan border. He had been a vigorous traditionalist, resisting the corrosive incursion of European culture and religion as best he could. Though several Christian sects had sought a foothold in his village, Benito made it very clear that they were unwelcome. He cooperated only as far as Brazilian law required, but no more. Usually, after months of no response from the people, the foreigners would leave. Within a year, though, another energetic group would appear to try their luck at converting the Baniwa. The missionaries all discovered quickly that Benito led the resistance to their efforts. It was his charisma and his knowledge of traditional ways that guided his people in their interactions with the intruders.

Reverend James Quinn of the All Tribes Missionary Institute was fighting for the souls of the Baniwa, and coming up on the losing end against Benito's persuasive eloquence, when a paralyzing stroke cut the headman down. Benito had been officiating at a ritual designed to placate the jungle spirits when he suddenly collapsed like a rag doll. The distressed cries of the crowd brought Quinn to the scene.

As Benito lay on the ground with only his eyes moving, the minister seized the opportunity to harangue the gathering. "You see for yourself the price that is paid for pagan idolatry. Where are his so-called spirit helpers now? God has struck him down as a sign unto you all. Continue to follow the ways of your witch doctors, and you too will end up groveling in the mud like this heathen."

Benito's hearing was unimpaired, and though he could not move, he seethed in rage at Quinn's words. His people murmured angry words against the missionary as they lovingly carried their fallen leader home. Soon word spread that the missionary had used witchcraft against the beloved Benito. When Quinn heard the rumor, he quickly had Benito air-lifted to a hospital in Rio Pilar run by the All Tribes Missionary Institute. Benito was placed in a bleak little room on the second floor. Reverend Quinn visited after the nurses had settled him in.

"We are going to spend a lot of time together," said Quinn. "God has given us this opportunity to do His will. God loves His children and wants all to love Him. I will talk to you of these things in the weeks ahead. You will learn that the religion of your parents is nothing but superstition and wicked rituals."

Benito thought of his mother and father, long since deceased, and a lump formed in his throat. He had loved them, and he knew they had loved him. They had taught him about the spirits of water, land, and sky. They had shown him that the world is alive, and that everything is part of the same great power.

" . . . and you will atone for your sins as God has intended, with your silenced body and voice. . . ." the reverend continued.

At that moment, in the dying light of day, Benito saw the *Wamu*, the Black Sloth, hanging upside down from a power cable on the far side of the hospital courtyard. A chill shot through him. The Wamu was known as the "Owner of Poisons" by the Baniwa, who believed that all the illnesses of the world resided in the Wamu's body. Wamu was death itself, and it was looking into Benito's room.

As the reverend droned on, Benito strained to communicate with his eyes. He stared first at Quinn and then out the window toward the Wamu. The reverend was too enraptured by his own lecture to notice Benito's frantic signaling. Soon, total darkness engulfed the courtyard.

Benito struggled to stay awake through the night. He could do noth-ing against the Wamu, but he certainly did not want to be attacked in his sleep. By the next morning, the Wamu had crawled along the power cable to within twenty feet of his room. It hung upside down in the dawn light, its tongue lolling, while thick, discolored saliva dripped from the corner of its gaping mouth. Benito could hear the mucusy drops splattering on the pavement in the courtyard below. The Wamu's eyes were viscous, and its hair hung filthy and matted.

Reverend Quinn entered Benito's room, fresh from his morning wor-ship service, and took the chair next to the bed. With the courtyard win-dow and the Wamu at his back, Quinn opened his Bible.

"Today we will consider the sacred word of God concerning your people's heathenish beliefs. You have fought the enlightened view of the church, and now you lay next to death, the fate of your soul in my hands."

The Wamu moved, ever so slowly. The reverend's words would pull Benito's attention away, and then a slight movement in his peripheral vision would turn his eyes back to the Wamu. It was drawing closer in its deathly slow pace. Reverend Quinn became more and more excited as he struggled with the word of God, his sword to slay the demons that controlled the heathen Indian who had been delivered into his hands.

Sweat poured from Benito, the Wamu crawled closer, and Reverend Quinn ranted. Benito could smell it now. The stench of rotten meat filled the room, but Quinn did not seem to notice, so enraptured was he with his preaching. The Wamu reached the window, staring with murderous intent into the room. Benito felt death near to him. He braced himself as the Wamu, in its maddeningly slow way, climbed through the window. Benito clamped his eyes shut and called on his mother's and father's spirits to meet him in the afterlife as he waited for his end.

A scream brought several of the staff into Benito's room. "Where is Reverend Quinn," one asked. "He was just in here a moment ago."

An orderly looked out the window. "Sweet Jesus! Look at this!"

Reverend Quinn, his throat ripped out, his frock in tatters, hung draped across the power cable over the center of the courtyard. Benito suddenly discovered that he could smile again.

The Arawak-speaking Baniwa people live in Brazil near the borders of Venezuela and Columbia. They number approximately 4,000 and occupy some ninety-three villages along the Icana River. Their subsistence centers on horticulture and fishing. They augment their diet by hunting small game in the forests with bow and arrow, and blowgun, and carry on a lively trade with neighbors. Like most of the tribes of their area, they define men first as warriors and second as farmers and hunters.

A central focus of Baniwa religious belief is *Kuwai*, child of the first woman. Kuwai's body was originally composed of all the elements of the world, and it is believed that the Kuwai's singing brought animals into existence. Kuwai was killed by *Iaperikuli*, the creator of the world, when the former was pushed into a fire and incinerated. From his ashes, poisonous plants and the sickness-giving spirit were created. The shamans call this spirit *idzamikaite iminali*, which means "owner of sicknesses," and say that its body comprises all the illnesses in the world. It is also known as *Wamundana*, a word constructed from *wamu*, meaning "black sloth," and *dana*, which suggests an invisible dark interior or shadow. The holy men of the Baniwa say that the Wamu is the owner of poisons and the shadow soul.

The Baniwa seek to protect themselves from their demons by performing ancient chants. During perilous times such as childbirth, demons and evildoers interfere, bringing about the need for many protective chants. For example, the Baniwa direct a chant called *Eenunai* toward friendly animal spirits that will attack evil animal spirits known to tie knots inside a woman who is giving birth, which cause her "biting" pain. The chant *Iraidalimi iakuna* is used against witches who attack pregnant women and cause internal bleeding and spontaneous abortions. The *Madzeekata keramu* is aimed at plant spirits that cause breech birth. However, even if one escapes death at birth through the power of primordial protective chants and navigates life successfully, always at the end awaits the Wamu, against which nothing can prevail.

Maereboe

FROM THE BORORO OF BRAZIL

Old Miguel was respected in his village. He was a Bari, a Bororo shaman who specialized in communicating with the *Bope*, spirits of death and decay. Some of the Bope were bringers of rain and thunder; others were masters of heat and cold. Old Miguel's job was to prevent the Bope from harming his people. He successfully battled them most of his career, and the people of his community, recognizing this, awarded him great honor. He walked in dignity among them and lived a peaceful life; that is, until the outsiders from Rio de Janeiro arrived one afternoon. They came—a man, his wife, and their three sons—in a fancy van piled with expensive luggage.

"City people," Miguel noted as he watched them step from the vehicle. The man and woman were dressed in fine clothes, and their gold jewelry flashed in the sun. The boys looked around at the village, and one said, not caring who heard him, "Yuck! What a crappy place!"

The woman complained, "Donny, why the hell did you bring us to this Godforsaken hole? I can't live here. These people are just Indians for goodness sake."

Her husband replied sharply, "Then go the hell back to Rio and see how long you last." More evenly, he added, "Look, Raquel, my grandmother is from this village, and I have some relatives around here."

"You never told me you were part Indian, Donny," Raquel whined.

"I wonder why?" he replied snidely.

In the days that followed, the old women of the village, all masters of information, pieced together the story. Donny had tangled with the head of a drug cartel in Rio de Janeiro and had to run for his life. Finding the airports and docks watched by his enemy's minions, he fled deep into the Amazon jungle to his family's ancestral home. Nobody knew his secret, not even his wife, until the day the family arrived in the Bororo village.

It was soon clear that the city people did not fit into the Bororo community. They were loud, pushy, and aggressive by village standards. Donny was soon ordering the local men around, and Raquel constantly complained about the "dirty, smelly Indians."

The three boys focused on Miguel, "the crazy old man," as a target for their harassment. They threw stones at him on the path to his thatched hut, which sat a hundred yards into the jungle. They released his chickens, and before he could catch them, half were eaten by the hungry dogs that roamed the periphery of the village. Then, they knocked down his garden fence. No one could help Miguel—the villagers feared Donny because he carried a gun.

When Miguel talked to the city people about the trouble their sons were causing, Donny ordered him to stay away from the boys. Miguel decided he would do exactly that. But one day when he had gone fishing, the boys broke into his house and killed his parrot, Mingo, his only companion. The distinct tracks in the sand from their expensive athletic shoes had given them away. Shortly after that, Donny raped a village girl and dared the villagers to do anything about it.

Late one night, a few of the old men sought Miguel's help as a Bari. After the boys killed his beloved parrot, Miguel was more than ready for revenge. He felt he had been provoked sufficiently to take the dangerous step of calling upon the *Maereboe*—the most evil of the Bope, one he had once known very well.

The following night, after the moon had risen high above the jungle, Miguel paddled his canoe to a bluff that overhung the little river that skirted the village. High above on a ledge sat a nest of vultures. Their droppings caked the mouth of a jagged crevice in the cliff wall.

Miguel beached his canoe at the base of the bluff. He set down a dozen or so hand-rolled cigarettes—the Bope's favored offering. Then, he chanted the primordial words that his teacher, his deceased father, had bequeathed to him. Miguel didn't even know the meaning of the words, but his father had assured him that the meaning was irrelevant—the correct sounds were the important thing. Within minutes, high-pitched voices pierced the darkness from all sides.

"They are yours," Miguel spoke into the night, indicating the cigarettes. "Come closer and take my offerings. I ask a favor."

A dozen small humanlike creatures appeared. They stood about a yard tall and had glassy-black skin. Their feet were cloven, their eyes jets of flame. Matted black hair grew in patches on their bodies. Hair even grew from their glowing eyes. Though Miguel had seen them often, he still grew tense as they came near to take the cigarettes, all the while uttering nervous, chittering sounds.

"I ask a favor of my friends," he said again, and pointed to the crevice above. "Bring the Maereboe, my father." At the sound of the terrible name, the Bope shrieked and hopped about in confusion. "Bring forth the Maereboe," Miguel ordered, his voice rising. "Bring it forth now!"

The Bope, now under the shaman's control because of their acceptance of the ritual gifts, pointed to the crevice where the Maereboe lay trapped beneath the vulture droppings and commenced a keening wail. The ground trembled and rocks and debris fell from the bluff face. Suddenly, the Maereboe burst forth.

"Greetings, Miguel," the Maereboe said.

"Greetings, Father," responded the Bari, suppressing a shudder as he gazed upon the hairy, leprous, oozing monstrosity that had sired him.

The Maereboe embodied the total evil of which a Bari was capable. In this case, it was Miguel's father. When alive, he used the power of the Bope to rape all the woman in a village in the same night and to slaughter their children before the sun rose. He left the men alive after castrating them, so he could enjoy their torment, grief, and anguish. Before he was captured by a group of Bari and penned beneath the vultures to die, he had emptied entire provinces of Bororo territory by his diabolical raids on peaceful villages.

"I know what you wish of me, my son," the evil spirit said. "Come with me, and I will show you my power."

Miguel and his father transformed into nighthawks and rose into the air. They flew to the house where the city family slept and returned to their original forms. Standing in the darkened front room of the sleeping house, Miguel's father instructed him to gather the husband's van keys, the wife's wedding ring, and the small suitcase filled with the boys' video games.

"Look, my son." The Maereboe pointed to the sleeping faces of the man and woman, which were twisted in anger and fear. In the other room, the boys whimpered in their sleep. "They know that we are here and what is happening to them. I have put that reality into the shape of their dreams."

"They experience us as nightmares," Miguel commented.

"Yes. But come. Now we will draw forth their souls."

Miguel and his father resumed the form of nighthawks and launched into the night sky, carrying the items the Maereboe had selected.

"Their souls will follow, my son. They are attached to these things we carry, and they will leave their bodies to retrieve what they so love."

The souls of the city family rose from their sleeping bodies and tracked the Maereboe and his son into the sky. The Maereboe put the keys, wedding ring, and video games into a wicker basket that Miguel had provided and chanted to the wandering souls: "Here are your beloved possessions. Come, take them."

The five souls entered the basket. As soon as the last was in, the Maereboe shut the lid. He spat fire, igniting the basket, and threw it to the earth. It fell like a shooting star, and only the Bari heard the screaming of the trapped souls. The flaming basket exploded when it hit the ground, and the Maereboe dove after it.

The wicked creature swallowed the souls of Donny and Raquel with relish, but when he turned toward those of the three boys, Miguel spoke, "Father, if you let me have the children's souls, I will not call on the vulture guardians to return you to your filthy prison beneath their roost. In fact, I will tell you where you can find a hunting territory beyond your dreams."

The Maereboe trembled, fighting his great urge to consume the children's souls, and said, "The children are yours, my son. Now, where do you send me to hunt?"

"The village is called Rio de Janeiro, and it lies to the south and east at the mouth of the great river," Miguel told him, not caring what would become of the people there.

The Maereboe howled joyfully and leapt into the sky. Miguel knew that it wasn't the last time he'd see his father. Then, he looked down at the charred souls of the three obnoxious boys, and he chuckled to himself.

The next morning, the maid found the city folk all mysteriously dead. Asking no questions, the villagers buried them quickly. That night they had a celebration. Everyone agreed that the feast was excellent, the best part being the delicious gift from old Miguel . . . three little suckling pigs.

The Bororo live in the highlands of Central Brazil, where they were first contacted by Portuguese explorers in the eighteenth century. They became known for their large circular or horseshoe-shaped villages located on the open savannah, for their physical prowess as hunters and fighters, and for the complexity and subtlety of their philosophical and cosmological thought.

The orderly life led by the Bororo most likely stems from their attempts to balance the *aroe*, characterized by elaborate codes of behavior that regulate human life, with the antithetical principle found in the belief in the Bope. The aroe represents the cultural side of life, while the Bope represents the natural. The Bope cause all things to reproduce and die. They are the principle of organic transformation and can manifest in natural phenomena such as rain, thunder, heat and cold, and light and dark. Although they can assume any shape they wish, moving from one form to another with dizzying speed, they most typically appear as humanlike creatures about three feet tall with red eyes, jet black skin, cloven feet, and long black hair covering their bodies or hanging in scabrous patches, even emanating from their eyeballs. Their hideous visage usually results in immediate death to those who contact them. The Bari, however, specialize in dealing with the Bope, who often appear to these shamans in the form of owls, finches, or hawks. When a Bari calls upon them for assistance in killing or healing, the Bope appear in their humanlike form and demand cigarettes.

The Bope can give the Bari the power to shape-shift, or they take on various animal shapes themselves and kill in these forms. Most dangerous of all the Bope are the *Maereboe*—souls of deceased evil Bari who became powerful Bope at death. The Maereboe attack individuals, families, or entire villages. They steal items that are dear to their victims so that the victims' souls will leave their sleeping bodies to search for their prized possessions. When a Maereboe captures a searching soul, it rises into the air and throws the soul to the earth in flames, after which the creature descends upon the cooked soul and feeds. The Maereboe have been known to steal the souls of young girls and copulate with them before eating them. They also delight in stealing children and turning them into animals. One experiences the Maereboe's attack as a nightmare from which he or she will never wake.

Yacuruna

FROM THE IQUITOS OF THE PERUVIAN AMAZON

Juan waded knee-deep along the muddy riverbank with his fishing spear on his shoulder and watched for the familiar swell of bottom-feeding fish swimming in the shallow water. He had hiked five miles to find an isolated area that had not been over-fished, but as he moved quietly through the water grass, he heard laughter upstream—girls' laughter. Smiling, he stepped ashore and set his spear against a tree. He pictured village girls bathing naked in the river and stealthily navigated the tangle of trees and brush that choked the bank.

Juan couldn't help himself. From the time he had been a small child, he had spied on his neighbors. He'd watched from his perch high in a tree as adulterers crept into the shadows. He'd lain silently next to the thatched walls of huts as husbands and wives made love. Juan got off on the fact that they did not know he was watching.

Then . . . there, through the trees, he saw them. Five beautiful young women swam off a small sandy beach. Their teeth shown like pearls against their smooth golden skin. Shining ebony hair flowed over their soft shoulders and ample breasts. Though he crouched in deep brush fifty feet from them, the five strangers looked as one, directly at his hiding place.

"Come into the river and swim with us," they sang out in a dialect that he understood but could not quite place.

Juan did not have to be asked twice. Throwing off his shirt and sandals, he sprang from his hiding place and splashed into the river. He waded toward the laughing girls. They swam around him in an ever-tightening circle, and Juan became dizzy following their movement. One of them broke from the circle and rammed him. Surprised, he stumbled backward in the waist-deep water, and when he put his hand out for support, he touched a . . . fin!

The girls thrashed around him, ramming him harder and harder. The roiling muddy water hid him, but their bodies seemed to be growing darker. Then one breached, jumping six feet into the air, and Juan realized that he was being attacked by the enchanted dolphin legions of *Yacuruna*, the dreaded river monster.

He screamed and fought, but the dolphins pushed him into deeper water where they entangled his arms and legs with long water grass. Bound hand and foot and drained from the struggle, he accepted the inevitable.

The dolphins dove with their prisoner through the gates of a bizarre city that rested upside down on the river bottom. Representatives of a thousand species of fish swam in a great circle, creating a gentle protective whirlpool over the city. Juan, breathing by the powers of the minions of Yacuruna, was ushered into the river monster's presence. The hideous creature looked like a giant frog with jagged teeth. Its legs and arms resembled human limbs, but were covered in the sleek green skin of a frog. The creature sat on the back of a huge snapping turtle who glared menacingly at Juan. Dozens of giant catfish with foot-long spiked whiskers huddled protectively around the living throne of the Yacuruna.

A long, slimy tongue snaked out of the creature's mouth and reached for Juan. When the boy screamed, the tongue slid between his lips and down his throat. It found his heart and squeezed. The monster's mind touched his own and Juan heard the words: "You are a pathetic little man. You live by watching. You are nothing but a sucking leech. No one will miss you when you don't return to your village this evening."

Juan knew that the words the monster spoke were true and fell to his knees. "Please don't kill me. I won't watch anymore. Please let me live! Please!"

Yacuruna shifted his weight slightly. "Oh, I will let you live, but your life is mine and from this day forward you will watch only what I want you to watch, and when not engaged in my business, you will be blind."

Suddenly, Juan felt as if he were floating, then swimming. Dozens of dolphins swam beside him. He gave a strong thrust with his wide tail and threw his body into the air, breaching in an explosion of spray in the bright sun. "I am alive," he exalted. Then all grew dark.

The Iquitos combine trade, farming, fishing, and hunting and gathering to make a living in Highland Peru. Although Christian missionaries have plied them with instruction for centuries, the villagers maintain many of their old beliefs. They believe that they live in a world populated by evil humans and the angry and spiteful spirits of the rivers and jungles.

Yacumama, the mother spirit of the river, attacks menstruating women who attempt to cross. Dolphins are sent to capsize an errant woman's canoe, and fish with their dagger-sharp teeth are directed to enter her vagina and cause hemorrhaging. Mother spirits of the forest will attack "unclean" women who walk through the forest by striking them with sudden pain, muscle aches, accident, or death. The *Tunchis*, spirits of the recently dead, carry a variety of illnesses and cause children to sicken and die. The forest is also home to the *Chullachaqui*, a Quechua word for "unequal feet," a creature with one spindly leg and one oversized leg who appears to a lone traveler as a friend or parent claiming to be en route to visit a loved one and invites the traveler to follow. If the traveler follows, he is doomed.

One of the most widespread beliefs in the Peruvian Highlands features the guardian spirit of the river, *Yacuruna*. His unusual form is that of a manlike amphibian, often a giant toad. Yacuruna can uproot trees with his bare hands; create inescapable whirlpools; and, when greatly angered, ascend into the sky to generate horrendous storms. His magnificent city rests inverted on the bottom of the deepest whirlpool.

Kwifi Oto

FROM THE KALAPALO OF CENTRAL BRAZIL

The *Kwifi Oto*, the Master of Darts, was running in the body of *Iso-goko*, the jungle wolf. The Master thrilled to the wolf's physical strength, and with its acute sight, smell, and hearing, he gleaned more information from the jungle night than he could in his human form.

A low growl bubbled in the wolf's throat when he came upon a newly cut roadbed. He caught the scent of strange-smelling humans. Then, up ahead in an area cleared of brush, he saw a group of them leaning against a mud-splattered bulldozer before a small campfire. They laughed and passed a bottle back and forth. One of the humans had finished cleaning his pistol and was putting the rags away.

Mike Johnson was the only gringo on the Trans-Amazon Highway road crew, the rest being Brazilian nationals. He had been bumming through South America, taking any odd jobs that allowed him to reach his next uncertain destination. Johnson carried his pistol everywhere for protection and occasional hunting forays.

"Hey, John Wayne," one of the workers said, "who you going to shoot with that thing?"

"More like *what* am I going to shoot," Johnson answered.

Old Carlos shook his head. "You are not in your home country now, gringo, where you can shoot at anything you want. In these forests there are things that you never saw before. Things that are unspeakable . . ."

"Oh, come on, old man," laughed a younger member of the crew. "Those old fairy tales don't scare grown men."

"Maybe you are not a real grown man until you know enough to be afraid at night in the jungle," replied Carlos with a snort.

The moon was high in the night sky when the men bid one another good night and headed to their tents, all except the gringo, who chose to stay up a bit longer. The Master of Darts, lying in the body of the jungle wolf, watched him with interest. He had seen and smelled the non-Indian humans before, but he had never encountered one like the man called John Wayne. His curiosity drew him closer to the lone man by the smoldering fire.

When the nearby insects and frogs grew deathly quiet, Johnson slipped the safety off his pistol and slowly pointed it toward the patch of stillness.

"Probably some local Indians looking for stuff to carry off," he thought to himself. "Maybe I should give them a little scare."

The Master of Darts, perhaps because he had neither seen a gringo nor understood his nature, was unprepared when the man suddenly ran toward his hiding place, waving his pistol and shouting, "Get out of here, you bums! Beat it! *Fuera carajo!*"

Johnson was almost on top of the jungle wolf when it rose from the thick brush. "Damn," he whispered, bringing his gun to bear on the wolf. The first shot creased the animal's skull, and the second buried deep in its left flank.

With gunshots splitting the otherwise silent night, the crewmen ran from their tents, and the mortally injured wolf crawled painfully into the jungle.

"What the hell is going on? What are you shooting at?"

"It's a wolf . . . or something like a wolf," Johnson stammered, still trembling.

Old Carlos crossed himself and whispered, "Mother of God."

Meanwhile, the Kwifi Oto was losing blood rapidly and used its waning powers to reach its village many miles away. Under the cover of darkness, it crawled to its son's house and pawed at the door. The boy had been trained from childhood in the arts of the witch of the Kalapalo. He had learned to manufacture the *kwifi,* supernaturally empowered darts, and to shoot them into his victims. He was on the verge of becoming Kwifi Oto like his father.

The witch's son cradled the wolf's head and bent low to hear his father's last words. They came out strained and blurred as the old man spoke through the muzzle of the wolf. "I want the strange one killed," the witch wolf moaned. "You must avenge me to become a real Kwifi Oto. My dying breath will give you the power to run as the night wolf. Call on the Itseke to help you."

"It will be as you wish, Father," the boy said sadly.

The wolf breathed its last breath and slowly transformed into a withered old man.

Before the moon set, the Master's son was looking for the *Itseke*—evil spirits that search out the dying to steal their souls at the moment of death.

"Oh, dark spirit," the boy sang outside the house of a woman who had only a few breaths of life left, "come with me to kill the strange one who has killed my father. You may have his soul in exchange for your help. We will ride to the kill in the body of my Isogoko."

The boy sickened at the approach of the Itseke. It was a living miasma of fever, sickness, and suffering in the shape of a man. Its only joy, its sole purpose in being, was to cause pain and death.

"Yes," it hissed, "we will ride the night wolf. We will kill."

The following midnight, the boy, the Itseke, and the Isogoko gathered at the crossroads north of the village and waited silently for the boy to chant his wolf-riding spell. A pale light flashed, and the Isogoko accepted the bodies, minds, and souls of the boy and the Itseke. With an unearthly howl, the jungle wolf leapt into the darkness.

At the road crew's camp, the men shut down for the night. The episode with the wolf the night before made them uneasy, and no one wanted to stay up late, no one except Mike Johnson. He laughed at the nervous behavior of the men, especially that of Old Carlos.

"As long as I have my pistol," he insisted, "no ragged old jungle wolf is going to scare me."

When the other men had quit the fire, Johnson retired to a makeshift bench in front of his tent. The moon was full, and a silver light played through the jungle. Crickets sawed away at the night, and frogs groaned and boomed in the darkness. Large tropical fireflies danced in the light, and the night-blooming flowers perfumed the air. Then all went silent.

The skin prickled on the back of Johnson's neck. He stood up slowly, and at the instant he reached for his pistol, a sharp, stabbing pain pulsed in his hand. In the muted light, he could see a three-inch dart so deeply imbedded in the back of his hand that the tip stuck out of his palm. When he opened his mouth to call for help, another dart pierced his throat. Johnson grabbed for the dart in his throat with his left hand while he shook his right hand to dislodge the other dart. Then, when three forms materialized in the moonlight, he froze in place. Two vaguely manlike creatures flanked a large jungle wolf—the old wolf's son. Both men carried darts in their hands. Johnson tried to run, but one of the men threw its darts and pinned the gringo's shadow to the earth. Johnson struggled but was glued to the spot. The wolf lunged and bit into Johnson's stomach. The other man threw a handful of his darts at the gringo, two penetrating his head, one his right eye, and one his neck.

The Itseke hurled a large harpoon-headed dart into Johnson's heart, and when he retrieved it, the gringo's soul was attached. The boy heard the Itseke's cry of victory and threw the remainder of his darts, wrenching all remaining animation from the gringo. Before the man's body hit the ground, the wolf was upon it, ripping it asunder.

The next day, the crewmembers searched futilely for their missing coworker, and a week later, when the construction company's man arrived to check on the road crew's progress, only the bulldozer and tents remained. The crew had vanished.

The brief report by the field investigator concluded with the following statement: "There was no evidence of foul play. Nothing was stolen. Nothing was burned or vandalized. There were, however, an unusually large number of what appeared to be very large dog tracks throughout the site."

The Kalapalo live in the geographic center of Brazil in the state of Mato Grosso near the headwaters of the Xingu River. They numbered only in the hundreds in the mid-twentieth century. Called *Aifa otomo*, meaning "people of Aifa village," by their neighbors, the Kalapalo are unusual for a number of reasons. While other groups in the area stress hunting and the aggressive male posturing that accompanies it, the Kalapalo believe that fishing, gardening, and only the occasional taking of capuchin monkeys and birds are the correct jobs for Kalapalo males. They hold pacifism and harmony, as opposed to violence and aggression, as the normal male demeanor. The Kalapalo people, though living in a world of social harmony, also dwell in a world of witches, the *Kwifi Oto*—the Master of Darts. This is not an ancient folkloric superstition. Between 1961 and 1968, seventeen people died in the Kalapalo village of Aifa. Of these, eleven deaths were attributed to witchcraft and three to Itseke.

The central tenet of witchcraft behavior among the Kalapalo is the manufacture of *kwifi*, magical darts, that *Oto*, a type of witch, hurl at their victims to cause a variety of effects from insanity to death. Sometimes the witch simply spins the kwifi to generate its magical effect, a whirlwind that can overturn houses. Witches teach the power of the Kwifi Oto to their children, who in time attain the power to fly, to make themselves invisible, and to transform into various types of animals, the wolf being a favorite vehicle. The Kalapalo believe that evil spirits known as *Itseke* can throw their own kwifi to cause illness and death. They are fond of creating skin diseases and attacking children with sickness. The witches often join forces with the Itseke, calling upon them to steal the soul of one who has been weakened by the witch's attack.

Winti

FROM SURINAME

Janine Rice—former Miss Jackson County, former homecoming queen, fourth runner-up in the Queen Tobacco 2000 competition—came from Biloxi, Mississippi, with her parents and brother, Patrick, to Paramaribo, where her father had been hired to manage a small bicycle factory. His contract provided an old plantation house complete with furnishings, several maids, a kitchen staff, and Komfu Bakra, the aged gardener.

The other servants stayed clear of Komfu. The proud old man descended from priests and chiefs of the Dahomey of Africa and communed with the *Winti,* strange and powerful African spirits. The household staff assumed a submissive posture and tone when dealing with the Rice family, but Komfu stood tall and looked into the eyes of those speaking to him, no matter who they were. Janine found him to be uppity.

"Mama, that nigra gardener looked at me funny this morning," she whined at breakfast a few weeks after arriving in Paramaribo.

Working with some border-shrubs beneath the open dining room window, Komfu heard the young woman's complaints.

"Now, darling, don't worry. These people know their place," Mrs. Rice replied.

"I just think something is wrong with his mind or something. He slinks around the garden like some kind of animal," Janine said.

"Well, you know how they are, dear . . ."

"Maybe Daddy and Patrick should go-upside-his-head or something to get his attitude straightened out."

Komfu slipped away to the secluded greenhouse in the back of the garden. He shook with rage, and his heart thundered in his chest. He dropped to the floor, traced mystical signs in the soil, and began the chant taught to him by his great-grandfather, the chant that when coupled with the magic symbols and his inherited powers would summon his Winti.

A rustling sound announced the presence of the mamba, a deadly African snake, the physical manifestation of Komfu's Winti.

"My, son," it hissed, "your anger is justified. The white girl has insulted us deeply and must pay for her stupid arrogance. Arrange for her to be present at the Winti dancing when the moon turns dark. I give you two pieces of opo so you can command the will of the insolent strangers."

The snake spat two tiny black balls onto the ground and withdrew into the shadows.

On the appointed day, Komfu visited the servants' quarter and ordered that one ball be put in the girl's breakfast and one in her brother's. He met Patrick at the stable and suggested that he take his sister to the "colorful native dance" being held that evening.

"The young miss seems bored in this old house," he said. "Why don't you take her to see the Winti ceremony? She might enjoy it."

Patrick, under thrall of the opo, mumbled, "I will obey."

Komfu waved his hand before Patrick's face and said, "You will not remember that we have spoken."

The young man responded, "I will not remember."

A few minutes later, Komfu found Janine sitting on a garden bench reading. Before she could speak, he waved his hand, capturing her with the opo.

"You might like to see the Winti dance tonight. Ask your brother to take you."

After instructing her captured will not to remember the encounter, Komfu returned to the greenhouse, and Janine went back to her book.

The Winti dance was held in an abandoned garden on the outskirts of Paramaribo. Some came to dance, possessed by their Winti. Others came to thrill to the magical and wondrous things that often happen when the possessed gather. Janine and Patrick stood on the edge of the crowd making snide comments to each other.

"I swear to God, Patrick, they look ridiculous jumping around out there."

Patrick laughed. "Hush, they might hear you."

"I don't give a hoot. They're just nigras."

Komfu, seeing Janine, whispered to the lead drummer, "It is time to call the snake possessed."

The drums shifted their seductive rhythms to the vibrations of the snake possessed. Young women moved onto the dance ground, and the men and older women stepped back.

Janine tugged Patrick's arm. "I'm going to walk around a little and see what I can see. I'm getting tired of just standing here watching this mess."

"Fine," he responded, "but be careful."

"Ain't nothing going to happen to me," Janine answered. "They're only field hands and maids."

"You just keep your eyes open," her brother insisted.

Janine wanted to move closer to the drummers and singers. She found that she liked the driving beat although she would never have admitted that, even to Patrick. She tapped her toe. Then her body gently swayed, and she hummed the repetitive melody of the chant.

A young woman screamed and fell to the ground. The possessed dancer thrust her hips from the ground again and again as if copulating with an unseen lover. As her cries of ecstatic release rang out, two other girls fell and commenced the same sensual motions.

Janine felt hot all over. Her body danced faster and faster to the compelling drums. She watched herself dance as if she were watching someone else. Then she was knocked to the ground. A scaled manlike creature with a flickering forked tongue lifted her skirt and entered her.

Janine went wild with excitement, moaning and shrieking in the dirt of the dance ground while the drums thundered. The others circled her in awe, watching the snake Winti work its magic. Patrick could not see what was happening; the crowd had thickened, forming a wall between his sister and him.

As the snake Winti rode her, Janine's blue eyes slowly turned brown, and her luxurious blonde hair turned to a rusty gray the consistency of straw. Next, her pale skin became splotched and wrinkled. When the snake Winti was through with her, it withdrew. Janine suddenly came to her senses. Her eyes were wild as she pulled her skirt down and screamed for her brother. She rushed toward him in the thinning crowd.

"Patrick, Patrick, help me," she cried.

Her brother pushed her away, seeing a hysterical old woman standing before him.

"It's me, Patrick, it's . . ."

The snake Winti entered her again, and she moaned and thrashed in his invisible embrace.

Patrick looked around and called for Janine. Unsuccessful, he ran toward the town to find help. When he had gone, the snake Winti withdrew from his sister, and she once again found herself partially clothed lying in the dirt.

"Come on, old woman. Get your butt up. The dance is done," said the head drummer, who hoisted his drum for the walk back to town.

"How dare you. You can't talk to me like . . ."

The drummer's slap snapped her head around. "Watch your mouth, crone."

Janine stumbled from the dance ground, pushing people out of her way, her only thought to gain the safety of her home and family. She gingerly ascended the front steps, wondering at the ache she felt in every joint of her body, and pounded on the door. A maid blocked the door when she attempted to enter.

"Get out of my way and let me in," Janine demanded.

"You be too drunk, old woman. You better leave before Mr. Rice come out here."

"I'm Janine, I'm . . ."

"You're a crazy drunk old woman is what you are," said the maid and slammed the door in her face.

Janine scurried around to the kitchen entrance and again found herself thwarted. The head of the kitchen staff confronted her. "You better get out of here. I can see you been to that heathen Winti dance, and you been mounted by the spirit. Look at the back of your dress. You been a' thrashing on the ground with the demons, a woman your age. You ought to be ashamed of yourself. Now get out of here."

"No, you don't understand, I'm . . ."

The snake Winti mounted her outside the kitchen door, and she danced and moaned, her teeth chattering and eyes closed, until one of the men who helped around the house drove her away with a broom handle.

Janine thought she was going mad. "Why are people being so mean? What is happening to me?" She bent over a little lily pond to splash cool water on her face but jumped back at the reflection of a withered hag staring back at her.

She heard a drum beat behind her. Komfu tapped lightly on a small drum, chanting the song of the snake Winti. Janine saw his tongue, now forked, flick and his skin become covered in scales. She felt her body respond to him, and he tore her blouse open and dragged her into the greenhouse.

Although the police searched for weeks, they never found Janine. Her father quit his job at the bicycle factory and prepared to return to Biloxi. In horror, Janine watched her family pack their belongings, but every time she tried to reach them, the snake Winti mounted her and she moaned, danced, and babbled until Komfu appeared to take her back to his greenhouse, where he kept her chained to a post.

"You are very kind, Komfu, to care for that poor, mad old lady," Mrs. Rice told him on the day the family left the house forever.

"I always do my best to help those in trouble," responded Komfu, standing straight and tall and looking directly into her watery blue eyes.

Suriname, formerly Dutch Guiana, is a small Republic on the northeast coast of South America. Its official language is Dutch, although there are also English speakers in the population. The lingua franca is a Creole language, Sranan Tongo, which is spoken by most of the population. Paramaribo, the seventeenth-century capital of Suriname, features a variety of architectural styles, which reflect the city's long and complex history. Dutch, Spanish, British, and French colonial buildings are joined by mosques and synagogues.

Among the more traditional of Paramaribo's Black population exists a belief in Kromanti, "African" spirits. Examples include *Opete,* the vulture; and *Tigri,* the jaguar; as well as spirits who live in the water, thunder spirits, and snake spirits. These spirits, called Winti, possess their devotees, entrance them, and cause them to dance. When under their control, believers are immune to bullets; knives cannot cut them, nor can fire burn them. Many believe that certain Winti are originally African and have moved through five generations in the New World. They can transfer from father to son, or mother to daughter, and they can possess whomever they wish.

The power and nature of a Winti is witnessed when a person dances while under its possession. This, of course, advertises to the community at large that meddling with such a person could draw the power of the Winti against them. Another power of the true believer is the ability to bend another's will through the use of opo. And yet another layer of horror is added when the *Wisi,* a witch who works through the control of spirits of the dead, is thrown into the diabolical mix. Woe to anyone who dares to harm a person possessing the power of the Wisi combined with that of a Winti in control of opo. The result is inevitable. There is no escape.

Kenaimas

FROM THE MACUSI OF BRITISH GUIANA

Mara's husband slapped her across the face, hard. She raised her trembling hands to cover her head, and he grabbed at them, pulling them away so that he could hit her again. The heartless blows stung, and hot tears erupted from her deep brown eyes.

"Why are you hurting me?" she cried, tendrils of hair falling across her weathered skin.

"Just giving you what you deserve," Natal sneered, clenching his fist. He advanced on her till she was backed up against the wall, and this time he punched her in the stomach.

She crumpled to the floor, while Natal reached for the sugar-cane liquor. Mara looked up into his angry gaze, his lips wet with liquor, and he yelled, "Some of the men said that you were talking about me to the women . . . showing me disrespect."

Mara stood shakily and moved toward him, "I never said any. . . "

He slapped her again, and her head snapped backward. She let out a piercing wail and tried to flee, but he caught her arm and shook it so violently that her legs buckled beneath her. Then, he advanced on her, slipping off his belt.

"Oh, no, please don't," Mara beseeched, cowering.

"I will teach you respect," Natal yelled and brought the belt sharply across her back.

Mara curled into a tight ball. The whipping exhausted the drunkard within minutes, but to Mara it had lasted an eternity.

"That ought to hold you until the next time you show me disrespect," he stammered through alcohol-numbed lips. He grabbed his bottle and walked out the front door.

Mara lay there for a moment. Slowly, her hurt, angry eyes opened, and she lifted her head with determination. The whisper that escaped her parched lips was barely audible: "No more. Never, never again." Blood filled her mouth, and her body burned. "No more."

She pulled herself up, trembling. How many years had she been letting this abuse go on? Far too many, she thought as she peered out the window at the front porch. Natal was lying on the bench, out cold, the liquor bottle on its side on the ground. She had expected as much.

"Dream on, you drunken scum," she whispered and turned away.

Mara walked purposely into the jungle and stopped at the tree where she had hidden *it*. Several weeks earlier, after one of Natal's beatings, she had paid a visit to the *Kenaimas*—the dreaded sorcerers—and had been given a small package. Possessing the tools of the Kenaimas was a capital crime among her people, so she was very careful not to be seen with it. She reached her bruised hand into a knot in the tree and pulled out a small parcel wrapped in red trade cloth and slipped it into her pocket.

Cautiously ducking into the shed behind the house, she rummaged until she found a good length of rope and paused to catch her breath, steeling herself for what she must do. She knew that she had justice on her side, even if she had been forced to deal with the Kenaimas. Since she and Natal lived alone so far out in the bush, there was generally no one nearby to come to her aid when he beat her. She had endured Natal's abuse alone. Her mother had told her years earlier that violence was typical of men, so she must put up with it. "But not anymore," Mara said, patting the small bundle in her pocket. "Not anymore."

The Kenaimas had instructed her not to open the package until she was ready to attack. Inside, the Kenaimas had told her, she would find the agent of death as well as brief written instructions.

Natal was still on the porch in a drunken stupor. Using newfound strength, Mara dragged him to the bedroom and onto the bed where she laid his body out. She tied his hands and feet securely to the metal bed frame. Then, she slapped him into consciousness. Hitting him felt good. She was dizzy with power.

"What . . . what's going on?" he stammered drunkenly.

Mara hit him sharply again and said through clenched teeth, "Wake up and prepare to die, you bastard."

Now fully awake, Natal struggled unsuccessfully with the ropes. His eyes glowed like hot coals as he let fly a string of curses.

Mara smiled crookedly, dried blood in the corners of her mouth, and held up the packet. "Do you know what this is, you disgusting, cowardly worm?" she asked. "No? It is a special death created just for you by the Kenaimas."

At the mention of the sorcerers, Natal's struggle intensified. When he realized that his efforts were futile, he tried reasoning with his wife, who up until now had been an obedient little mouse. "Mara, you must be crazy. Come on and untie me and get rid of that evil thing before something bad happens."

"Oh, something bad has already happened," Mara told him, still dangling the package. "But after tonight, it will happen no more."

She opened the package and found a two-inch bamboo tube plugged with a bone stopper. A string tied around the tube secured a small piece of paper. Mara unfastened it, read the tiny print, and erupted in hysterical laughter.

"Mara, stop that," Natal said, near hysterics of his own. "You sound crazy. What are you laughing about?"

She held the paper near Natal's face so that could read the words: INSERT IN EAR.

Mara pulled the stopper from the tube and looked inside. "Ooh, nice."

Natal thrashed, trying to free himself. "What are you going to put in my ear? Let me go! I'm going to kill you if . . ."

Mara placed the tube on the pillow beside Natal's head, and he frantically tried to pull away from her.

"This is wonderful," Mara said, entranced, and tapped the tube with a jagged fingernail. A house cricket walked out onto the bed sheets.

Natal's screams became maniacal howls. Saliva bubbled from the corners of his mouth, and blood dripped from his wrists and ankles where he was bound. Mara enjoyed Natal's attempt to escape his fate for a while, but finally, she picked up the cricket and stuck it in his left ear. At first it just tickled, but then Natal's eyes widened, and he lost all control as he could feel the bug eating its way into his brain. He thrashed with such force that he dislocated both shoulders and elbows, and he uttered sounds that had no analogy in the human world.

"I want to watch you roll around in your own waste, but I am getting tired of your screeching." With that, Mara stuffed a wad of roof thatching in his mouth, but Natal's pain was such that his screams didn't require his mouth to be heard.

The Kenaimas' cricket spent several days chewing through Natal's brain—the tortured man writhed in constant pain. It finally exited through his forehead. Mara took care of her now lobotomized husband by allowing him to sleep in lice-infested blankets in the shed and feeding him the pigs' leftovers. She didn't bother him too much because she was paying off her debt to the Kenaimas with her new hobby—collecting crickets.

Wide rivers meander through the swampy coastal areas of British Guiana, through deep jungle, and finally onto the savannah, a vast open area interspersed with mountainous terrain. This is the homeland of the Macusi—a world that they exploit through hunting, fishing, gathering, and small-scale horticulture. The region is perilous, populated by hordes of ghosts, witches, and evil spirits.

The Macusi believe in the *Di-da*, Water Mama, who lives in deep pools and lures innocents to their abode to drown. The *Omar*, pictured as a huge crab or sometimes a gigantic fish, also dwells in these deeps and, like the Di-da, kills his victims by drowning. A relatively unique belief of the Macusi is that spirits possess certain rocks. Some rocks house giant white were-jaguars; others, the souls of those who have drowned in the vicinity.

The central tenet of the Macusi religion, however, focuses on the relationship between the Kenaimas and the Peaimen. All bodily afflictions, from injury to illness to death, are believed to be the work of a *Kenaimas*— a type of sorcerer who can work evil with his body and his spirit. He has the power to separate his soul from his body and to travel, typically by flight, in his spirit form. He flies by night in search of victims. The Kenaimas like to take their victims alive, bind them, and torture them to death either by rubbing a slow-acting poison on their skin or by violently dislocating their joints. The Kenaimas can place his spirit in various animals or insects to accomplish his aim—always the death of his victim. These sorcerers kill mainly for enjoyment, but also can be hired to kill. Against these demons, the Macusi turn to the *Peaimen*, the shaman who battles the forces of the Kenaimas with his own powers.

Karaisaba

FROM THE WARAO OF VENEZUELA AND BRITISH GUIANA

Peccary hunting was great fun—a sport, however, best suited to young men, which explains why old Jolopa's request to accompany the young hunters was at first laughingly refused. He argued that as an old man he had knowledge to offer them, but they claimed that he wouldn't be able to keep up with the chase.

"Well, then," Jolopa said, "just let me start out with you, and if I can't keep up, the issue is settled." Jolopa knew that he wouldn't have to keep up for too long. He knew that this hunting expedition would end before the sun rose the next day. His master had told him this and many other things.

After some grumbling, the hunt leader said, "Just don't get in the way, old man."

Jolopa bowed and smiled grimly, and the small band set out for the thickets that crawled over the flanks of a worn ridge. The men hiked through the rainforest for hours, conserving energy by their silence. Jolopa walked last in the line.

The shadows of late afternoon settled like a mist over the tangled jungle floor, and the hunt leader called a halt for the day beneath a giant silk-cotton tree.

"This will give us some cover if it rains tonight," he said.

Jolopa thought, "There is nothing in creation, young man, that will give you cover from the rain that will fall on you tonight when the Master comes."

"Hey, take a look. A pot of banana pudding," someone shouted.

The men gathered around a large pot. "I wonder who this belongs to," said the hunt leader.

One touched it and said, "It's very cool to the touch."

Another dipped his finger in and tasted. "Just like my mother used to make." He smacked his lips and took another bite. Soon they were eating the pudding with their hands—all but Jolopa, who sat apart from the rest, pretending to mend his arrow quiver.

After the pudding feast, hammocks and mosquito nets were set out. The night was beautiful. The men commented on the great size and unusual clarity of the full moon, while night birds whispered in the treetops. Within minutes, all but Jolopa slept, having been mesmerized by the moon.

Jolopa's master, the *Karaisaba,* with a large light glowing in the center of its forehead, descended to the ground. He moved next to Jolopa, who stood motionless before his master's inspection, and sniffed his breath. Not finding the telltale banana odor there, it shuffled to the next hammock, raised the mosquito netting, and smelled for a trace of the pudding. Detecting it on the sleeping man, he placed his mouth against the sleeper's left eye and sucked it out of his head with a pop; then he did the same with the right eye. The entranced man did not awaken. The Karaisaba continued until he had sucked the eyes from all of the men who had eaten the pudding.

When the creature was finished, it spoke to the old man. "You have arranged my meal well, my student. You, in return, will receive everything you are capable of receiving."

The Karaisaba touched Jolopa's head, and the old man, in a burst of light, understood how he would attain his desires.

"Thank you, great jungle lord," Jolopa responded with sincere gratitude.

The Karaisaba left and Jolopa awakened the men as he had been instructed. After they had calmed enough to hear him, he explained that a Karaisaba had eaten their eyes but had passed him over because he was old and weak. The young men moaned over their fate while Jolopa placed them along a rope by which he would lead them *home.*

"Everybody hold on," he told them.

On the second day of their journey, Jolopa announced that they were within sight of home—that to their left about a foot out was a little stream narrow enough to step across. The men turned to their left and boldly stepped into a river teaming with hungry piranha. Jolopa laughed as the killer fish chewed the blind men to shreds, turning the water into a bloody froth.

That evening, Jolopa stumbled into the village and pretended to collapse. "It was awful," he moaned. "The Karaisaba killed the young men." Forestalling the obvious question, he quickly continued, "But it didn't eat me because I am so old and stringy."

He fell to the ground in feigned grief. "Oh, why couldn't it have been me? I'm just a useless old man. Why did it have to be those fine men?"

The young widows gathered around Jolopa and hugged him, sharing one another's grief. As he consoled the young women, Jolopa reflected upon the fact that the young widows were left without men, and he contemplated that the land parcels owned by the men were now up for grabs. The moon rose behind the trees, and Jolopa bowed toward it with gratitude as the wails of the grieving young women rent the night.

The Warao of Venezuela have lived in the Orinoco Delta since prehistory. Deep swamp dwellers, they used their environment as a shield and managed in the several centuries before contact by Europeans to keep their more predatory neighbors at bay. The swamps gave them fish, game, fruits, vegetables, an endless supply of fresh water, and, as noted, protection. Then in the eighteenth century, the "Spanish Warao," a Spanish colonial designation for those Warao living in British Guiana, were forced out of their territory by the Spanish military. The "Spanish Warao" fled into the interior forests, where they have lived at peace with their neighbors for the past two centuries.

Many demons stalk the jungle nights in Warao country. The *Rattle Jaguar* is an evil spirit that takes the form of a jaguar reclining in a hammock. As he rests, he plucks the hammock strings with his claws, making a sound suggestive of a rattle. The sound is so peculiar and hypnotizing that sometimes Warao will approach it out of curiosity. The sight of the jaguar in a hammock is bizarre enough, but the real impact is felt when the doomed traveler sees the human bones that cover the ground beneath the jaguar's hammock. Then there is the *Maihisikiri*, a jungle spirit that specializes in assuming the form of absent husbands and having sexual relations with their wives. That would be bad enough, of course, but the Maihisikiri takes it several steps further into the horrible. The victim becomes hopelessly enamored of the Maihisikiri and will run into the jungle in search of her demon lover if not tied down at night. If the entranced wife cannot be controlled, her liaisons with the Maihisikiri will in time dissolve her bones completely but leave her its conscious toy.

However, the *Karaisaba*—also known as Ogre Big-Eye, Ogre of the Moon, Ogre Moon-Eye, and Ogre Eye-Extractor—is the major concern of the Warao. Even today, the Warao are frightened of walking alone in the jungle at night for fear of encountering this demon.

Hekura

FROM THE YANOMAMO OF VENEZUELA AND BRAZIL

Jimenez, the village Shabori, or shaman, was communicating with the Hekura, several of whom dwelt in his chest. The people respectfully watched from their hammocks as he staggered around, shouting incomprehensible words and pounding himself. He seemed insensible. Strands of green mucus hung from his nose, and saliva dribbled down his chin. From time to time, he returned to the fireplace where Chagni sat with a two-foot bamboo tube and a bag of a green powder, a hallucinogenic drug derived from the ebene tree.

Jimenez squatted before him, and his assistant placed a pinch of ebene powder in the tube. Jimenez inserted the tube into his nose, and Chagni blew the drug into Jimenez with a strong burst. The Shabori stumbled backward, shivered, and began his dance, once more calling on the Hekura.

Mothers ordered their children to stay clear of the Shabori as he danced across the large communal yard formed by the circle of the Yanomamo huts.

"Come from my body," he murmured. "Come from the jungle. Harken to me. Obey my command." Around his feet and seen only by him, his *Hekura,* tiny humanoids about five inches tall, pranced and giggled, attending to their Shabori. Jimenez took more ebene from Chagni and intensified his spirit calling. "Come from the jungle. Come be my warriors. Obey my commands," he chanted.

The Hekura pointed to the sky, and Jimenez saw a band of Hekura floating to the ground like falling leaves. Each carried a small bow and quiver of arrows. These Hekura were sent by enemy Shabori to attack the children of Jimenez's village, to steal their *noreshi,* or souls.

One landed on a child's head, and Jimenez hit it soundly with his bow. The child rubbed his head and ran screaming to his mother. The Shabori ran from child to child, fighting the Hekura as they attempted to bore holes into the children's heads to snatch their souls. Likewise, the Hekura who lived in Jimenez's chest attacked the enemy Hekura. Of course, the villagers saw nothing but Jimenez chasing the children and hitting them on their heads with his hardwood bow. Children ran in all directions. Some hid behind their mothers while others ran into the gardens or the jungle to hide.

At last, the enemy Hekura were gone—no longer falling from the sky, no longer sitting on the tops of children's heads. The Shabori knew where they went. Calling his Hekura to him he said, "My warriors, we must attack the enemy Hekura before they reach their home village and the support of their Shabori. Rise into the air, my warriors, and carry me to the enemy."

The villagers watched Jimenez lying semiconscious on the ground, twitching and babbling; however, in his spirit form, he and his Hekura were on the attack.

He flew above the treetops toward the enemy village until he spotted the swarm of enemy Hekura. "My demons, it is time to destroy the child killers sent by our enemies. And then it will be time to destroy our enemies." Jimenez shouted and dove on the fleeing enemy Hekura. Tiny bows and poisoned arrows were brought to bear, and soon the air was choked with the deadly little missiles. The Shabori wrapped himself in the power of his noreshi and in the shield provided by the Hekura of his chest. His presence made the difference. In minutes, the enemy Hekura lay stunned, wounded, or dead on the jungle floor. Jimenez's Hekura swarmed over the defeated demons and ate them.

"Quickly, take up their bows and arrows," he ordered.

When all was ready, the shaman and his Hekura flew to the enemy village. The Shabori of the enemy village saw the Hekura with tiny bows and arrows dropping from the sky and announced that the raiding party had returned in triumph, thus setting the stage for an attack by men. Although the people could see nothing, they came out of their huts and cheered. The enemy Shabori danced and called his Hekura to him, but joy turned to terror when the Hekura, instead of entering his chest, alighted on the children and shot their poisoned arrows into the tops of their heads.

"Noooo!" screamed the enemy Shabori, who rushed from child to child to remove the raiding Hekura. But it was too late. The arrows of the tiny monstrous raiders drove into their brains, and the children fell to the ground writhing, foaming at the mouth, and finally dying.

The Yanomamo of southern Venezuela and northern Brazil call themselves "the fierce people," and their behavior lives up to this startling self-appellation. A culture very involved with martial behavior and warfare, the Yanomamo are still actively raiding today. They fight for revenge. They fight to protect their gardens, the major source of their subsistence in an environment largely devoid of big game animals. They raid to capture women. The Yanomamo feel that it is natural for men to fight—that it is of divine origin, since in mythic times, blood from the moon fell on the ancestral humans, making them fierce.

The Yanomamo believe that the cosmos comprises four layers, or worlds. The upper-most world, *duku ka misi*, is empty and likened to an abandoned garden. The Yanomamo pay little attention to this realm; it is void and of no significance. The second layer is *hedu ka misi*, the sky layer. Here, an exact replica of normal life is acted out by spirits of the deceased. The bottom side of hedu ka misi is what we see as the sky. Humans dwell below the sky on *hei ka misi*, this layer. The lowest layer is *amahiri-teri*, a community of dangerous spirits of deceased Shabori, or shamans. The evil shamans of amahiri-teri, in coordination with the malevolent shamans of "this layer," send demons or go themselves to capture children to eat.

The Shabori must always be on guard for attacks by enemy demons against the children of his village. To strengthen himself for this work, he seeks contact with the Hekura, tiny, amoral creatures of supernatural strength, and dangerous sources of power to which certain men are drawn. The Hekura are generally first contacted in ebene-induced visions. Under the influence of this drug, a Yanomamo Shabori can see the Hekura and invite them to live in his body or entice them to attack the children or the adults of enemy villages. The Hekura, deadly when not under control, can, when their powers are harnessed, assist the Shabori in healing.

Chochoi

FROM THE YUQUI OF CENTRAL BOLIVIA

Fernando and Chato, Yuqui from a village on the east bank of the Ichilo River, were enjoying the morning coolness. The sun had just risen, and songbirds and butterflies flitted about. The night before, hunters had reported a possible bee tree in the far reaches of the jungle in the swamp north of the village, but the dusk had forced them to abandon their search. Honey was a special treat for the Yuqui, so Fernando and Chato decided to leave early and go in search of the tree. But by the time the sun was straight up in the sky, the heat and humidity had clamped down hard on the hunters. Swatting flies and mosquitoes, the pair moved slowly. An overwhelming stillness shrouded the jungle as they ambled into the swamp.

They soon came upon the dead body of an opossum, its eyes missing. It showed no signs of violence, and oddly enough, no flies swarmed over the carcass. It was clearly a fresh kill. Puzzled, the hunters squatted beside the animal. Fernando poked it with a stick. "What do you think, my friend?"

"God has given us lunch," answered the other, laughing.

"Perhaps," pondered the hunter. "I wonder what killed it?"

"It may have been its time, that's all," his friend answered. "Ants must have eaten the eyes out after it died."

"You're probably right. I'll skin it and cut it up while you gather wood for a fire. We'll have a good meal and a nap and look around for the tree when the sun drops."

As they walked, neither of the hunters noticed the shadow that darted among the bushes beside their camp.

The opossum tasted good, and with their stomachs full, Fernando and Chato found a shady spot for a short siesta. The soft humming of insects and the warming of the day soothed them and rapidly brought them sleep. A little while later, the snap of a twig awakened Fernando. He raised his head slowly and listened. Another snap. Without waking Chato, Fernando picked up his rifle and slipped into the brush. He thought it might be another opossum or some other tasty morsel.

Fernando concentrated. Another sound immediately ahead drew him forward. Strange noises all around him, coming from one direction, then another, confused the experienced hunter. Soon he had walked far from the camp. Lengthening shadows finally convinced him to cut off his pursuit of the animal, which always seemed to be just out of reach.

Fernando had almost reached the camp when a dark shadow dropped over him like a net. A thick slime enveloped him, moving over his body of its own will. He clawed at the black stuff that oozed into his ears and eyes and up his nose, finally suffocating him.

Chato awoke to a shrill scream. He called out for Fernando and looked around the camp for tracks, which were hard to find in the growing dusk. Then, the peculiar screeching wail came again, and he noticed that it had moved closer. A chill rippled up his spine. He started to run, when, looking over his shoulder, he saw the shadow close behind. With a jolt, he understood; it was the *Chochoi*—a shape-changing shade. The screech sounded directly behind him, and he whirled, his gun raised. A black cloud hovered low in the air. Chato fired into it with no effect. Two tendrils shot out from the evil mass and entered his eyes. He screamed in pain as bloody fluid flowed from his pierced eyes. The Chochoi slashed into his brain, and Chato's scream died with him on the jungle floor.

Villagers came upon the hunters several days later. Like the opossum, their bodies bore no marks, and insects had avoided the decaying flesh. Their eyes, however, were gone. An old man, wise in the ways of the jungle, said, "We must let their bodies be and leave this area quickly. . . ." A piercing scream broke the stillness. The old man whispered in a trembling voice, "Now."

The Yuqui, who refer to themselves as *Bia*, meaning "people," descend from the Guarani Indians, who migrated into Bolivia from northern Paraguay about 300 years ago. When they were first studied in the early twentieth century, they were among the most technologically undeveloped societies known, living as nomadic hunters and gatherers. Contemporary observations find them somewhat more advanced.

In the spiritual world of the Yuqui, the dead garnish most of the power. They move between earth and their homes in the sky, and they can possess the bodies of humans as well as animals. When a person dies, his or her spirit divides into two entities, the *Biague* and the *Yirogue*, both of which present danger to humans. The Biague is the more feared of the two. It causes death, insanity, illness, and all manner of misfortune. It is believed to be intimately connected with rain and storm, thunder being considered by the Yuqui as a drinking party of the dead. The Yirogue is invisible but can appear as two small birds, the gurai and the tiruru. Considered an ogre and cannibal, this entity can take up residence inside a snake or jaguar.

Even more feared than the Biague and the Yirogue are the shape-changing *Iguanda* and *Chochoi*. Invisible except to elders, they come in the night, at dusk, or at dawn to abduct the unwary. The Chochoi is specifically identified by its hideous, shrill wailing call and its tendency to attack through its victim's eyes.

3. Demons of the West Indies

Ghede

FROM HAITI

After three long years, Regina left the Sisters of Charity and moved to Boston to stay with her brother and his wife. The Mother Superior understood Regina's reasons for leaving the convent, but Regina still felt guilty, and over the weeks, she sank into a bleak depression. After a month of watching his sister mope around, Regina's brother bought her a plane ticket to Haiti. She would arrive just in time for Carnival—a time of merry-making and feasting just before Lent.

"What you need is a week or so of old-fashioned partying to blow the convent dust out of your system," her brother told her. He had never approved of her choice of vocation.

At first, Regina only reluctantly agreed to accept the ticket, but as the trip grew closer, she began to look forward to getting away and letting go. "I'll fly down to Haiti and have myself a ball," she told herself, "and if I'm lucky, I'll leave 'Sister Regina' there."

The flight down was short and uneventful. But when Regina found herself in the wild world just outside the airport at Port-au-Prince, she was anything but disappointed; in fact, she was thrilled. Boisterous singing and jubilant shouts bombarded her as revelers in outlandish costumes and grotesque masks danced wildly through the streets.

Regina quickly unpacked at the hotel and enjoyed a few courtesy rum drinks in the lobby before joining the revelers in the streets. She felt wonderful and free. She danced and sang, and even accepted drinks from a couple of men who saw that she was without an escort.

By two in the morning, the crowds had thinned, and Regina stumbled down the dark streets in search of her hotel. She ended up at a crossroad on the edge of town. The moon was riding down an empty sky, and frogs and crickets droned in the tall grass. She was tired and dizzy and could go no farther. She slumped to the ground against a road sign and fell asleep.

Regina awoke abruptly when someone tapped her bare foot with a cane—somehow she had lost her shoes—and she looked up at a tall man dressed all in black wearing a top hat. She gasped at the sight of his skeletal visage, but quickly realized that it was a mask—a death mask.

"Hey, girl," he laughed, "here you be sitting when the best party in all of Carnival is starting just down the road. Get up on your good foot and come along with me."

His proposition was irresistible and soon Regina was dancing once again, this time down the street behind the man in black as he twirled his cane and sang snatches of Carnival songs in a crisp, mesmerizing voice.

The man led Regina to a mansion set in a grove of ancient, moss-covered oaks. Inside, a band played, and couples danced in the large ballroom, which was lit by long, tapering white candles—there must have been a thousand of them to light the room so brightly in the absence of electric lights.

The stranger took her arm and led her up the marble steps.

"I don't even know your name," Regina chuckled.

As the elegant white doors opened, the stranger turned to her and said, "Some call me Baron."

Regina's bare feet carried her to the dance floor where she joined the dancers, and the Baron looked on in approval. Handsomely attired men in expensive antique Carnival costumes vied for the opportunity to dance with her.

"Sister Regina doesn't live here anymore," she thought with a sense of joy, a weight lifting from her shoulders. She danced with all of them and laughed in tune with the music as she twirled around.

When the crow of a rooster welcomed the first hint of dawn, the music stopped abruptly. The dancers froze in place. Confused, Regina looked around for the Baron, who had stepped up behind her.

"The party is over, Sister Regina," he said in a silky voice.

"How do you know my name?" she asked, alarmed.

"Hush, girl, I have a bit of business to take care of," he said harshly.

And as Regina watched in horror, the Baron walked among the dancers, tapping each one with his cane. As he did so, they turned to statues of milky-white dust.

"Watch this, little virgin," the Baron said. He blew on one of the statues, and it crumbled to the floor, the dust intermingling with the expensive costume and jewelry. He blew on one after another. When the last one fell, he said, "And now for you, little sister."

Regina, who'd been paralyzed until now, drew her hands into claws and went for the Baron's eyes, but his mask came away in her hand, revealing another hideous face. She ripped that one away, too, only to find another horrid visage staring back at her. Again and again she tore at his face, and each time he laughed wickedly when one face after another appeared in its place.

"I don't understand," she sobbed, at last giving up.

"I am the corpse of the first man, and my faces are the faces of all the dead that have ever been. I am Baron Ghede, Lord of Death."

Regina cried out and realized the futility of flight.

"Yes, daughter of Christ. It is best that you surrender to my will," he said, moving toward her.

He tapped her trembling hand with his cane, and to her horror, it turned to dust. At the second tap, the particles floated slowly to the floor. Regina screamed and grabbed the stump. Then, the man in black tapped her arm, and it too turned to dust and fell away in a cloud. When she tried to run, the Baron tapped her leg, and she fell to the floor. He danced around her, touching her here and then there with his cane. She screamed for mercy, but none came.

"Now, Sister Regina, the sun is pushing up, and it's time for me to go home and sleep, so I must say goodbye until next year."

The Baron threw open each window in the ballroom, and the morning breeze stirred the dust on the floor. Regina's dust blended with that of the other dancers. She had entered Ghede's world. From then to the end of eternity, she would dance each year at Carnival for the Lord of Death.

Haiti's culture, based on agriculture, is rich and complex. The original native group, the Arawak, called their homeland *Hayti,* meaning "mountainous land." By 1525, the natives had nearly disappeared under the onslaught of diseases—smallpox, measles, and influenza—brought into the area by the Spanish and later the French. To fill the void left by the destruction of the Indian labor force, European plantation owners brought in almost 3 million slaves from the Congo, Ibo, Nago, Mandique, Ara, Dahomey, and other West African cultures. Slave revolts in the late 1700s ultimately led to the proclamation of independence for the colony by Jean-Jacques Dessalines on January 1, 1804.

The traditional religious orientation of the islands is divided between the Roman Catholic elites and the voodoo religion of the ordinary citizen. Voodoo incorporates cultural and religious ideas from African sources and from the Roman Catholic pantheon of saints and angels. The Catholic Archangel Michael is venerated as *loa*, or spirit, as are the Blessed Virgin Mary, Lazarus, and Saint Joseph. Beside them, fully equal in power and attraction, are loa that clearly find their origins in Africa—giant serpents, lords of death, human-headed animals, and many more.

Ghede and his entourage—Baron Samedhi, Baron Cimitiere, and Baron la Croix—are associated with death. The origin of the name *Ghede* is uncertain, but one of his titles, Ghede Nimbo, is very closely related to an African cult that centers on death and resurrection. Ghede is generally pictured standing at crossroads dressed as an undertaker. He is the keeper of cemeteries—a clown and a trickster, wise beyond all because he embodies the knowledge of the dead. He epitomizes death, sex, and irreverent humor. Ironically, although Ghede is the Lord of Death, he is also the protector of children. He does not like to see children die; likewise, he is the last resort of the ill in healing since he is the one who decides the fate of the sick.

Several years ago, a group of voodoo priests, known as Hougans, possessed by Ghede and wearing his black attire, forced their way into the presidential palace in Port-Au-Prince and demanded food, drink, and money. Rather than calling in the military, the president's staff gave the spirit-possessed priests what they wanted. No one was willing to challenge the power of Ghede.

Ligahoo

FROM THE REPUBLIC OF TRINIDAD AND TOBAGO

The official letter from Mr. Pierre Beauchamp of Beauchamp, Beauchamp, and Fitzjames, Attorneys at Law, caught Angelique's eye in the stack of bills and junk mail that she removed from her mailbox. The firm's address placed it in Port of Spain, Trinidad. Angelique had not thought of her hometown—more accurately, the town of her birth—for many years. Her mother had moved with her to New York when she was very young, and Angelique had grown up a certified New Yorker. She could not remember her island relatives, but her mother did her best to remedy that by regaling her daughter with rollicking tales of family history.

She sighed heavily. "Mama is gone now," she thought wistfully.

Snapping out of her funk, she briskly opened the cream-colored envelope. There were two letters—one a cover letter from the attorneys and the other a letter from a person named Paul Renard. The cover letter explained that the firm had been contracted to send the enclosed letter upon the demise of Paul Renard, whose letter read simply: *Come to Port of Spain and collect your inheritance.* There was no signature. No date. In addition, the letterhead was very peculiar—a two-inch drawing of a chain with thirteen links centered a quarter-inch from the top edge of the paper. She couldn't recall ever having heard the name Paul Renard.

She discussed the strange letter with some of her friends. The consensus was that she should make the trip. It would be romantic, it would be mysterious, and most of all, it might be lucrative.

"An inheritance, Angelique, just think of it," one of her friends had said, and Angelique did, quite often.

Two weeks later, she faxed the firm in Port of Spain to tell them that she would be coming, and they forwarded her message to another Mr. Renard—the son of the newly deceased Mr. Renard—so that he could make arrangements for her arrival.

Her Trinidadian relative proved very efficient. Angelique flew first class and was picked up at the gate in Port of Spain by a vintage black limousine, which delivered her to a picturesque old hotel located across the street from the beach. In her room, a large buff-colored envelope waited for her on her pillow. It was a letter from Mr. Renard. On top of the page was a simple line drawing of a man carrying a coffin on his head. The note read: *I will come for you this evening at nine o'clock,* and was signed, *Your Cousin, Paul.*

"Hmmm. Can't wait until morning, I guess," she said aloud. Then, a barely perceptible force urged her to open the zippered pocket of her suitcase and retrieve the letter that had come with the attorney's letter weeks ago. She held the old letter and the new letter in each of her hands, wondering why she was doing so. She felt compelled to tear the drawings off the letters so that she could view them side by side, the tops facing north. She sensed an energy—something that was yet too weak to emerge into . . . into what? Within seconds, the odd energy faded, but Angelique was left with the feeling of something missing. A third image? Yes. She didn't know why, but she felt the need to find the third image. She put the two pictures in her purse. The experience, whatever it was, exhausted her, and thinking of chains and men carrying coffins, she drifted off to sleep.

A muffled tapping on her door awakened her.

"Who is it?" she asked, struggling to consciousness.

"Mr. Renard's driver, miss. I'm here to take you to him," came the gruff reply.

She asked him to wait while she readied herself. She felt giddy as the thought of her inheritance washed away the experience with the letterhead pictures. Soon, she found herself being driven out of the city and into the mountains.

"How far is it?" she asked, but the driver did not answer. She cleared her throat. "I asked how much farther," she said louder this time.

"Two hours more," rumbled the bearded old man who hunched behind the wheel in a moldy chauffeur's uniform.

Angelique looked out the window into the enveloping darkness. "Where exactly are you taking me?" she asked, and the driver pointed toward the highest peaks in the distance.

The moon slid from behind a cloud, giving Angelique a better view of her destination. The mountains looked faintly ominous. They didn't have the noble heights of the Rockies or the ancient, rolling swells of the Blue Ridge, but looked full of decay—jagged and rotten. "Up there?" She gulped.

She considered telling the driver to turn around, but she remembered the promise of an inheritance and kept her mouth shut. With nothing else to do, she admired her long well-manicured fingernails and passed the time fantasizing about what luxuries she would buy with her inheritance. Soon the limousine rattled up a cobblestone road and stopped in front of an ancient three-story plantation house. A tall, thin man stood on the veranda.

"That's Mr. Renard, your cousin," the driver told her.

"Welcome," said her cousin, his voice dry and raspy, as he held open the car door for her.

"Peculiar," she thought. "Just a moment ago he was standing on the veranda." She took his arm, and he escorted her toward the house. "I wonder if this is part of my inheritance," she thought to herself as they mounted the veranda steps.

"No," Renard said without looking at her. "Your inheritance is much more than this. Much more."

Angelique gasped. She hadn't said the words aloud, had she?

A light meal was served by a silent old black woman, and while Angelique ate, Renard told her stories about the history of the house and the family that had lived in it since the first occupation by the Spanish. Between sentences, he sipped a thick, deep red wine.

"My grandfather's grandfather told him that the house sat upon a sacred site of the Arawak Indians. An early Spanish governor built the house on the sight to show the Indians that he was not afraid of their spirits."

Finished with her meager meal, Angelique grew restive. "Mr. Renard, I was called down here about an inheritance. When are we going to talk about it? I don't mean to be insensitive, but I have a job I have to get back to in New York, and . . ."

"You will have no need to labor for the rest of your life," he told her.

Her heart beat quickly with excitement, but she maintained her composure. "That's fine, but why can't we just sign the papers and get on with it?" she asked, dropping the linen napkin onto her plate for effect.

Renard's thin lips curved into a smile. She would do fine. Her anger lay just below the surface.

He looked at his watch. "We will deal with the papers at 12:37 if you still want to at that time."

"What do you mean? Why are you dragging this out?" Angelique asked, her alarm rising.

Renard again looked at his watch, stood up, and strode from the room with a glance back at Angelique. "Come with me quickly and bring the pictures in your purse."

Angelique stood to follow, but then stopped. "How do you know about the pictures in my purse?"

He let out a a short barking laugh. "Child's play, really."

Renard opened a door in the hall that led to the spiral staircase which would take them to the top floor. Angelique followed. The room had no furniture. No carpet. No wall decorations. One rectangular window supplied the only illumination, a slightly irregular square of moonlight.

"The exact time is known," Renard mumbled excitedly. "Sit there at the top of the square of light. Hurry," he ordered.

Angelique quickly sat where he had indicated. She could hear the faint whispers of warning deep in her mind.

"Now, take the pictures out of your purse and place them here, tops facing north." He indicated the exact spot on the moonlit square. "Place them in the upper left- and right-hand corners of the square of moonlight."

Angelique shivered, beads of sweat rolling down her back. When she set the pictures where Renard had ordered, she felt a jolt of vertigo and fell backward onto the hardwood floor.

"Help me. I can't get up," Angelique cried. It felt as if something was holding her down. "What's happening?"

"Rest still, my little redeemer," Renard said as he pulled an envelope from his pocket and removed a small slip of paper.

"The third picture," Angelique whispered. "I knew it."

"This picture is of a bat. The three images, when placed in the right order, at the right time, in the right light, will invite the Ligahoo to come," Renard said.

"Ligahoo?" Angelique asked, struggling. "What are you talking about?"

Ignoring her, Renard reverently placed the third piece of paper in its proper position and raised his hands to the sky. "Please, please release me. I've suffered enough. I have served you for a hundred years. Ride your new steed. I have brought her for you. She is a daughter of the line. Awaken her to who she really is. Grant her the inheritance of the Renards—the power of the Ligahoo!"

Angelique's muscles tightened, her arms and legs cramped and trembled. She screamed, or rather howled, as her nose and mouth transformed into a muzzle. Coarse brown hair sprouted all over her body. She looked at her hands and growled low in her throat at the long yellowed claws. She could hear the soft flight of the bats outside and the far-off song of night birds with a clarity that she had never experienced before. She tilted her head back and inhaled. The odors of the room and of her cousin brought massive amounts of information to her fevered brain. She could sense her cousin's fear. That message came through her eyes, her ears, and her nose, and through senses she had never ever known—the senses of the wolf.

Renard cringed in the farthest corner of the room. He knew that the manner in which he handled Angelique in the next few minutes would determine whether he would live or die.

"So this is my inheritance," she growled. "You have brought me here to escape your curse, and . . ."

"No, it's not just my curse, cousin. You are in the line. It is a curse on all the Renards. Years ago, an ancestor of ours grievously affronted a powerful witch who placed a curse on our family forever. When the moon cycle returns in exactly this way, at exactly this time, under exactly these conditions, you may bring someone to replace you."

"How many years do I have to wait before these conditions are again present," she snarled.

Renard whispered, "One hundred years."

Angelique hissed through clenched canine teeth.

"But," he hastened, "you will have the power of twenty men. You will be able to fly, to be invisible, to take on any shape you wish." He laughed a little madly and said, "You should thank me."

Angelique, now the Ligahoo, was beginning to experience her abilities and said, "There is more to this ghastly situation, dear cousin. Tell me all of it."

Renard stood slowly, his back pressed against the wall. "You can consume no food or drink that ordinary men do."

"How the hell am I supposed to survive the hundred years of the curse if I can't eat or drink?" she barked.

"I didn't say you couldn't eat. I just said . . ."

Angelique pounced on him in a split second, her claws around his throat. "You will tell me the truth now!" she growled threateningly.

Renard stared at the square of moonlight and recited, "You will live off the flesh of people you kill. You will drink only the blood of your victims. None of your powers will serve you if you do not kill at least once every waning moon."

Renard's heart turned to ice under Angelique's wolfish gaze. She licked away a thin line of saliva that oozed from the corners of his mouth.

"Very interesting folklore, cousin. You have such a way with your little stories."

Angelique paced the perimeters of the empty room and came to stand in the square of light, her feet shuffling the pictures out of their precise alignment.

"You have given me my inheritance, cousin. You have paid to have me flown down here. You paid for a nice hotel room, but there is one more thing I want."

"What is that, cousin?" Renard asked.

"A real meal," she said, licking her lips.

No one ever saw Paul Renard again. When Angelique moved into the mansion, she told the attorneys at Beauchamp, Beauchamp, and Fitzjames that her cousin had gone to the United States to collect an inheritance.

The Republic of Trinidad and Tobago encompasses the southernmost islands of the Caribbean. Tobago, a small twenty-six-mile-long island, lies north of Trinidad. Its population is approximately 50,000, while nearly 2 million people live on Trinidad. The Republic boasts mountains, coral reefs, rainforests, and miles of beaches.

The original inhabitants of the islands were the Carib and Arawak people, but the Spanish occupation of the islands, which began in the late fifteenth century, saw the end of the native people. Today, the ethnic profile of the Republic is rich, with the majority of the population being of African and East Indian origin. The Republic's cultural mosaic is reaffirmed by the number of major religions that have found adherents there, including Judaism, Islam, Hinduism, and Protestantism.

The Republic's diverse cultural tapestry has contributed numerous demonic images to the beliefs of the islanders. Flavors of Africa, Spain, France, England, India, China, Syria, Lebanon, Portugal, Holland, and Latvia mingle to form new images and reinforce ancient ones. There is *Mama Dlo*, "Mother of Waters," who is half-woman, half-anaconda; *La Diablesse*, with her ancient costumes and cloven foot, who waits for lone travelers so she can eat them; and the *Soucouyant*, who speeds through the night as a ball of fire. And, of course, there is the *Ligahoo*, sometimes called Loup Garou, a Caribbean werewolf. The werewolf is found in almost all cutures, but a unique characteristic of the Caribbean werewolf is that it can, in a sense, haunt family lines—it can be inherited.

La Diablesse

FROM THE REPUBLIC OF TRINIDAD AND TOBAGO

All of us are at times gifted by a warning from the gods. But sometimes we fail to comprehend the gift or its importance. The message can come in many ways. We may hear it from a stranger or read it in a book. Perhaps we convince ourselves that we have created it from whole cloth, but we don't gracefully receive the gift of prophecy. We miss the signal, which for Kenny Saint Peu was the faint jingling of chains.

Walking along the beach one evening, he heard a tinkling sound, a hint of an aural mosaic airbrushed by the wind and the waves. The image barely had time to register when he heard behind him, "Young sir. Young sir, wait a minute please."

Kenny slowed and a woman approached. Although there seemed to be something unusual about her, she was hard to see in the palm grove shadows.

"Young sir, you dropped your ring back there," she said, extending a shiny gold ring to him on her index finger.

Kenny blinked. The ring hung from a claw! She dropped it in his hand, and the claw curled back into the shawl that she clutched in the evening damp.

"Did I see what I thought I saw," he wondered. "No. It had to have been just a long fingernail," he convinced himself.

He cleared his head with a deep breath of salty air and handed the ring back to the woman.

"This is not mine, madam," he said. "I've never seen it before in my life."

"But it'll look very good on you, young sir. You must be meant to have it, and I must have been meant to return it to you." She pushed the ring back to him.

Kenny felt coldness in her touch. But no claws, he noticed. He remembered thinking that she seemed older when she first spoke to him. Now, she was clearly young and very beautiful.

"Please take the ring. All you owe me is one kiss," she said in a lilting voice.

"Well, I . . ."

The woman moved toward him. Then he knew why she had looked peculiar to him earlier: Her manner of dress was several hundred years out of date. Something drew his attention downward; something odd about her feet caught his eye. His breath froze in his throat. From beneath her long blood-red dress protruded a cloven hoof!

"You're so pretty, young sir. Come over here and kiss me," she beckoned.

Kenny stumbled backward. "What are you?" he gasped.

"Take off your clothes, and I'll show you," she whispered.

"Get away from me." Kenny raised his fists.

"Ooh. I like them fiery and spirited. Remove your clothes," she demanded.

Kenny took another step away from the woman. "Look, whoever you are, I . . ."

The moon slipped behind a cloud, and Kenny watched in horror as the young woman instantly transformed into a hideous crone. She shouted at him, her voice harsh and shrill, "I have had it with you, you stupid man!"

She dropped her shawl and exposed her clawed hands for the kill.

"I've been trying to tell you how to save yourself, and you just can't hear me. I'm the one that sent you the jingling chains," she cried, advancing on him.

"The what?"

"The warning, you fool," she moaned. "My master, El Diablo, caught me trying to steal from his treasure chest. As punishment, I must warn my prey of my approach and tell them how to escape my attack before I can sink my teeth into their tender young flesh or torture them—whichever suits my fancy at the time." She looked him over as if he were an expensive cut of meat. The following words came haltingly, as if they were being torn from her: "Now take your damn clothes off and put them on backward, and I cannot harm you."

The devil woman's babble clouded Kenny's mind, and he knew that he must try to escape. It never occurred to him that the sinister woman's instructions on how to thwart her rang true. Then, to Kenny's relief, the call of a night bird distracted the witch-woman for a moment, and he bolted. He raced into the palm grove, his efforts to lose the foul creature in the underbrush spurred on by her bestial howls of rage.

Then the yowling stopped. Kenny strained to hear her, though his labored breathing interfered. Not knowing where she was proved just as terrifying as knowing. Then something flew at him, and he averted his eyes just as a cloud of powdered human bones hit the side of his face.

"You are mine," the evil woman shrieked and closed in on him.

Kenny gagged and vomited and ran deeper into the palm thicket. The devil woman leapt from the darkness and landed on his back. A few swipes of her clawed fingers ripped his spine from his body. Shrieking with delight, she threw it into the sky. Up and up it went, a gore-dripping spinal column twisting in the moonlight, and it never came down.

Information about the culture and spiritual beliefs of the people of the Republic of Trinidad and Tobago can be found on page 122 under Ligahoo. Please refer to that section for some insight into their ways.

La Diablesse is the demon woman. She seduces and kills young men for no other reason than that she likes to. Those who have seen her describe her as a withered hag who comports herself as a young girl. She wears the clothes of several generations previous, but they are always scarlet. She flits in the shadows, and with coy movement and soft voice, attempts to lure young men to their death. If a potential victim does not run before she touches him, he is doomed. When confronted by La Diablesse, you can survive by undressing, turning your clothes inside out, and then redressing.

Mama Dlo

FROM THE REPUBLIC OF TRINIDAD AND TOBAGO

Harry Gorn was furious. "What do you mean *the men no mo work?* How can they *no mo work?* We're almost there with this project. The government people are happy with my work on their damn airport, but they've been very blunt about wrapping the whole thing up as soon as possible. So . . . as you can understand . . . I don't want no mo *no mo work*. Do you understand what I'm saying?"

The foreman, Anton Peavey, shuffled his feet. "I can't make them work if they don't want to."

Gorn grabbed the map of the job site and spread it across his cluttered desk. He scanned it quickly. "We're only talking about five acres of swamp. Clear and fill it. What's the problem?"

"The men say there's something in there, Mr. Gorn," Peavey said haltingly.

"Something in there? What the hell are you talking about, Peavey?"

"Some kind of . . . thing, sir," came the reply.

"So you're telling me that the men aren't going to do their job because there is a . . . *thing* . . . in that little swamp? Is that what you're saying?" Gorn asked angrily, fumbling with the map as he tried to refold it.

Peavey hung his head. "I am telling you all I can, sir," he mumbled.

"Look, Peavey, I don't want anymore ex . . ."

Peavey interrupted. "You are not from the islands, sir." He took the map from Gorn and folded it adeptly.

"Obviously." Gorn snatched the map from Peavey's outstretched hand.

"Therefore, you're unfamiliar with the kinds of . . . beliefs about . . . things . . . that the people have here."

"Are we talking about boogiemen and things that go bump in the night?" Gorn asked, slamming his desk drawer shut. "Because if we are . . ."

"No, sir! We are talking about the. . . . Well, the men say that it is Mama Dlo—she lives in that swamp. She owns that swamp."

"Mama who? Are you talking about some old lady?" Gorn seemed relieved. "Just pay her the hell off and get her out of there."

"No, sir," Peavey said, a hint of exasperation in his voice. "Mama Dlo, *they* say, is a demon with the head and shoulders of a beautiful young girl but with the body of a giant snake, an anaconda, *they* say, thirty feet long." Peavey stared into space for a moment before adding, "I myself heard the crack of her tail on the water while I was walking along the shore of a swampy lake."

Gorn snorted. "You, too, Peavey? Ah, you're as bad as the whole damn bunch of them. I guess the old saying, 'if you want something done right, you got to do it yourself' hits it right on the head in this case." He opened his desk drawer to look for the key to the equipment shed.

Keys in hand, he pushed past Peavey and said, "Yeah, I may as well do it myself."

Peavey watched him go. He didn't try to stop him.

The shadows were lengthening as Gorn hefted two five-gallon cans of gasoline into the back of his mud-covered pickup truck.

"If I step on it, I can get this done and maybe get a good solid day of work from this superstitious bunch of ignorant . . ." He continued to rant to himself the entire mile-and-a-half ride to the swamp.

All around him was cleared land. His men had cut and burned the old forest to prepare the site for the new airport.

"If it weren't for this damn piece of swamp, I'd be on schedule," he mumbled when he reached his destination. He looked around for dried grass or deadfalls that he could use to start the fire and then checked the wind to ensure that it would push the flames in the right direction. Gorn poked around and finally found the perfect spot about a hundred feet into the swamp.

He returned to the truck and hefted the gasoline cans off the back, but was brought up short by a loud cracking sound coming from a little pond. He slowly set the cans on the ground. The sound came again. *Snap! Snap!* Something stirred in the bushes about twenty feet to his left. He strained his eyes to penetrate the gathering shadows in the dank bog, then blinked. No, he wasn't seeing things. He clearly saw the face of beautiful young woman with golden skin and flowing black hair.

"Miss!" he called out. "Hey, lady!" The woman disappeared into the gloom. "Damn! Damn! Damn!" Gorn hissed through clenched teeth. Now he had to find the woman and get her out of the swamp before he fired it.

"Hey, damn it," he shouted, "Where the hell are you?" He knew that he had to get out of the swamp before dark, otherwise he wouldn't be able to steer clear of the quicksand pits throughout the area. He shouted again, "Lady! Where are you?"

"Here," the clear, melodic voice said from behind him.

He turned. There she was again—an alluring woman standing behind an elderberry bush. In truth, Gorn saw only her head and shoulders. The rest of her was hidden by the thick bush behind which she stood, or crouched; it was hard to say which. He wondered if the rest of her was as bare as her gleaming shoulders.

"Look, miss," he began, "I got to burn this patch here. My so-called men won't do it, so that leaves me. This job is under contract with your government, so I got authority to tell you to leave this property right now. If you need something to cover up, maybe I can find something in my truck." Secretly he hoped to catch a glimpse of all of her.

"Silly man, now why would I leave my sweet home?" the woman asked. A slight lisp gave her words a hissing sound. "And why would I allow you to burn it?"

"Are you threatening me, lady?" Gorn laughed. "I got a right to be here and you don't, so . . ."

"Were you born here?" she asked.

"I don't have to be born here, lady. I work for your government. While I'm working for them, it's the same thing . . ."

"No, it isn't, mortal," she whispered. Her head swayed from side to side.

"Mortal? Who the hell are you calling . . ."

Though it was growing difficult to see in the dusk, Gorn watched as the lovely head rose into the air . . . on the pillar of an anaconda's limbless body. He stumbled backward, fell over a slick root, and was on his back gasping for breath when Mama Dlo slithered up beside him.

"Husband," she hissed in his ear. Her breath was sweet like jungle flowers.

Gorn fought to regain his breath as she reached down and kissed him with a long, forked tongue. Her body engulfed him in its coils, and he writhed to free himself.

"Yes, yes, my husband," Mama Dlo moaned.

Her coils tightened, and Gorn felt the piercing pain of a snapping rib. He cried out while the creature moaned in pleasure and spasmed in ecstasy. Gorn was crushed in her embrace.

Mama Dlo rested until the moon rose. Then she leaned over Gorn's body and said, "Once more my husband." She put her mouth over his and breathed into him.

Gorn's eyes popped open. Once again, she draped her heavy coils over him. Her tongue flicked out to taste his terror, and she again made him her husband. As she squeezed him one more time in her spasm of pleasure, she whispered, "For the rest of your life, you are mine, husband . . . as well as for the rest of your next life."

Gorn had a brief moment of awareness before he was once again crushed to death by the hideous creature, his eternal wife.

Information about the culture and spiritual beliefs of the people of the Republic of Trinidad and Tobago can be found on page 122 under Ligahoo. Please refer to that section for some insight into their ways.

Mama Dlo, the Mother of Waters, is an eternal enemy of all men. Her lovers must die, experiencing the crushing of their body each time she enjoys them. The extra horror is that she will also revive them in order to kill them over and over again, for all eternity. If Mama Dlo stands in your path, take off your left shoe, turn it upside down, and leave it on the ground. Then quickly leave the area, walking backward all the way to your house.

Soucouyant

FROM THE REPUBLIC OF TRINIDAD AND TOBAGO

Brothers Joseph and Henry Devereux walked along the beach that edged a fishing village on the main island of Tobago. The soft Caribbean surf whispered at their feet, and far on the horizon, a smudged black line announced the coming of a storm later in the day.

"I bet she's got a lot of good stuff in that old house," Joseph said.

Henry just shrugged.

Joseph didn't want to let it go, so he pushed. "That old lady's been here forever, and she's probably collected lots of stuff over the years—expensive stuff."

"Ah, that's bull," Henry muttered. "She's just some crazy old bat . . . probably dead and dried to dust. Her stuff's probably turned to dust, too."

"She could be dead," Joseph said, as if the thought had occurred to him. "Nobody has ever seen her. There could be jewelry in there . . . maybe silver stuff, too. Silver plates and tableware—just laying around. Maybe some fancy pictures you could get a good price for. First person who stumbles on the dead lady's stuff will take it all away, and we'll be left with nothing."

"And what if she's not dead?" Henry asked, incredulously. "You want us to wait around here until she dies?"

"If she's not dead," Joseph began, "we'll help the natural, God-ordained process along. I'm just an agent of the Lord."

Henry raised his thin eyebrows. "Yeah, right."

Joseph glanced up at the sky. "We'll wait until dark, and then we'll take a good, close look inside."

"Whatever," Henry said, planning to go along with his brother's devious scheme only because he had nothing better to do.

To pass the time, the brothers went to a bar on the beach. One beer led to another and another and another until they decided that it was time to return to the old house. They parked their rundown car a half-mile away and walked, taking care to move in the shadows. The wind picked up, and lightning flickered in the distance. They approached the back of the house through the weed-choked yard.

"Henry," Joseph's voice was hushed and tense, "look up."

Henry peered up into the branches, almost all of which were festooned with large bats rustling in the trees. The night creatures flexed their wings, and the rising wind pried them from their perches.

"Come on, " Joseph whispered. "Let's get inside before they start tearing around out here. Some of them things got rabies, you know."

The back door was unlocked, and they slipped quietly into the darkened house.

"Now what?" Henry asked.

"Shut up and listen," Joseph said, pointing his finger threateningly. "Hush."

They stood rooted to the floor, listening.

"There. Do you hear it?" he asked.

"Yeah, sounds like somebody's upstairs," Henry whispered.

"It's got to be the old woman shuffling around," Joseph guessed. He picked up a dusty, heavy candlestick and motioned as if he were hitting someone over the head with it. Henry understood and nodded.

They slowly climbed the decrepit staircase, the moans of the warped steps masked by the thunder and thrashing wind.

"There," whispered Joseph, pointing to a room at the end of the hall.

A faint light shone through the cracks in the rickety door. The brothers approached quietly, and each pressed an eye to one of the cracks. They watched as the old woman moved from behind a heavy green velvet curtain. She reached into an ornate cabinet for a mortar and pestle and placed it on a table. Then, she returned the pestle to the shelf.

Without averting his eyes, Henry whispered, "Let's beat it, Joe, while we can. I don't feel right about this."

"Are you afraid of a ragged old woman? She don't matter, so don't get . . ." his voice died away.

Through the cracks, the men watched as the old woman slowly peeled the skin from her arm as if it were an opera glove. Fiery plasma flickered in the shape of the arm as she placed the wad of wrinkled skin in the mortar. She looked at the door, almost as if she could see right through it, and the brothers were jolted backward by an electric shock. Joseph dropped the candlestick. Scrambling to their feet, they ran for their lives, stumbling down the old steps and leaving the way they had come in.

The old woman smiled in anticipation of the feast she would have. She'd been observing tonight's dinner from the moment her bats had warned her of their presence. Wasting no time, she peeled off her right ear and placed it in the mortar. Fire crackled where her ear had been. Soon, the flesh filled the mortar, and the *Soucouyant* stood in its true form—a blistering ball of fire. Like a bullet, it shot up through the chimney and into the night sky.

The sizzling roar of its flight set the village dogs to howling piteously. The villagers, snug in their beds, pulled their blankets over their heads and tried not to think of what might be abroad in the night.

Henry and Joseph, meanwhile, raced back to the village, but had no luck persuading anyone to give them sanctuary. Their wild pounding on cottage doors reinforced the villagers' reluctance to respond, and encouraged them to burrow deeper under their covers.

Joseph grabbed Henry's shoulder. "I have an idea!"

"Well, get it out quick," Henry shouted. "That . . . *thing* is after us."

"That old lady, her arm was made of fire, right?" He shuddered to think that her whole body was made of fire. "Well, water puts out fire. Let's get us to the water!" Joseph said urgently.

Henry sprinted for the beach with Joseph right behind. They made it to the strand and were within several yards of the surf when the Soucouyant appeared. The sizzling fiery ball hovered in the air, blocking their path to the water. Its nearness made them uncomfortably hot.

Joseph impulsively kicked sand at the Soucouyant and dove for the water. The flaming ball shot after him and brushed the side of his head. Joseph screamed and fell to his knees, holding his face in his hands, rocking back and forth in pain. When Joseph lowered his hands, Henry gagged when he saw what was left of his brother's face—half of it cooked like well-done meat. His left eyeball had been boiled in its socket, and his ear was seared from his skull.

A hissing voice sounding like steam under pressure came from the flaming ball. "Smells good."

Then, it swooped at Henry's feet, causing such ghastly pain that he bit off the tip of his tongue. Blackened stumps replaced his feet.

"I do love fried feet," mocked the voice.

Thunder rolled through the night, and heavy, dark clouds slid across the moon.

"Damn!" the voice cried. "The rain comes to spoil my picnic."

The storm swept over the mountains and hit the beach within seconds. The Soucouyant hissed and popped as rain struck it.

"I will come for you again," the Soucouyant warned and shot up into the sky.

Some fisherman found Henry and Joseph in time. Though horrific, their wounds were not life threatening. Joseph's face became almost bearable to look at with plastic surgery, and Henry was fitted with artificial feet. They built a shack as close to the beach as possible and kept buckets of water all around—in case of fire. They slept during the day and kept watch through the night. They never again went near the old woman's house.

If the drinks are free and the pitchers of water are handy, Henry and Joseph will tell you about their encounter with the Soucouyant. Don't laugh and don't mention the sizzling sound you heard in the sky last night when your barking dogs woke you up from a deep sleep.

Information about the culture and spiritual beliefs of the people of the Republic of Trinidad and Tobago can be found on page 122 under Ligahoo. Please refer to that section for some insight into their ways.

The Soucouyant is an evil fire, a kind of witch, that robes itself entirely in the skin of an old woman to hide its true identity from neighbors. It is often said that it slips the skin off and stores it in a jar when it hunts during the dark moon. Even if one finds the witch's skin and destroys it, the Soucouyant simply waits for the death of an elderly woman and steals her skin.

4. Demons
of Africa

Kalengu

FROM THE KAPSIKI OF NORTHERN CAMEROON

The Kalengu raiding party crept through the tall grass outside their enemies' village. There were five of them; more were not needed. They were very tall, very thin young men with elongated heads, extraordinarily long arms and fingers, and mesmerizing, unblinking eyes.

They moved quietly to the enemies' sorghum field and sat in a row facing the crops. Each removed a black sack from his belt, held it open, and chanted softly. Moments later, the sacks expanded, while at the same time the life force seeped out of the sorghum field. When the unearthly raiders tied up their sacks and crept away, the previously lush green field was devastated—the plants dry, withered, and gray.

Upon returning to their village, the Kalengu emptied the sacks containing the stolen life force onto their own sorghum fields and watched their fields turn an even darker and more vibrant green. When people from other villages marveled at the lusciousness of their fields, the Kalengu, who kept their ways secret, demurred and credited their agricultural success to modern management practices. They even cited their own thin bodies as evidence that they worked from sunup to sundown to create lush gardens and fat, sleek herds.

One day, Talenda and his brother Bima were hunting in the forest near the village when they came upon these five Kalengu. As one, the gathering faced Talenda, opened their sacks, and began to chant. Before Talenda could call out to Bima for help, the Kalengu had drained the life energy—his soul—from his body. The hunter fell where he stood, a dry, gray husk. The Kalengu held the sacks close to their mouths and slowly inhaled the stolen human life force within. In this fashion, they could extend their lives indefinitely.

A shotgun blast from Bima ripped through the foliage where the Kalengu stood, but they had already moved as one to the left.

"Die, you evil things," Bima shouted as he readied to shoot again.

The Kalengu stepped aside a fraction of a second before the second blast tore through the recently vacated space. He aimed and fired again and again, but each time, the Kalengu seemed to anticipate the direction of the next shot and deftly moved out of harm's way.

Finally, Bima understood what was happening, and said, "You know what I am . . ."

" . . . thinking," one of the lanky creatures finished for him. "Yes, always."

The shotgun was snatched from Bima's hand so quickly that he barely felt it leave his grip. He considered his chances at making a break for it, but one of the repulsively gaunt things stepped behind him at that very moment.

"Don't waste your energy," the Kalengu sneered. "And don't count on anyone coming to your aid."

Bima knew that he was trapped and hung his head.

"Yes, that's better. Conserve your energy so our feasting on you may be richer," one of the creatures said.

Bima was tied to a tree with one Kalengu left to guard him. The other four took advantage of a few more hours of night to raid a nearby chicken coop to steal the chickens' souls, which would invigorate their own flock.

After a while, the guard nodded and fell asleep. Bima knew that if he could not escape, he wouldn't have much longer to live. Then, an idea flashed across his mind. It was obvious that they could read his thoughts, but could they actually read—letters, books, and the like. Bima had not progressed far in the village school, but he could read and write. If he imagined himself looking at a page in a book and suppressed his emotions as much as possible, perhaps the Kalengu would be momentarily confused when they could not anticipate his behavior. And in that moment, perhaps. . . .

"Not good enough," Bima thought. The men outnumbered him, and he didn't know what other powers they would be able to launch against him. He thought harder. Then, an interesting idea occurred to him. What if he could somehow use their mind-reading powers against them?

He focused his mind and visualized a blank page. He quieted his thoughts until he could see the page clearly. Then, he pictured five Kalengu sacks on the page. Once he was able to hold that image in his mind, he added a short message to the bottom of the page, which read: ENEMY BEHIND YOU! And just in case they couldn't read, he added a picture of a fierce lion about to pounce on the Kalengu from behind. Then, he covered the imagined words and picture with a strip of white tape that he could remove quickly, all in his mind's eye.

His creative work done, Bima cleared his mind except for the page he had created, and worked at the ropes that fastened him to the tree. While doing so, he imagined every detail of his page over and over. Soon his captors entered the clearing, their sacks bloated with chicken souls, and awoke the guard, admonishing him for having fallen asleep.

As one, they turned toward Bima. Although Bima's thoughts, focused on the page, confused the Kalengu, they could still picture what he was thinking.

Five sacks came through, and each unconsciously touched his soul-carrying sack. At that moment, Bima mentally ripped away the tape exposing the words ENEMY BEHIND YOU! and the image of the leaping lion. Having loosened the ropes sufficiently to break free, he dived into the brush.

When the Kalengu turned around and instinctively opened their sacks to catch the soul of the lion, the stolen chicken souls rushed out. There being no chickens around, the souls were confused and entered the nearest living beings—the five Kalengu.

When all was silent for a few minutes, Bima peeked out from his hiding place in the brush. The Kalengu were still in the clearing, their empty soul-catching sacks in heaps. One of them scratched the ground with his toes, while another collected bits of grass and twigs. Two others crouched close to the ground, trying to lay an egg.

The leader of the Kalengu glared at Bima, but "cluck, cluck" was all he said.

Some experts consider the Kapsiki-Higi to be one ethnic group although they are known as Kapsiki in Cameroon and Higi in Nigeria. Usually, this group is simply referred to as Kapsiki. *Kapsiki* means "to sprout" and refers to the treatment of sorghum grain in making beer. The Kapsiki live on the central plateau of Cameroon in horticultural villages, and numbered about 25,000 in the mid- to late twentieth century.

As is typical of the majority of African horticultural village cultures, the Kapsiki possess a complex religious system, which combines ancient native traditions with a core of Islamic beliefs. In addition, the Kapsiki believe in a world of witches, sorcerers, and wandering ghosts that often possess people during special rituals designed to evoke them and bring them into secular life. The possessed ones then deliver messages from the dead or utter prophecy.

The most feared entity in Kapsiki life is the *Kalengu*—spirit walkers—who possess the power of the evil eye. The evil eye gives them an awareness of future events, making it very difficult for ordinary mortals to outsmart them. The Kalengu also have the ability to steal the life energy from crops, cattle, chicken, and goats, and add the stolen energy to their own. Therefore, the Kalengu can often be identified by the unusual vibrancy and health of their crops and animals. Another identifying feature is that they tend to be very tall and thin. Their thinness, it is said, comes from the fact that they never rest, working by day, stealing by night.

The Kalengu, although entirely capable of attacking members of their own village, are more typically interested in attacking enemy villages, and are therefore seen by citizens of their home village as warriors who engage in noble exploits for the good of the community. The *mehele*, or character, of the Kalengu is passed from father to son, although women, in ways that are not completely understood, can also become spirit walkers.

Yamo

FROM THE LANGO OF UGANDA

Everybody liked Duntwasi. He was even-keeled and never spoke harshly about anybody. He made a good living for his wife, Mariki, who doted on him, and for his three little boys. But all the villagers, including his wife, agreed that Duntwasi was not very bright.

His younger brother Taka, on the other hand, was a prodigy—intelligent and imaginative. He was creating songs to entertain his playmates when he was three years old, and by his teens, he had developed into a talented storyteller. People would say things to him like, "How do you think up those stories, Taka?" and "You have a tremendous imagination."

It was true. When others saw a turtle or fish in the clouds, Taka pictured ancient gods from the beginning of time battling sky monsters. Yes, it was true that Taka was very, very bright and had a wonderful imagination. And he knew it. In fact, he reveled in it, particularly when he was around his elder brother. Since they worked together at their father's lumber company, he had the opportunity to taunt his brother daily.

"Hey, brother, how many fingers can you count?" Taka said and held up three fingers.

"You got three fingers up," Duntwasi answered.

Taka quickly added a fourth finger. "No, you're wrong again. I have four fingers up."

Duntwasi persisted, "You had three fingers up. I saw them."

"Prove it," Taka responded.

"Well, I don't know . . ."

Taka interrupted, "Have you thought about what we were talking about three days back? You remember, don't you?"

"I don't think so. Maybe it was . . ."

Taka again interrupted. "Well, then why are you on my property? Go away. You're fired."

Duntwasi's head spun. "Now . . . wait a minute . . . I . . ." his lips continued to move, but nothing more came out.

Taka smiled condescendingly. "You just don't have it upstairs, do you, Dunt? All you can see is what's right in front of your face."

"Well, right in front of my face is usually where I'm going," Duntwasi replied.

"See, that's exactly what I mean," laughed Taka.

Duntwasi looked at his watch. "Time to close up."

The two went through a routine familiar to them since they were little boys. But while Taka counted the receipts in the office and Duntwasi turned off the lights and power tools, a ratlike creature about six inches tall crouched behind a pile of two-by-fours in the parking lot. It was one of the *Yamo*—the dreaded "Winds."

When Taka locked the front door and the two brothers stepped into the night, the Yamo emerged from its hiding place. Duntwasi looked down at the strange little rat with the three gleaming red eyes and, not quite believing what he saw, rubbed his eyes thinking, "It's been a long day . . ."

Taka also looked down at the odd creature, which seemed harmless enough. But his imagination worked quickly as it usually did, and while Duntwasi rubbed his eyes, Taka thought, "If those three red eyes were flickering flames licking out of empty eye sockets and those paws were thick-scaled appendages with razor-sharp claws . . ." The creature seemed to transform into his imaginings right there in front of him, and his eyes widened.

"I must not imagine that it could get larger," Taka thought, but the creature tripled in size and made a lunging assault against his right calf. As he shook it off, he tried desperately not to think of the creature getting larger still. "No," he cried to himself, "I must not think!" But for Taka, not thinking was an impossibility. And, of course, the creature grew in size, and Taka found himself staring up into the face of the rat-thing, drool dribbling from its open mouth. The Yamo lunged at Taka's face, biting it off. With a second bite, it swallowed his body whole, clothes and all.

That's when Duntwasi lowered his hand and opened his eyes. Seeing the rat still in front of him, he crushed its skull with the heel of his shoe.

The Lango live in northern Uganda in a homeland that covers approximately 6,000 square miles, including several hundred miles of open water and swamp. The predominant native growth is elephant grass, which reaches a height of six feet. Like most of their tribal neighbors—Acholi, Teso, Ganda, and Nyoro—the Lango are horticulturalists and pastoralists living in scattered villages. Their slash-and-burn type of horticulture, coupled with the incessant need for firewood, has resulted in major deforestation of their territory. At present, only forests within parks and reserves protected by the Ugandan government remain.

Ancestor worship, though common throughout the area, is not a major theme of Lango religion. The spirits of the deceased are of significance only for the harm they bring to the living. The *Tipu*, the shadow of the dead, brings all the negatives of life from sickness to quarreling, impotence, and death. The Tipu is the embodiment of greed and unbridled desire. It loves music, dancing, and fine food, and, of course, all to excess. The Lango believe that all people have a fragment of *Jok*, or God, within their being and this is Tipu. A short time after birth, it is thought that the Tipu splits, one part taking up residence in the head and the other in the heart.

When someone has thwarted the desires of the Tipu, or sometimes for no apparent reason, it enlists the aid of the *Yamo*, the "Winds." The Yamo can assume any form, but are usually seen as elflike or ratlike creatures about half a foot tall. In fact, the only limitation on the form they take is the imagination of the one who sees them.

Adro

FROM THE LUGBARA OF AFRICA

Mila's parents were proud of their beautiful daughter. Her skin reflected the color of rich polished mahogany, and her teeth gleamed like the brightest stars. When she walked through the village, the boys followed her, vying for her attention, calling out to her, shyly offering her gifts of flowers.

"That one will marry well," said the elders, "and it's almost time."

One elder, however, did not share the affection most felt for Mila. She, in fact, was jealous of the attention paid to the girl, and the gushing pride of Mila's parents stirred her anger. She was Amokat, an *Oleu*, one who walks at night—a witch. Seldom seen during the day, Amokat spoke to no one when she did appear in the village. Her face had a grayish tint, and her eyes were always bloodshot. Most people simply stayed away from her.

One day, Amokat overheard some old women talking about Mila. They praised her parents and grew poetic describing her beauty. Amokat felt sick to her stomach and knew the time had come for action. She slipped behind a fence and turned herself into an owl. On silent wings, she flew to Mila's house and alighted on the roof, where she turned back into Amokat. Crouching close to the roofline, she crept to a point directly above the front door. Using her Oleu powers, she projected the voice of Mila's best friend.

"Mila, Mila, come see what I've found," she called out.

Mila stepped through the door, and Amokat gathered the saliva in her mouth to spit upon her head. Her spit would cause the girl sickness and death. But Mila's father, who had been behind her, saw Amokat's shadow and pushed his daughter aside. Amokat's spit missed them both, but barely. Mila's father ran into the front yard and picked up a large stone. He hurled it at Amokat, hitting her on the side of the head. Momentarily stunned, she tumbled from the roof and landed in a heap on the ground. Mila's father was on her in an instant, kicking her and calling to his neighbors for help. The Oleu gathered her powers and transformed herself into a sleek leopard. She struck at Mila's father with her clawed paw and raked long gashes down his arm before fleeing into the jungle.

The Oleu ran until she was exhausted. Blood flowed down her face, and she touched her ribs gingerly where Mila's father had kicked her. She went to the river to quench her thirst and wash her wounds, trembling with rage.

"How dare they?" she hissed through clenched teeth. "I will kill that precious girl. I will maim her, and . . ."

"No," came a voice that Amokat recognized as that of her master, Adro. "Bring her to me."

She pressed her face to the ground, not daring to look into the terrible visage of evil itself, and whispered, "Yes, Master."

That night, Amokat, in the form of a small black snake, slipped into Mila's house. The lovely girl slept soundly, not a care in the world. Like a shadow, it slithered to Mila's feet and vomited blood on them. Then, it slid to the girl's mouth, sealing it shut with a touch of its forked tongue.

"Come with me," Amokat said to the scarlet puddles on Mila's feet.

Suddenly, Mila's eyes opened. Her feet were twitching oddly. She felt a powerful compulsion to stand, and before she knew it, she did. Without volition, she walked into the darkness. She tried to call out to her sleeping parents for help, but her mouth would not open. Her feet carried her from the village, and no amount of struggling could stop them. About a mile away on the path that led to the river, a jaguar appeared to her.

"Behold the power of Adro," it said.

The elephant grass on both sides of the path burst into flames, and Mila, suddenly freed from the enchantment of Amokat, ran back toward the village. A whirlwind dropped into the fiery grass and blew blazing debris into the air through which Mila could not see. She heard someone crying and twirled in the flaming chaos, not knowing what to do. Squinting into the maelstrom, she saw a man standing partially behind a tall termite mound. He pointed and said, "That way to the river, my girl."

Mila ran as tongues of flame licked the air around her. The man watched her flee, and if Mila had looked back at that moment, she would have seen half of a man balanced on one leg—a man that looked as if he had been ripped in half from head to toe. He threw himself into the flames and rose into the stifling air, on fire.

Something whizzed past Mila as she neared the river bank. She watched in puzzlement and horror as a flaming half-man disappeared beneath the water in a cloud of hissing steam. Feeling the heat on her back, she knew the fire was closing in on her, but now she feared stepping into the river with the half-man beneath its waters.

She ran along the bank in the direction of the village and cried in terror when human-looking arms seemingly composed of water reached for her from the river. As she ran, the arms grew longer, and more of them lunged for her. The fire pressed her toward the water, and the grasping hands forced her toward the fire.

Something wet and powerful gripped her ankle, and she fell forward into the mud. She tried to rise, but another watery hand grabbed her foot and pulled. She clawed at the ground, trying to find something to grip to keep herself from being dragged into the river. But she found only mud. She screamed into the crying fire when she felt the cool water touch her leg, then her waist, and finally her neck.

Mila dug her fingers into the muddy ground of the river bank, fighting to keep her head above the water. Then Amokat appeared, backlit by the flames.

"Please help me," Mila begged.

"Of course, little sister," said Amokat as she reached out one foot and stepped on the girl's fingers. In pain, Mila released her grip and disappeared beneath the river's surface.

The next morning, Mila returned to her family's house. Her beauty was gone. Her drawn face had a gray tint, and her eyes were red. She stood in the yard, unmoving, still as death, with mud, slime, and water grass hanging on her.

Mila's father took one look at her, went into the house for his shotgun, and blew his daughter's head off.

The Sudanic-speaking Lugbara live along the Nile-Congo divide between modern-day Uganda and the Belgian Congo. Numbering over a quarter million, they are primarily horticulturalists and pastoralists, with population centers on the almost treeless uplands of the Nile-Congo watershed.

A major focus of Lugbara religion is ancestor worship. Those who have begotten children are called *a'bi*, meaning "ancestor." When they die, they become *ori*, ghosts, and special shrines known as *orijo*, ghost houses, are erected by their families in their honor. The Lugbara believe that ghosts live under the huts that once housed them or in the sky. The ori have awareness of everything that the living do, and the living attempt to maintain good relations with their deceased ancestors through prayer and offerings.

Some people known as *Oleu*, witches, invoke hostile ori for their own evil ends. The Oleu are known as the ones who walk at night and are believed to be capable of shape-shifting, with leopard, wildcat, snake, jackal, owl, and monkey being favorite animal forms. These evil beings have been known to slip into their victim's house at night, perhaps in the form of a snake, and vomit blood on their prey, thus initiating the process by which their souls will be eaten. Some witches are called spitters. These Oleu spit on children's heads, causing them to waste away. Some Oleu have the power of the evil eye and can harm with a gaze. The Lugbara believe that when the Oleu fly, fire emits from their wrists and anus.

The traditional Lugbara belief is that God has two aspects. The positive is *Adroa 'Ba*, meaning the "God of the Sky," while the negative is *Adro*, "God of the Earth." Adro lives in rivers, appears as a whirlwind, can be heard crying in a grassfire, possesses young women, causes sickness and death, kidnaps people and eats them, and is considered the epitome of evil. Adro often takes the shape of a pale or almost translucent humanlike entity that has been torn in half, leaving half a face and the arms and legs on one side of the body. Adro, believed by the Lugbara to be the inversion of Adroa 'Ba (Good), is thought to be the master of witches and wizards.

Genie

FROM THE MENDE OF SIERRA LEONE

Senje had never traveled the Bome River trail, which had seldom been used since the new road connecting his village with the capital, Freetown, had been built. The new road was, however, a slower route because it meandered through numerous villages along its track. Some in Senje's village insisted that the old trail was completely overgrown and impassable, while the old-timers assured him that though there were rough stretches, he would be able to make it.

Senje needed to reach Freetown as soon as possible to register his claim on some frontier land, which he believed held deposits of bauxite. If it did indeed contain the ore, the land could make him rich.

Although the new road to Freetown was safer to travel, the Bome River trail would be quicker. So, with a newly sharpened, long-bladed bush knife, a sleeping mat and blanket, and provisions to last several days, Senje struck out on the Bome River trail early one morning.

By midday, Senje had ventured deep into the jungle and, to his concern, found that the trail had indeed become so overgrown that it was increasingly difficult to find. By late afternoon, he realized that he was hopelessly lost. That's when he saw an old white man sitting on a stump watching him with an amused smile on his face.

"Why are you so lost, young man?" asked the man.

Senje was momentarily startled by the question. "Why am I lost?" he repeated dumbly.

"Repeating the question is not an answer to the question," the old man said. He rose from his seat. "That's one for me, don't you agree?" the old man said happily.

"One what?" asked Senje.

"Ah, there you go again. That's *two* for me." The white man took a step toward Senje. Then he asked, "How many ways are there to Freetown?"

"Well," said Senje, "there is the old Bome River trail and the new road to Freetown."

"Ah, but what if one person takes the new road to Freetown and walks faster than another who takes the Bome River trail? Is that the same way or a different way?"

Now that the novelty of seeing an aged white man in the middle of the jungle had worn off, Senje grew irritated and said rather harshly, "Sir, if you can direct me back to the Bome River trail, I would greatly appreciate it."

"The answer to my question first," the man replied.

Senje resettled his pack on his shoulders. "I'm tired of your questions. I've got business to take care of in Freetown, and you are wasting my time."

"You are free to go anywhere you wish, young man. But then again you are lost, so one can't say that you are going anywhere if, in fact, you don't know where you are." The man took another step toward Senje.

Although the old man looked quite frail, Senje felt a vague feeling of uneasiness. He scanned the area and thought he saw a trail cutting off to the north.

"I'll leave you to your pondering, sir," he said and pushed into the brush crowding the trail. The old man's dry chuckle followed him into the brush.

For several hours, Senje fought his way through the thicket. The sun descended, and it occurred to Senje that night would overtake him before he reached his destination. Night in the deep jungle was not a situation that Senje relished, and he drove himself harder, cutting away at the thick brush.

"Hello, again," came the familiar voice. The old white man sat on a low branch beside the trail.

Senje was dumbstruck. "How . . . how did you get here?"

"Oh, good, a question for me," answered the old man. "Let's see. I must be careful how I answer." He jumped lightly to the ground in front of Senje and smiled. "Perhaps I was here all along, young man."

"No, you weren't. I was talking to you a few hours ago back up the trail somewhere," Senje said, his breath coming quickly.

"But how could I have been there when I have been here all the time?" quizzed the old man.

"That's not possible," insisted Senje.

"Tell me what is possible." The old man moved slowly toward Senje.

"I don't know . . . anything that is possible is possible," replied Senje.

"Tautology! Tautology!" the old man shouted. "I win."

"You win what?"

The old man stepped closer, stroked his beard, and answered, "I think for my prize I will take your left hand."

Moving faster than was humanly possible, the mysterious man opened his mouth extraordinarily wide, revealing several rows of pointed teeth, and snapped Senje's left hand from his arm. The young man grabbed the bleeding stump to his chest, eyes wide in shock.

"Now tell me quickly. Where is a mouse when it spins?"

Senje whimpered, trying to wrap his shirt around the end of his bleeding arm.

"No answer?" the old man asked.

Senje looked pleadingly at him. "Please don't . . ."

In a blur of motion, the man bit off his right hand. Senje fell and numbly watched his life's blood drench the jungle floor.

"Now tell me, young man. If a two-handed man manages to lose both his hands, how many hands does he have?"

Senje's eyes glazed over as his life slipped away.

"Come now," said the old man, "that was an easy one. Don't leave me yet. I have more questions." He leaned over and bit off Senje's right foot. "Now tell me. What is higher than the highest thing in all existence?"

Senje was dead. The old man kicked the corpse a few times. "Young people today just aren't what they used to be," he mumbled and dissolved into the night.

The Mende comprise 30 percent of the population of Sierra Leone—a country on the west coast of Africa. The coastline stretches for 300 miles. Along this shore and extending approximately 70 miles inland is a belt of low-lying land that gradually rises as one moves westward. Agriculture is the main occupation of the people, and about 80 percent of the manpower in Sierra Leone is directed toward this work.

Muslims comprise 60 percent of the population, while 10 percent are Christian, and 30 percent continue traditional religious practices. The central thrust of the composite religion of the Mende is the health and augmentation of agricultural activity. Allah, Jehovah, and the traditional clan and nature gods are invoked to provide ample rain for the crops and to direct storms and floods away from the Mende's children. The second theme in the Mende religion is the vitality and continuance of clans and families.

The Genie encountered by the hapless hiker, Senje, reveals a combination of cultural elements. The Genie is found wherever Islam is found. Originally, these beings were specifically identified as patrilineal ancestral protective spirits, but in time, they became generic spirit beings, some of them good, others evil. The Genie among the Mende is described as a type of nature spirit. Some are spirits of the forest while some are associated with water. All are dangerous. The fact that the Genie in the story is an old white man who confuses people is easily seen to be the result of the not-always-benign relationships between the native population and the Europeans, who began incursions in the seventeenth century.

5. Demons
of Asia

Oyasi

FROM THE AINU OF SAKHALIN

The villagers of Takeo Kohen were ready for drastic measures. Although the name of their village means bamboo garden, it was hardly a garden at all when the infestation of rats began several months earlier. The villagers resorted to ancient rituals to drive the vermin away. They burned rat effigies. They made sacrifices to the local *kami*, spirits. They consulted the Shinto priests and the spirit mediums, but none of their advice worked, and the rats only seemed to increase in number. The chittering of the rodents in the night kept people awake; those who did manage to fall asleep had nightmares. The rats even attacked sleeping infants—in one case, a baby's eyelashes were chewed off before its screams could rouse its sleeping parents.

After much debate, the village council concluded that the time had come to shift tactics—they would hire professional exterminators from the city. Some of the village elders on the council warned that killing the rats in such a way would bring danger, but the younger councilmen ignored their concerns and suggested that they should appreciate the miracles of modern vermin extermination. Outnumbered, the elders gave in, and the exterminators soon came with ferrets, snakes, dogs, succulent poison baits, lethal gases, and sweet deadly liquids.

The exterminators proved successful, and in the following days, the dead and dying rodents were piled in the village square. Soon, the mound stood eight feet high, a pulsing mass of rats. Gasoline was poured over the mound, and the crew's foreman ignited the conflagration with the toss of a match. Bystanders retched from the stench of sizzling rat fat. The high-pitched screams of the dying rats rose in the putrid air, and people covered their ears to shut out the horrific cacophony.

Despite their discomfort, the villagers cheered the destruction of the rats; however, a large bird with long claws, eyes like a wildcat, and golden-flecked black feathers perched itself high in a tree overlooking the square and hissed in rage. It watched the crime against the rats, and a tremendous anger burned in its evil heart. The creature was not a bird at all, but rather an *Oyasi*—a demon that had created the imposing bird as a conveyance and disguise.

Early the next morning, a large rat—invisible to those in the town square—observed the people bustling happily about, going to school, doing the day's shopping, and chatting with their neighbors. The Oyasi absorbed the malevolent energy of the slaughtered rodents from the remains of the smoldering fire, and the horror started without preamble.

First, the Oyasi rat bit the hand off one of the men. People screamed as other appendages were gnawed from bodies, ragged holes appeared on faces and arms, and gouts of blood spewed. The Oyasi rat chewed through the panicked townspeople until it was exhausted. Then, it transformed into an ordinary gray rat, which the people could now see. Its mouth was covered in blood.

Understanding that the rat had somehow caused the horror in their village, the people rushed toward it with one angry roar. Using the energy of their rage, the Oyasi multiplied itself a thousand times over, and rats boiled out of thin air, attacking everyone in sight. The slaughter of the townspeople was complete within minutes. For the remainder of the day, hordes of rats swarmed over Takeo Kohen, carrying shreds of humans to their underground lairs.

The town was never resettled. Locals came to call the place Oyasi Kohen—the monster's garden. Sometimes travelers on the road late at night claim to see lights in abandoned houses, and a few report unusually high-pitched squeaking sounds when they near the edge of town.

The Ainu of Sakhalin descended from the original inhabitants of Japan. They lived as hunters and gatherers, harvesting the produce of the land. Today, they continue their ancient way of life with additions such as horticulture, lumbering, business, and herding. They are identified by the profundity of their epic poetry and the aesthetic sensitivity expressed in skillful woodcarvings by men, and weaving and needlework by women. They also possess a botanist's knowledge of their local flora.

As with many ancient populations, religion enters every facet of their life. All the world is spirituality alive to the Ainu. Spirits, gods, heroes, and demons roam the landscape—beings derived from ancient beliefs, as well as from later Shintoist and Buddhist religious ideas. Everything the Ainu do must be understood in terms of maintaining good relations with the supernatural. Opening a gate, disposing of trash, celebrating birth, all have rituals that must be adhered to.

Ainu demons, which they call *Oyasi*, exist as two basic types—intrinsic demons and estranged-soul demons—and can be either visible or invisible. People with proper sensitivity can "feel" the presence of invisible demons. Intrinsic demons are simply born as demons, whereas estranged-soul demons become such because of mistakes made by the living. For example, bungled funeral arrangements may create an estranged-soul demon. Further, since everything—including inanimate objects—is spiritual, or contains a spirit, to the Ainu, an estranged-soul demon may be accidentally created by any seemingly everyday act. For instance, a man moving to a new house must be careful to locate all his tools and to break the ones he is abandoning in order to release their spirits. If a tool is left behind unbroken, its spirit will become angered and will seek to kill the tool's owner.

The Ainu say that Oyasi specialize in masquerading as birds—generally with unusually long talons, catlike eyes, and gold-flecked feathers. They can also become demon night birds, whose nocturnal calls cause insanity. In all their manifestations, the Oyasi possess incredible strength and are capable of picking up a house and turning it upside down. Although humans are powerless against the Oyasi, they do have warnings of the demons' presence—the skulls of sacrificed puppies are said to bark when an Oyasi is near. Since the Ainu believe that they have no power whatsoever to defeat the evils of demons on their own, they hope that these warnings will suffice.

Huli Jing

FROM CHINA

Man-Yu, a scholar, prided himself on his level-headed, rational approach to living and assailed what he considered fuzzy-headed thinking at every opportunity. He would say such things as, "He who does not keep the search for truth foremost in his mind sows the seeds of his own destruction," and "All answers must be received with doubt until they have survived the cauldron of rigorous analysis." And when asked about the impact of the *Kuei*, evil spirits, he would laugh and say, "Mature people refuse to see their own shadows as ghosts. Mature people know the difference between the real and the unreal."

The scholar was much loved in his village, but he was loved most by his beautiful young wife, Ching-Wah, the joy of his life. Just thinking about her radiant smile would illuminate his day. She was as soft as a flower and as graceful as a fawn. He would hold her in his arms at night and whisper, "You are true. You are real," and she would sigh with delight knowing that these words reflected Man-Yu's highest possible praise.

Then she died. While carrying his noonday meal to the village school, a tile fell from the roof of the community temple and split Ching-Wah's head open. Man-Yu was devastated. He tried to understand his loss through logic and analysis, as was his way, but nothing could overcome the dark depression that gripped him. He quit teaching and wandered the streets crying through the night. His lonely walks always ended at the cemetery, where he would throw himself upon Ching-Wah's grave and howl in mad despair.

One winter night, as the moon hung in a hazy sky, Man-Yu entered the cemetery on leaden feet and walked numbly to the grave. A movement, a rustle in the grass, caught his eye. Astounded, he watched a fox emerge from the neglected grave next to Ching-Wah's. It didn't crawl from a hole in the ground, he noticed, but rather simply materialized as if rising through the earth.

"My grief has affected my mind," he thought. "I'm dreaming while I'm wide awake."

"No, scholar, you are seeing truly," the fox spoke. "And isn't that what you want to do—to see truly?"

Man-Yu's knees buckled, and he dropped to the ground. Kneeling before the fox, Man-Yu asked in a trembling voice, "Who . . . who are you?"

"I am whatever you want me to be, scholar," replied the fox.

"You are not real," Man-Yu said as if the statement in itself had power. The fox jumped forward and nipped his finger. Man-Yu pulled his bleeding digit back and stuck the tip in his mouth.

"Real enough for you, scholar?" the fox asked.

"Let me alone," Man-Yu said. "Haven't I suffered enough? Go and harass someone else. I have nothing you want."

The fox sat before Man-Yu. "But I have something you want, scholar."

"The only thing I want is beyond my reach," Man-Yu cried. "Oh, Ching-Wah, I miss you so much."

The fox nipped Man-Yu again. "Stop your whimpering, scholar, and listen to me. I can give you what you want. All you have to do is ask."

Man-Yu shook his head. "You are a nightmare. You are not real. You..."

"What's all this nonsense about my not being real? What do I have to do to convince you? Chew your whole arm off? You rational people are such idiots," the fox said. Then his body shimmered, and to Man-Yu's amazement, Ching-Wah stood before him.

Instead of running into her beckoning arms, Man-Yu fainted. A few minutes later, he came to with the fox licking his face.

"What? Where?" the scholar mumbled and looked around for Ching-Wah.

"True or not true? Real or not real?" asked the fox.

"I . . . I . . . all right, yes. It's true," he conceded. "Bring Ching-Wah back to me."

"Ah, very good, scholar. Now you go back to your cottage and wait. Tomorrow I will bring back your beloved and also set before you wealth and fine food. It was easy, wasn't it? But once again, tell me, scholar. Am I real or not real?" the fox prodded.

"You are real. That is obvious, or I wouldn't be talking to you," Man-Yu admitted.

"Then again, you have been under a lot of stress, and perhaps you might be dreaming," said the fox.

"I don't care. Don't torture me. I want her back," the scholar pleaded.

"Then go home, and I will cast a sleeping spell over you and you will rest. Tomorrow you will receive all that I have promised." With that, the fox vanished.

Just after dawn the following day, Man-Yu awoke abruptly. Beside him lay Ching-Wah, soft and warm and smelling of subtle perfume. Man-Yu kissed her, and she responded passionately. The morning passed in bliss.

Toward noon, Man-Yu walked into his front room where the table was set with a sumptuous feast for two, and hundreds of gold coins were strewn about. He called to Ching-Wah, and she joined him at the feast. After eating the fine meal and counting their newfound wealth, they again made love and slept. All night, Man-Yu dreamed of Ching-Wah and his amazing good fortune. He awoke to wet kisses. But it was not Ching-Wah—it was the fox, licking his face.

"Good morning, scholar, defender of the real and true."

Man-Yu looked around quickly and sighed with relief when he saw Ching-Wah sleeping beside him, the remains of his meal and the golden coins glistening on the table.

"You scholars are such fools," the fox said.

"You have given me everything that I want, fox. Why now do you insult me?" Man-Yu asked suspiciously.

"You have what you want? Is that what you're telling me?" asked the fox.

"Oh, yes. Everything is . . ."

"You idiot," the fox barked. "Look upon your real and true love, your real and true food, and your real and true fortune." The fox indicated Ching-Wah with his paw. She was still there, but in her real condition—a rotting corpse. "Behold," said the fox, pointing to the table. The wonderful food had, in fact, been enchanted chicken droppings, and the golden coins were rocks.

Man-Yu retched, his mind reeling.

"The true. The real," said the fox with a sneer.

Man-Yu sat still, his jaw slack.

"I have another gift for you, scholar," the fox said, waving his paws in the air, and a knife materialized in front of Man-Yu.

"What do you see, scholar?" the fox asked.

Man-Yu stared at the knife. "I see a jade pendant," he said thickly.

"Very good, scholar. Now feel how cool the jade is. Touch it to your face," prodded the fox.

The scholar did, and blood flowed from the cut.

The fox went on, "Now rub its cool softness across your throat."

The scholar obeyed, and the blood from his jugular gushed down his chest.

"Is it real, scholar? Is it true?" the fox asked.

"Oh, yes, it is real, and it is true," replied the scholar with his last breath.

"Idiots all around me," the fox laughed and scurried out of the house and into the bushes.

China has always been a nation of farmers. Cattle play little or no part in the economy and never did. Rice is king, or rather, emperor. The great dynasties that have led China to matchless cultural developments were all based on the ability of the peasant populations to provide food to feed soldiers and armies of workers who in turn built great canals, temples, walls, and cities, and who maintained the defense of China for thousands of years.

With perhaps the longest continuous history of any nation on earth, China possesses a rich legacy of demonic images. Buddhism and Taoism provide tales of evil spirits and devils. The various ethnic groups found along the western edges of the nation contribute to the wide variety of Chinese spiritual beliefs. One of the most ancient and widespread beliefs centers on the *Kuei*—ghostly demons who bring death, insanity, or illness. They strike at humans in anger because either they died unjustly or their graves were disturbed or neglected. Of the Kuei, one of the most dangerous is the *Huli Jing*—the Fox Fairy.

The Huli Jing is a shape-shifter. It may appear as an animal, an old man, a seductive young woman, or a long-dead relative or friend. It takes special delight in attacking scholars because they are thought to be especially virtuous and reasonable people, qualities that enrage the Fox Fairy. Although immortal, this demon requires the souls of humans to maintain this state. Of particular interest to the Fox Fairy is the vital essence expressed during sexual orgasm. To ingest this power, it will change into a beautiful woman or a handsome man and seduce its prey. If the mortal succumbs to this temptation, he or she will soon wither and die. In addition to its power as a shape-shifter, Huli Jing can enter houses through walls, fly, and become invisible at will. It delights in making people believe the opposite of what something really is—what is seen as beautiful is, in fact, repulsive, and what is experienced as sweet is actually sour. Fox Fairies emerge from the earth in graveyards after dark and prowl on rooftops, waiting for the arrogantly virtuous or the unbearably rational to come along.

Tamboree

FROM THE DUSUN OF BORNEO

Ponapeh wanted to end it before things got out of hand. Jinka was his neighbor, after all, and they were both Dusun, he reminded himself. The two had fought. They had been drinking and had disagreed over something minor. They exchanged provoking words, and Jinka swung at Ponapeh and split his lip. Ponapeh, younger and stronger, shook off Jinka's punch and floored him with a solid right cross. Some men at the party separated them, and after a few more drinks, both passed out.

Ponapeh woke the next morning, his head pounding. It took him a moment, but he reconstructed the night before and the fight with his neighbor. "Alcohol does that to people," he thought sadly. Further rumination convinced him that he should go to Jinka and apologize, maybe offer him a small gift. It was bad for neighbors to be angry at each other. The village wasn't that big, and tension between two people could affect everyone. Ponapeh was a good Dusun, so he decided to visit Jinka and try to resolve their spat.

Jinka was sitting on a bench beside his house when Ponapeh approached. He didn't look up.

"Hello, Jinka, how are you today?" Ponapeh started uncomfortably.

Jinka just stared at the ground in front of him.

Ponapeh removed his bracelet and placed it on the bench. "Here, my friend. Please take this gift. Let's not fall out with each other. We are neighbors. We are Dusun."

Jinka brushed the bracelet to the ground.

Ponapeh looked down at Jinka sadly. "If that's the way you want it. . . . I'm sorry you feel that way." He closed the gate behind him.

As soon as Ponapeh left his yard, Jinka went inside, stepping on Ponapeh's bracelet on his way. In the space vacated by the two men, the ether vibrated with a chilling evil. Fed by the hostility Jinka felt, the *Tapun*—the evil force that harms any person who refuses an act of friendship—grew. Sensing Tapun, the *Tamboree*—disease-givers—came.

Jinka understood that something was amiss that evening when he left to visit his friends. He stepped out of his front door and fell over something. When he turned to look back at it, there was nothing there. Shaking his head in puzzlement, he unlatched the gate and stepped through it, only to rip his shirt on the latch. Then he stepped on his cat, whose yowl alerted a dog, who attacked it. The angry cat climbed Jinka's body for safety, which it found on his head. By this time, Jinka's antics had drawn a small crowd of neighbors. His neighbors laughed hysterically as the poor man went from one mishap to the next. No one knew that he was being toyed with by the Tamboree; they thought he was drunk.

Trying to remove the terrified cat from his head, Jinka backed into the garden fence and fell over it, flipping backward to the ground as the cat jumped off. The swelling crowd laughed and applauded. Then, Jinka felt something crawling up his legs. He slapped at his pants and danced from foot to foot. The crowd clapped along, keeping time.

"Damn you all," Jinka screamed. "Somebody help me!"

His face turned red. He tried to speak again, but without success. Then his mouth opened wide, as if someone had pried it open against his will, and out came, "I am up the down puddle pig knuckle go for empty." His jaw clamped shut, then he shot out, "What am I happening? Who do I mean?"

Jinka was the Tamboree's puppet, and he struggled futilely against its power. The evil spirit forced him to undress before the crowd and caper like a madman. Finally, the Tamboree tired of this game with the hapless mortal and struck. Jinka's temperature rose rapidly with fever. He dropped to the ground, and sweat poured off his body as he crawled in the dirt. The Tamboree stuffed a piece of filth from Jinka's coat into his mouth, and the doomed man coughed and hemorrhaged. Lesions covered his face. He could feel his life slipping from him. His neighbors stood back; no one in the crowd was willing to touch him.

They now understood all too clearly that Jinka had not been an amusing drunk, clowning for their enjoyment, but rather a man who had incurred the state of Tapun and all the horror that accompanied it.

Three-fourths of Borneo, the world's third largest island and home of the Dusun, is jungle. Swamps, coastal plains, and mountains with elevations between five and six thousand feet are also part of the Dusun's world. The Dusun subsist by gardening, with a great emphasis placed on rice cultivation, both wet and dry; by continuing their ancient hunting and gathering practices; and by gathering raw materials for an array of manufacturing projects. However, these projects are circumscribed by an incredible collection of customs and rules.

The many rules of Dusun life are enforced by the demons of their world. *Tamboree*, disease-givers, are very difficult to differentiate from ordinary people unless one has *second sight*, the ability to see spirits. They are the owners of all aspects of nature—water, air, rock, trees, plants, soil, mountains, animals, and humans. Existing from the beginning of time, they are always ready to punish humans for violations of the natural world. The Tamboree not only attack and kill humans but also enjoy making their victims look like fools before they die. They are often aided in their mayhem against humanity by the *Ragun*, souls of the dead. These beings have been cursed by the creator god to wander the earth, subsisting as cannibals. The Tamboree and the Ragun are drawn into cooperative action against humans when the demons sense *Tapun*—a negative spiritual state that is offensive to the demons. Refusing a gift offered in friendship can bring about Tapun.

Oni

FROM JAPAN

Ten-year-old Billy Johnson, with his big blue eyes and light blond hair, was a big hit with the people of Japan. They would stop him and his parents on the street to exclaim, *"Kawai desu, neh?"* which roughly means, "What a beautiful child." Billy's mother, Imogene, would nod and smile warmly, clearly understanding the compliment.

Billy's stepfather, Frank, on the other hand, had no use for any of it. Frank blamed the Japanese for his father's death during World War II, and he was not in Japan for sightseeing or cultural enrichment or to listen to these backward people compliment the kid. He was there to complete some legal work for the Japanese operations division of the engineering firm that employed him. He found Japanese food disgusting—"seaweed, rice, fish, and a bunch of stuff you can't even tell what the hell it is."

Frank bullied his way through meetings with his Japanese counterparts, and when they invited him out to dinner, he always found an excuse to decline. But one day, he was invited to bring his family to a small rural community outside Dazaifu for a local festival. His boss, having heard ever so subtly of Frank's prejudice, strongly suggested that he take Imogene and Billy to the festival and that he act as if he were enjoying himself.

The family of three boarded the train in Fukuoka, and Frank grumbled the entire trip, but Imogene and Billy enjoyed the adventure.

The golden rice fields of autumn sped by, and Billy pointed to the ancient Tori gates on the mountainside. "What is that, Mom?" he asked.

Frank answered before Imogene could open her mouth. "Just some crap, some Japanese crap. Now, shut up and read your book."

Billy didn't like his stepfather but tried to be a good boy for his mother's sake, so he kept quiet for the rest of the trip. He leaned against his mother's shoulder while she read the English language brochure about the festival that Frank's boss had given them. He examined the pictures of the strange-looking buildings and men carrying huge colorful statues. According to the brochure, the festival parade would begin on the grounds of a large Zen temple and wind its ways through the narrow streets of the town.

Soon, Imogene was guiding her irritable husband and delighted son to the front of the temple, where hundreds of boisterous, celebrating people had already gathered.

"Big frigging deal," said Frank.

"Mom, can I look around?" Billy asked.

Imogene looked at Frank, but he was busy ignoring everything around him. "Yes, dear, just don't go too far, and check back with me every now and then. If you hear a big bell ring, come back right away. The pamphlet says that they ring the temple bell before the parade starts."

Billy took off. He liked the friendly, laughing people who crowded the path to the temple and found the decorations and costumes "totally cool." He watched some men performing martial arts for a while, then bought himself a soft drink at one of the many concession stands that lined the approach to the temple.

People rushed here and there, shouting happily to one another and preparing the floats that would be carried by large groups of men along the parade route. Several times, he was moved gently out of the way and was told to stay clear of the big floats in case one accidentally fell over. He didn't understand what they were saying, but he could tell that they were trying to help him somehow. Next, he decided to walk deeper into the garden surrounding the temple to see what the people were doing back there. Along the way, he found a stream full of *koi*, giant goldfish, and he drifted along watching their skin glisten in the sunlight.

Someone spoke to him. *"Kawai desu, neh?"* That, he understood.

It was a young woman dressed in a brightly colored kimono. She beckoned him, gently took his chin in her fingers, and smiled. She smelled like flowers. Suddenly, a frown lightly touched the young woman's brow. At her feet, a tiny frog sat on a patch of moss. Bending down, she squashed it with her palm and put the gooey remains in a silk handkerchief that she pulled from her kimono sleeve. Stunned, Billy stared up at her with his mouth agape.

"Now, pretty little boy, you must do as I tell you." She handed the folded kerchief to Billy and said, "There will come a time today when you must take this magic charm and rub it on your tummy." Billy didn't notice that the woman spoke to him in English, nor did he notice that her lips did not move. "You will know when the time comes for you to do what I say. Do you understand?" Billy nodded dumbly.

One more time she touched his face and sighed, *"Kawai desu, neh?"*

Billy watched her as she continued down the garden path to a dark, old building that sat deep in a bamboo grove. The ponderous boom of a temple bell rumbled over the town, and the pretty woman was gone. Billy absent-mindedly stuck the kerchief holding the smashed frog into his pocket and ran to find his mother and Frank.

He arrived as the first float was carried out the front door of the temple. People cheered, and some threw buckets of water at the men who carried the elaborate floats on their shoulders. Some held statues of samurai warriors, which Billy recognized, but most were strange images that he did not understand. Then, as the last float passed, he smelled flowers, and tugged on his mother's arm.

"What does the pamphlet say about that one," he asked.

Imogene leafed quickly through the pages. "Oh, that one is called an Oni. It's some kind of bogeyman, you might say."

"Some kind of silly crap, you might say," Frank mocked.

Billy stared at the statue transfixed. It was about five times taller than he, with green skin and horns and big sharp teeth in a mouth that spread from ear to ear. The monster carried a long, spiked metal staff. Its face was flat, with three eyes, one of which winked at him as it passed.

"Mom, it winked at me! Did you see it? Did you?" Billy asked.

"What, dear?"

"That Oni thing winked at me."

Frank slapped the top of his head. "Don't talk like an idiot."

Suddenly, chaos erupted. The Oni statue began to move and people screamed as it jumped into the crowd. It grabbed Frank and twisted his head off. Imogene fainted. Panicked people ran in all directions away from the Oni, which was ripping through the crowd in a killing frenzy. When Billy watched it pick up several children and chew out their belly buttons, he knew the time was right. He opened the silk handkerchief and rubbed the gory remains of the frog on his stomach. No sooner had he finished than the Oni plucked him from the ground and brought its terrible mouth toward his stomach. But, with a grunt of disgust, it pulled its gruesome face back and tossed him, unharmed, into the shallow river. Then, the Oni disappeared into the forest beyond the temple garden.

Billy heard the wailing of the sirens, and soon ambulances were collecting the human remains that littered the street. He wandered through the frazzled crowd looking for his mother. To his relief, he found her being cared for by a nurse. In English the nurse said, "Don't worry little boy. Your mother will be fine. She just needs to sit here for a minute and rest."

Assured that his mother was going to be okay, Billy wound his way through the rescue workers and tried not to look at the bloody remains as he stepped over them. He was drawn back to the stream where the giant goldfish swam. Someone called to him, and the beautiful young woman in the bright kimono walked from the dark building in the bamboo grove. She dabbed at a red stain in the corner of her mouth as she approached. Billy smelled flowers when she touched his face. *"Kawai desu, neh?"* she whispered. And she disappeared.

From the beginning of time, monsters have stalked the islands of Japan. The native religion, Shinto, the way of the Gods, was heavily influenced by shamanism and the belief in *kami*—spirits that occupy all unusually powerful things, including humans. According to tradition, Prince Shotoku introduced Chinese Buddhist influences into Japan in 660 BCE, and with them came more spirit and demonic images of Chinese and Indian origin. In 1543, a Chinese cargo ship carrying three Portuguese traders ran aground on the Japanese island of Tanegashima, introducing the era of Japanese contact with the cultures of the West. Several years later, St. Francis Xavier entered Japan to spread the Christian religion. Each of these cultural waves added new elements, which were manipulated by the Japanese people into acceptable cultural forms and integrated into their way of life. It is not surprising, then, that Japanese lore includes numerous dragons, ghosts, monsters, demons, and fairies—some more obviously influenced by outside contact than others.

The Oni has some classic worldwide demonic traits, as well as some uniquely Japanese elements. In its fully developed form, it is seen as a giant ogre with horns, large sharp teeth, three eyes, talons at the end of its three toes, and claws instead of fingernails. The Oni can have a variety of skin colors—pink, blue, black, red, or green, with green being the most common. They are often depicted carrying a *kanabo,* a large spiked weapon. They have the power to reconnect body parts that may be hacked away in a fight, to fly, to change their forms at will, and to inflict disease, insanity, and death. Their favorite food is human flesh, and they delight in causing societal breakdown, quarreling, and confusion. Intelligent yet grotesquely uncouth, the Oni are gluttons for food and drink. They are associated with the wild and untamed regions but also reside in cities, often in the guise of a beautiful young woman.

Pisatji

FROM THE JAVANESE OF MODJOKUTO

Abdur Suwanto, the banker, walked home from work through the cool bamboo grove. He had taken the same path thousands of times since inheriting the bank from his father twenty years earlier. His mind wandered over the transactions of the day, and he was pleased. There had been a few rough patches, but bankers have to expect that the local population doesn't always understand what bankers have to do to make a living. Sometimes it is simply time to foreclose on a house; other times a loan must be refused or someone who owes back rent must be evicted.

Abdur enjoyed the power. He actually liked pushing the little people around. Of course, sometimes the little people pushed back. Fortunately, he had the means to deal with that eventuality. He thought of the old cobbler who had failed to pay back a small loan. When Abdur showed him the contract that morning and explained that he must vacate his small shop because it now belonged to the bank, the old man became enraged.

"I signed nothing that said you would own my shop if I couldn't make the payments on my loan," the cobbler argued.

"Ah, perhaps you didn't read the language under subsection three," the banker said condescendingly. "It says here . . ."

"I worked with you in good faith," said the cobbler, "and now you treat me like a child . . . with no respect."

"It is not my fault if you don't understand business and banking procedures," responded the banker. "Perhaps you don't even deserve to have a business if you are so ignorant of basic . . ."

"Ignorant?" yelled the cobbler. "You . . . you . . ."

"Be off my property by nightfall," the banker responded icily and left the shop, leaving the cobbler behind trembling in rage.

"Lies to me, shows me no respect," he mumbled to himself. "I'm old enough to be his grandfather, and he treats me like a child."

The cobbler knew what he had to do. He locked up the shop and hurried off to find Madam Sardijito, a *Dukun*, a sorceress of great power. She would be able to help him. After presenting a small gift of tobacco to her, the cobbler complained about how the banker had cheated him, lied to him, and treated him like a child.

When the cobbler mentioned being treated like a child, the Dukun smiled and raised her hand. "Ah," she said, "have you not seen the *Pisatji*, the wandering spirit children, playing around the cemetery?"

"No," said the cobbler with an involuntary shudder.

"Yes, yes," said the Dukun, "they wait and watch, wait and watch. They hide in the shadows and are hard to see for those without the proper gifts."

"Wait and watch for what, Madam?" the cobbler asked.

"They watch for an adult to enter," she told him.

The cobbler had heard these stories since he was very young. Spirits of many types existed in the Javanese countryside, but he had never thought much about them.

"But what does this have to do with me?" the cobbler asked, perplexed.

"Ah, don't you see? The banker has a soft life. He lives in a fine house. He eats well. He has whatever he wants . . ."

" . . . because he steals from honest people like me, and . . ."

"Yes, of course," interrupted the Dukun. "What I am telling you is that the wanderers must be told of this banker and perhaps they will take him as their own."

"What will happen to the banker?" asked the cobbler.

"When the Pisatji take him, he will become as a small child, and he will stay that way until the Pisatji grow bored with their human toy and move on in search of another," the woman explained.

"How do I arrange this, Madam?"

"You must go to the cemetery late tonight. Take some toys with you and some candies. Find a child's grave and sit on it; then spread the toys and candy on the ground around you. When you see them move, it means the wanderers have come to play. It is then that you ask them to do what you want and promise them more toys and candy if they succeed."

Late that night, the cobbler slipped into the cemetery and found the grave of a child who had, according to information on the grave marker, died at the age of ten. Sitting upon the child's grave, the cobbler spread the toys and candies around him and addressed the darkness. "Come, my little ones. Come play with me and receive my gifts. Come to me."

The cobbler heard a noise. Light footsteps approached from the shadows. He strained to see in the darkness but without success. The steps came closer. "Come to me, my wanderers," the cobbler intoned. "Come play with me."

Suddenly, an invisible foot smashed one of the toys. The cobbler froze. The candy likewise was violently flattened by something unseen. Then the remaining toys rose from the ground and flew, as if thrown, into the overgrown hedges surrounding the cemetery. The cobbler's breath caught in his throat when he saw a small girl, dressed in rags, materialize before him. Her eyes were wide and unblinking. She bestowed a hideous smile upon him as she approached.

"No," cried the cobbler. "Not me!" He stumbled to his feet and tried to run, but his feet were somehow stuck to the grave upon which he had been sitting. The little girl, gibbering mindlessly to herself, floated up to the cobbler and touched his heart. In that instant, she disappeared, and the cobbler fell to the ground unconscious.

Early the next morning, villagers on their way to work found the cobbler sitting in the dirt next to the cemetery road. He babbled to himself and played with little balls of mud. When he noticed the bystanders' attention, he smiled and said, "I call this one Bibi, and this one is Yohoha, and this one is my mommy, and this one is my puppy."

People shook their heads and walked on. "The poor man is crazy," they said.

Around noon, Abdur Suwanto, the banker, walked past the graveyard with an associate, a secret partner in his bank. "Ah, look at the poor cobbler," he said. "His mind is gone. Poor, poor man." He laughed. "Now what do you suppose happened to him?"

"The same thing that will happen to anyone who threatens one of mine. Isn't that right, banker?" replied his companion, the Dukun.

"Yes, Madam Sardijito," the banker replied, proffering a respectful bow.

Set in a land of irrigated rice paddies and mud-walled villages bordering streams that flow through the countryside, Modjokuto is home to about 18,000 Javanese, 1,800 Chinese, and a small contingent of Arabs, Indians, and other minority groups. A combination of Hindu, Buddhist, Muslim, and local shamanic beliefs and practices forms the pattern of religious behavior in the area.

Central to most beliefs, however, is the existence of three types of spirits: *Lelembut,* the ethereal ones; *Tujul,* familiar spirits; and *Memedis,* the frighteners. Lelembut are invisible spirits that take great pleasure in causing illness or driving people crazy. Their unique characteristic as possessing spirits is that they enter their victims through the soles of their feet. Highly localized, they dwell in clumps of bamboo or in large and interesting-looking rocks. Tujul are often spirit children, or "children who are not human beings," not to be confused with the Pisatji discussed below. The Tujul can help humans attain wealth and power if they are dealt with correctly.

Memedis, on the other hand, like to terrorize people, and are capable of taking various forms. A common Memedis is the *Sundel Bolong.* This Memedis appears as a beautiful, desirable young woman with long flowing hair that covers a large hole which penetrates the middle of her body. If a man succumbs to her seductive attacks, she will castrate him and leave him paralyzed to bleed to death. Another very common Memedis is *Gendruwos.* Although usually merely playful, Gendruwos can also be dangerous. One of their ploys is to imitate a woman's husband and sleep with her. Resulting children will be monsters. Other Memedis include the *Djrangkong,* a man "with his flesh off"; the *Panaspati,* whose head is where his genitals should be and who walks on his hands breathing fire; the *Uwils,* former Buddhist soldiers; the *Setan Gundul,* bald devils; and the *Pisatji,* the wandering spirit children. The Pisatji, some say, are the spirits of aborted children materialized through the powers of the Memedis. Others think that the Memedis spirit children are the souls of lost or abandoned children. In 1960, a large, black, and curiously misshapen child in the village of Modjokuto was said to be a Pisatji. Belief in these beings is so real that traditional Javanese villagers will generally not walk abroad at night.

Rai Na'in

FROM THE TETUM OF EASTERN TIMOR

Life for Hanu and his family was good. He had many pigs and his wife's gardens produced a surplus of yams and other vegetables. Peace and plenty tended to be conducive to family growth, and soon Hanu found himself with three sons and two daughters. He was running out of space for a garden sufficient to feed his family, so through the village council, he arranged to trade his land for a larger piece on the fringes of the village.

The new site was perfect, and he moved his family as soon as he had made preliminary arrangements. The first night they slept under the stars and whispered to one another in the dark about what kind of house they would build.

"Tomorrow, the rest of our lives will begin," Hanu whispered to the night.

He roused his family early the next morning. "Big day today. Come on, sleepyheads, get up and get at it."

The family ate a frugal breakfast. Hanu could not eat much; he was too excited about staking out the foundation for his new house. He shouldered a spade and walked about a hundred yards south to the site where the house would be built. It was a perfect spot, a bit overgrown, but he and his sons would tend to that the first day. He was about to drive his spade into the earth when a strangely accented voice stopped him.

"I wouldn't do that if I were you, sir," the voice warned.

Hanu beheld a short person—man or woman he couldn't tell—who swayed from side to side on stubby legs. It wore a ragged loincloth and had unnaturally meaty, probably very powerful arms that were a third longer than normal. Hanu's attention was drawn to the intruder's hands— huge, big-knuckled hands.

"I don't know who you are," said Hanu, "but the village council assigned me this land. If you have a problem, take it to them."

Hanu raised his spade, and once again he heard, "I wouldn't do that if I were you, sir," but this time, the voice was soft and pretty. The little person with the strange hands and arms was gone, and a young woman stood in its place.

Hanu raised his spade, keeping his eyes on the young woman; and suddenly, where she had stood, there lay a large snake, its tongue flicking as it hissed, "I wouldn't do that if I were you, sir."

Finally, Hanu dropped his spade and ran back to the camp. Meanwhile, Hanu's eldest son, Ranat, had reached the pine grove where he had been directed to cut the poles for a large tent the family would use until their new house was built. After adding a sharpening touch to his axe blade, he raised it. But before he could swing, a voice said, "I wouldn't do that if I were you, sir."

Ranat saw no one. "Who's there? Step out here where I can see you."

The voice came again. "I wouldn't do that if I were you, sir."

A short, squat little person stepped from behind a tree about ten feet away.

Ranat hefted his axe and replied, "I don't know who you are, but this is our land now, and we can do anything we want."

The strange little creature turned into a giant spider and repeated, "I wouldn't do that if I were you, sir." This time, Ranat dropped his axe and ran back to the camp.

Later that night, as the family huddled around the fire, Hanu regained his courage.

"Those ghosts, or whatever they are, didn't really do anything to us, did they?" he said to Ranat. "They just scared us a little. That's all."

"Yeah," said Ranat, "we just won't pay any attention to them tomorrow. They're just ghosts. Just like smoke."

"That's right, they can't hurt us," Hanu said, and the father and son joked with each other and explained away their unsettling encounters.

Three of the squat, long-armed creatures waited patiently outside the firelight of Hanu's camp until the family had been sleeping for a few hours. Then they approached, with their long arms and big-knuckled hands serving as another set of legs in the manner of apes. Before the family knew what was happening, one of the creatures grabbed Hanu's wife around the neck with its large hands, lifted her off the ground, and shook her like a rag doll. Another seized Hanu's throat and squeezed until the man passed out.

Sometime later—he could not judge time at this point—Hanu regained consciousness. He felt pressure on his chest. He opened his eyes and stared into the face of one of the creatures, a *Rai Na'in,* who crouched on his chest with its big hands poised at his throat. Before Hanu could speak, the little lord of the earth clamped its beefy hands around his neck and squeezed again until he was unconscious. This occurred several times throughout the night. But finally, the creatures grew tired of their game and withdrew into the darkness.

The next morning, Hanu and his family, all of their necks black and blue from ear to shoulder, packed their belongings as quickly as they could and left without a word.

The Tetum people occupy Eastern Timor and number about 150,000. Their territory straddles the equator and features a variety of environments—mountains, swamps, beaches, and rolling inland plains. In their gardens, they grow sweet potatoes, yams, beans, corn, and green vegetables, and each family has an areca tree for the nuts it produces. Dry rice is planted in March and is harvested in August. Some families cultivate coconut palms. Timorese pigs serve as a valuable source of protein.

According to Tetum belief, the island's bounty belongs to the *Rai Na'in,* lords of the earth—demons who live in sacred realms but descend into the secular to hunt souls and kidnap children and women to torture and eat. Each Rai Na'in has a home in the secular world that parallels its abode in the spiritual world. These demons occupy bamboo groves, ancient trees, strange-looking rocks, whirlpools, swamps, caves, hills, chasms, and forests. It is through these secular world realities that the Rai Na'in enter the world of humans.

6. Demons
of the Pacific

Nokondisi

FROM THE GURURUMBA OF NEW GUINEA

Wamdani's mind drifted as she herded her mother's pigs along the steep mountain wall. She understood in some small way the importance of pigs in the life of the Gururumba, but as with all adolescent girls, her attention was focused elsewhere. The pigs meandered leaderless, and Wamdani, thinking of the village boys, wandered with them into an abandoned garden as they rooted for small yams that had been left behind during the harvest earlier in the year.

A rustling in the trees interrupted her daydreams. "Shush," she ordered the pigs.

The sound came again. Wamdani shaded her eyes to scan the tree line. Then a light thud drew her around, and a man jumped down from a tree branch.

"I should have seen him up there when I passed," the girl admonished herself.

The glaring afternoon sun and sharp shadows obscured the stranger's face, but she could distinguish the long, woven cape that fell just below his knees.

"What are you doing in my garden?" a reed-thin voice demanded. The stranger's lips seemed not to move.

"I'm sorry," Wamdani said. "My mother said I was to bring her pigs up here to root in the abandoned gardens. We thought no one was using them."

She looked around. Weeds grew everywhere; no one had planted this patch for a couple of years. She addressed the strange man. "How can this be your garden? There's nothing here."

"Are you calling me a liar, little one?" the apparition whispered.

"No, sir," the girl responded. "It's just that you seem to be tending an empty garden."

"You have invaded my sanctuary, my pretty little bird," the shadowy figure whispered into the still air.

"Sanctuary? This is a patch of weeds, sir. And who are you to have a sanctuary anyway? You don't act like a god or spirit."

"And you would be the village expert on gods and spirits, little nothing-girl?" the man snapped.

Wamdani became irritated with the obstinate man. She whistled to her pigs and walked away, but the pigs didn't follow. She whistled again, and when they still didn't move, she picked up a switch and hit the one closest to her. The switch snapped in two against the large rock that had previously been the pig. Wamdani, in a panic, went from pig to pig, touching each and finding that all of them had turned to stone.

"What have you done?" she shouted.

"Don't raise your voice to me!" the man warned. "Now, let me see, what shall your punishment be?"

"Punishment?" Wamdani asked incredulously.

"Well, of course," rasped the stranger. "You have defied me, argued with me, annoyed me by your presence, and you wonder why I consider your punishment?"

Wamdani stared in disbelief as the man slowly dissolved and then disappeared altogether.

"Where did you go?" she whimpered, wondering how should would explain to her mother that all the pigs had been turned to stone.

Something she could not see grabbed her tapa cloth skirt and pulled it from her body. Wamdani screamed, fighting the invisible hands that slapped and groped her and pushed her to the ground. The stranger then reappeared standing above her. With a flourish, he threw off his cloak to reveal a large set of bat wings, and he grinned at her with a mouth full of sharp, pointed teeth.

Wamdani struggled but was no match for the *Nokondisi*—an evil nature spirit. He ravaged her and afterward amused himself by nibbling small pieces from her arms and thighs. That evening, when her brothers were looking for her and their mother's pigs, they found Wamdani, naked and bleeding.

Wamdani had survived the attack, but she never spoke another word. During the day, she would crouch in her mother's house whimpering, and at night, while the others slept, she would wander the darkened forests. In the mornings, she would sometimes find bite marks on her flesh. A year after the attack in the abandoned garden, Wamdani died giving birth to a baby . . . with the face of a bat.

About thirty households comprise the Gururumba village of Miruma in the Asaro Valley of New Guinea. The cool, damp weather of the mountains and valleys provides a lush environment for the villagers to successfully garden and keep small domestic animals, chiefly pigs, dogs, and chickens. Yams are by far the most important crop. The people of Highland New Guinea have over ninety words for the yam. Their diet is so nutritious that the native doctors are little developed among them.

Warfare was chronic in Gururumba society until recently, and warriors held high status. Today, in the absence of war as a road to prestige, most men aspire to the position of *Tonowi,* or "Big Man." Such men, through manipulation of wealth, attempt to exert political sway over their neighbors.

Gururumba religious life is replete with numerous supernatural entities and a wide variety of rituals designed to appease the forces of evil and enlist those of good. Most feared are the nature spirits—the *Nokondisi* and the *Gwomai.* The Nokondisi live in upland forest zones, while the Gwomai hover along riverbanks and lowland areas. They are difficult to see, often appearing as beings of smoke, mist, or haze. The nature spirits are male and can materialize in a number of fantastic forms, such as half-man/half-bat creatures or fur-covered men with long claws on their hands and feet. They are also capable of presenting a human appearance to their potential victims. The Nokondisi and Gwomai are believed to have enormous sexual appetites, which they satisfy with human females since there are no female nature spirits. Very territorial, they dwell in specific clumps of reed along a stream, in the crevices of a particular assemblage of boulders, or in the tangled roots of an old tree. Anyone wandering into the territory of a nature spirit will be attacked.

The nature spirits, no matter how dangerous, are motivated by ideals of reciprocity. Some people even enter into mutual relationships with them. Many farmers build a small fenced enclosure called a *ropo'ne,* spirit house, in their gardens. The domed hut features a miniature entryway and a small earthen oven by the front door. The garden owner thus provides a house for the nature spirits, as well as food and gifts. In return, the Nokondisi or Gwomai takes a proprietary interest in his patron's holdings and will attack any who disrupt the garden or steal the patron's pigs. However, since the nature spirits are so treacherous, capricious, and difficult to read, this relationship may turn dangerous if the patron inadvertently angers the nature spirit by some ritual slight involving housing, feeding, or gift-giving.

The Gururumba's attitude about their "nature spirits" is captured in this statement by Philip L. Newman, who studied them in the 1960s.

> When walking with the Gururumba outside their village or gardens, or especially through unfamiliar territory, one notices that they are quite cautious. They seldom stray from the clearly marked paths and manifest little interest in exploring the countryside. This is partly because they still retain some fear of being ambushed, partly because they want to avoid straying onto someone else's property, and partly because they fear being attacked by nature spirits.

Tege

FROM THE KAPAUKU OF NEW GUINEA

Mildred Cupfurer accompanied her husband Ted to New Guinea when the Dutch engineering firm sent him to oversee a dam-building project on the Asmat River. The living conditions were very primitive, but Mildred tried not to complain. She couldn't help thinking longingly of her home in Virginia, but she did her best to adapt to Ted's working world, at least in the beginning.

The project, which he had assured her would be over in a year, stretched to two, then to three years. When Mildred became pregnant, she pleaded with her husband to take her back to civilization, but he put her off by saying that they would take a few months leave when he passed a crucial point in the project. Mildred realized that her husband had become so involved in his work that he was not thinking of her or the baby. Seven months into her pregnancy, Mildred lost the baby but found an abiding hatred for her husband.

In the succeeding months, Mildred lay in her darkened room, refusing to speak to anyone except for a Kapauku woman named Ukwan, whom Ted had hired to look after her while he was in the field. Having lost a child of her own and deeply touched by Mildred's mourning, one day Ukwan broached the subject of *Kego Tai*—sorcery.

"You long to see your lost baby, is that not so, Misses?" Ukwan asked as she swept the bedroom. Mildred nodded, and Ukwan went on, "I know how it feels since I lost my first child, too."

Mildred laboriously pulled herself up to lean against the headboard. "I'm sorry, Ukwan," she said with sincerity.

"Thank you, Misses," Ukwan replied. She looked around to make sure that no one was nearby and whispered, "The Kego Epi Me of my village allowed me to see my dead child, to hold her in my arms, and to say goodbye to her." Tears welled up in the eyes of both women. "Perhaps he might help you, too."

Mildred began to sob. "Oh, yes. Anything. I'll do anything to hold my poor baby."

Ukwan made the arrangements, and Mildred paid the first of many visits to the *Kego Epi Me*—the village sorcerer. As Ukwan had promised, he performed a ritual, chanted magical formulae, and gave Mildred a rancid-tasting liquid to drink. She fell into a narcotic swoon, and suddenly, there before her, stood a lovely little girl who Mildred instantly knew was her daughter.

They embraced, and the child said, "I would be with you now instead of in the cold, dark world of the unborn if it weren't for my father. He is responsible for my death and your heartache. You must kill him for me. You must kill . . ."

Mildred's eyes popped open. Across the fire, the Kego Epi Me stared at her.

"My daughter said that I must . . ."

"I know what she said, woman," he answered brusquely. The old man reached behind him and pulled out a crude basket in which grew a sapling of the Otikai tree. The sorcerer stroked the small leaves tenderly. "Do you want your husband dead?" he asked.

"Oh, yes," Mildred said, and ground her teeth. "More than anything."

The Kego Epi Me handed her his bush knife. "I want you to picture your husband in your thoughts, and when you do, cut this sapling in half." Mildred did as she was told. "Now," said the sorcerer, "go away from me and prepare to mourn your husband like a proper widow."

Several days later, news came from the dam project that Ted Cupfurer had died in a horrible accident. A steel cable had snapped and cut the engineer in two. Although her husband's company offered to fly her home immediately after the funeral, Mildred chose to linger. As soon as propriety allowed, she eagerly returned to the Kego Epi Me.

"Teach me your ways," she said.

The Kego Epi Me was glad to have a new disciple. But first, he had to put Mildred to the test. "I will teach you," he said, "after you dig up your husband's body, burn it, and scatter his ashes in my hog pen."

When her task was complete, Mildred again approached the Kego Epi Me. "Teach me," she begged.

And he did. Over several years, the Kego Epi Me taught Mildred of the Tege—the evil spirits who live in certain plants. He taught her how to invoke them to make herself powerful against her enemies. Together, they wandered the Asmat swamp collecting strange, innocuous little plants, and late at night when they imbibed the sorcerer's drink, the Kego Epi Me summoned the plant spirits who helped mold Mildred to the practice of Kego Tai—the arts of the black sorcerer.

After five years, Mildred's teacher told her it was time for her to return to her home country, and, of course, she obeyed. In her home town of Raphine, Virginia, she opened a plant nursery offering a wide range of ornamentals, trees, and shrubs, but specializing in the exotic plants of New Guinea. She initially had competition, but after Mildred visited other nurseries to introduce herself and present them with one of her exotic plants from the Asmat swamp, the competitors faded away. She always waited for a number of months to evoke the Tege so that no one would connect her visit with the bizarre deaths that befell nursery owners in the Raphine area. One owner had died when an air-conditioning unit fell from a second-story window and crushed his skull. Mildred had arranged for this to happen by calling for the Tege and stomping on a plant of the same species she had given the man. Another competitor drowned in a three-inch puddle behind his store after receiving one of Mildred's gifts. The night it happened, Mildred had placed the plant's mate in a bucket of water and weighed it down with stones. The third owner had seemingly burst into flames after Mildred sprayed the mate of the plant she had given her with lighter fluid and set it on fire.

By the time Mildred died many years later, she owned the bank, two car dealerships, a hardware store, a restaurant, and several farms where she grew exotic plants. On the day of of her death, all of Mildred's plants died, too.

The Kapauku are Papuan speakers living in the central highlands of western New Guinea. In the early 1960s they numbered about 45,000. Rugged mountains, swamps, and forests isolated them from contact with Westerners until 1938, when a small Dutch outpost was established at Paniai Lake. Japanese military action in World War II interfered and contact was not reestablished until several years later. Cultivation of sweet potatoes, their dietary staple, also provides food for their pig herds—the core of Kapauku economy. Power in this society depends not upon political or religious status, but on the accumulation and redistribution of capital. Control of capital, in turn, forms the basis for political and military power.

This power, however, must be viewed in terms of the role of the

Tonowi, or "Big Man," which all men aspire to be. Such a man wields influence, but not authority. The key to wealth among the Kapauku lies in giving it away. Elaborate gifts position others in one's debt. Kapauku men also battle one another with *Kego Tai*—the practice of sorcery. When economic persuasion fails, the less moral of the community will appeal to the *Kego Epi Me,* the sorcerer. This man, feared and hated by everyone, employs *Tege,* the souls of his ancestors; powerful spirits; magical spells; and the magical use of certain plants to have his way.

A variety of powerful and decidedly evil spirits roam the Kapauku consciousness. *Tege,* the most feared of the forest demons, are associated with plants. If one knows the correct procedure, the Tege can be sent from its plant abode to kill in the same manner that the sorcerer employs. Other spirits include *Ukwania,* the wife of the Tege; *Madou,* a water demon; and *Makiutija,* ghosts of the earth. Sorcerers consort with these despicable beings and allow themselves to be possessed. The Kapauku recognize this transformation by the high-pitched, staccato delivery of the possessed sorcerer. Since the psychological skill of manipulating men, as well as the ability to cure, is much prized, some sorcerers become public and powerful people.

Bolrizohol

FROM THE KUNIMAIPA OF NEW GUINEA

All night long, eerie whistles coming from the forest kept her awake. And this morning, sitting in front of the women's house, Sapia heard leaves rustle when no wind blew. Every little sound became a bone awl prodding the inside of her stomach. It had been hurting for the last several days, ever since she'd eaten the offering. Once again her mind went over what had happened. . . .

It had been a long walk from the flat rocks, where Sapia's mother and aunts had been burning brine-soaked banana leaves to produce salt-ash—a necessary accompaniment to meals in the Kunimaipa village. Sapia knew better, but the day was hot and she was very hungry, so she decided to take a shortcut to her mother's house—the forbidden overgrown path her brother had shown her years earlier.

After walking for an hour or so, she came upon a cool, mossy bank beside a rivulet and sat down. The day was still. A crudely constructed bamboo table about eight inches high had been set in the tangled roots of a nearby tree. She recognized it as an offering to a local spirit, an offering that had no doubt been made earlier that morning. The superstitious old people put them up where they thought Bolrizohol lived. A small swatch of bright cloth and a handful of beads had been arranged with small cups containing milk and tapioca pudding. Sapia knew it was food for the spirits, but she was so hungry that she couldn't resist. The milk was gone in one swallow, the pudding in the next. Then, Sapia continued on her way.

Startled back to the present, Sapia thought she heard a small animal behind her, but when she turned, nothing was there.

"I wish I could stop thinking about that spirit offering," she thought with a small pang of guilt. In an attempt to make herself feel better, she reasoned, "When the elders find the cups empty, they will be happy because they will think that the spirits took their offerings." Then, another thought struck her. "I can search out spirit offerings, take the gifts, and make people happy because the spirits accepted their prayers." She continued on, forgetting for a moment the pain in her stomach. "Then, the spirits will be pleased because the people will believe in them more. And when people believe in them more, they will place out even more offerings that I can eat up. Everybody wins!"

"You will be sorry for such thoughts, little unbeliever," came an angry voice.

With a gasp, Sapia turned and found herself face to face with a monstrous pig-faced manlike creature with patchy black bristles growing on his pinkish-purple body. His sharp tusks and tiny obsidian eyes mesmerized her. In his strangely deformed hand, he carried a branch from a thorn bush.

Sapia backed away, but a quick slash across her face with the thorn branch brought her down screaming. She could taste the blood from the many small rips in her cheeks. Pushing through the pain, she struggled to her feet. The demon stood still, smiling at her, encouraging her to run with a flick of the thorn branch and a nod of his head. Not believing her good fortune, Sapia ran, but the creature lashed at her feet with the thorn branch, and once more she fell. Again, the pig-man stepped back and encouraged her to flee.

Realizing that he was simply toying with her and that she could not possibly escape, Sapia screamed as loud as she could. Snorting and slavering, the pig-man tossed away the thorn branch and was upon her, thrusting his twisted index finger deep into her navel. It pushed through her stomach, penetrated her intestines, and touched her backbone. Sapia felt a painful pressure on her stomach, then realized with a shock that the pressure was coming from inside. Her stomach was inflating!

The pig-man laughed and shook his head, scattering drool in all directions, as he pulled his finger from her abdomen with a *Pop!*

Sapia screamed until her expanding stomach blocked her lungs. Her face turned red, then purple, then white, and she exploded like a popped balloon filled with confetti.

The pig-man snorted happily and licked the tapioca pudding-flavored gore from his ragged coat.

The Kunimaipa follow the New Guinea highlands horticultural lifestyle. Domestic pigs are the main source of meat, but are more valuable as items of exchange, more akin to money than to hamburger. Yams are the basic root crop and are present in all meals. Pigs are eaten only when they are given as gifts in wedding, funeral, or military ceremonies. Men endeavor their entire lives to become rich and powerful, and will seek this end through trade as well as warfare.

Kunimaipa territory is ancient and is crowded with the living and the dead, as well as a variety of spirits, most of whom are dangerous. They believe that three kinds of *Rizohol*, or spirits, inhabit their environment. The *Baltakari* are spirits of dangerous or forbidden areas—places that the Kunimaipa call "Baltak." These spirits attack and attempt to kill all who enter their area. Baltakari may be owned by those brave and strong enough to challenge and defeat them. Then there are the *Rizopu*, human spirits. They appear as shades or odd reflections, and are thought to be a feature of the human soul. The third type of spirits are the *Bolrizohol*, pig-spirits, who live in pools, caves, certain stones, and streams. An area may have ten or twenty pig-house streams or pig-house stones. They appear either as "soft" or "sharp" in nature. Soft Bolrizohol do little harm, while the sharp Bolrizohol are greatly feared. One who is experiencing an acute gastro-intestinal attack is thought to be under attack by a Bolrizohol.

Kopuwai

FROM THE MAORI OF NEW ZEALAND

"**G**randpa! Grandpa! Look what I got!" Hopu shouted, rushing to his grandfather.

Miwali gathered his grandson into his arms. "Calm down, Hopu, before you bust. Now tell me what you have."

The little boy opened his fist to reveal several spring berries. "These are the best berries I've ever eaten. They are probably the best in the whole world. Here, try one," he said.

Miwali popped a few into his mouth. "Yes, Hopu, they are very good, but I don't know if I would say that they are the best-tasting berries in the whole world."

"Sure they are. You tasted them. They are great," insisted the little boy.

Miwali smiled at his precocious grandson. "Let me tell you a story about spring berries, and then we can see if these are the best in the whole world."

Hopu resisted. "Ah, Grandpa, I'm not a baby. I don't want to hear a story about berries."

"Well, it also has Kopuwai in it," his grandfather said.

That attracted the boy's attention. *Kopuwai*—a scale-covered, dog-headed demon—was said to roam the land in search of human flesh with his pack of two-headed demon dogs.

Miwali began, "This story didn't happen too long ago. A man told it to my father, and my father told it to me. So maybe what I'm going to tell you about happened around 1920 or so. Anyway, this Maori man named Wakii went on a fishing trip in the mountains along the north coast. He had been working hard in town and decided that he needed a break.

"The weather was good for the first several days, and he enjoyed himself. On the third day, clouds moved in, and by noon a heavy rain had started to fall.

"Wakii saw the mouth of a cave through the driving rain and ran for it. Safe inside, he found some dry twigs and shortly had a fire going. His teeth chattered, and he stripped and held his wet clothes before the fire. Soon he was dry and warm. Feeling a little better, he rooted around in his pack for his canteen. That's when he noticed the animal tracks in the soft dirt. His eyes widened in surprise. They looked like dog tracks, but some of the paw prints were about five or six times larger than normal. They pointed toward the rear of the cave, but there were no tracks coming back out. That meant that whatever had made the tracks was still in the cave.

"The howling of the storm subsided for a moment, and Wakii heard a low rumble. It grew more intense, and he realized it was the throaty growl of an animal. He peered into the darkness, and Wakii saw two fiery eyes glowing in the shadows. When a bolt of lightning lit the entrance to the cave, Wakii saw Kopuwai—the dog-demon—crouched in the back of the cave. Attending him were four two-headed dogs only slightly smaller than the Kopuwai.

"Thinking quickly, Wakii reached into the fire with his bare hands and picked up handfuls of burning twigs and threw them at the demons. Then he ran for the mouth of the cave. Only momentarily impeded by the shower of burning twigs, the Kopuwai and his pack were fast on Wakii's trail. Their blood-chilling howls warned him of their pursuit.

"Wakii ran blindly into the rain, driven by the terror that bore down upon him. Unfamiliar with the territory, however, he soon found himself at the edge of a cliff. Behind him approached the Kopuwai, walking on his two hind feet like a man. The monster barked orders to his pack, and they split up, two on either side, in an effort to flank Wakii's escape. The demon bared his sharp canine teeth and ambled toward a trembling Wakii.

"Wakii heard barking from below, and he glanced over the edge of the cliff. More of the Kopuwai's pack had gathered at the bottom, throwing themselves against the cliff wall in a frenzied effort to reach their prey.

"The Kopuwai approached, full of menace and evil, as the wind howled and the rain drove down on the terrible scene. But Wakii was Maori, a son of many generations of warriors. He had been taught to choose death when all else failed. He stepped closer to the edge of the cliff, and the Kopuwai leapt at him. Then, Wakii bravely stepped over the edge. Above, the Kopuwai snarled down at him, and below, the two-headed demon dogs waited to eat him. It all seemed like a bad dream to Wakii. A tree root sticking out of the side of the cliff broke his fall, and he held onto it with all his strength. The demon dogs howled in frustration, furious with their prey, which dangled just out of reach.

"The root slipped through the dirt, and several inches came tearing out of the ground and then stopped. Wakii knew it was only a matter of time before he fell to his death. Then he noticed growing in the same scant patch of soil, a stunted spring berry plant with one berry. The tree root slid out a few more inches. Wakii reached for the berry just as the root came free of the cliff. As Wakii fell, he put the berry into his mouth and bit down. He tasted the berry's sweet juices and laughed."

Miwali grew silent. Hopu watched him for a moment and blurted out, "Well, what happened?"

"He died, of course, torn to shreds by the demon pack. But I think that the berry Wakii tasted as he fell to his death was the sweetest berry in the world. What do you think?"

The word *Maori* is used here to indicate the original population of New Zealand, although the term is somewhat misleading in the same way that the word "Indian" is a misleading name for the original inhabitants of the New World. In both cases, many different cultural groups exist, often with varying dialects and customs. Maori tradition asserts that about a thousand years ago, a man named Kupe set sail from his home, Hawaiki-roa. He sailed south and west until one day he sighted a huge white cloud hovering low on the horizon. He knew from long seafaring experience that a large body of land lay under the unusually large cloud. Kupe named the island *Aotearoa*, meaning "land of the long white cloud," the name still used for New Zealand by the Maori. Centuries later, others left Hawaiki-roa and found their way to Aotearoa.

In time, a general cultural pattern based on horticulture, gathering, hunting, and fishing evolved. Because of chronic warfare, the people lived in *Pa*, fortified villages. They organized their societies in a complex manner—Iwi (tribes), Hapu (sub-tribes), and Whanau (clans). Each individual belonged to one of the four classes—nobles, priests, common citizens, or slaves. Men of high position were heavily tattooed, a custom called *Ta Moko*.

Most Maori religions focused on *Io*, the Supreme Being, although there was considerable variation from tribe to tribe concerning the particulars of Io's nature, and, indeed, some Maori tribes did not possess belief in a supreme being. The one area of belief shared by all, however, was the acceptance of the existence of demons. Maori traditional religious life was a delicate balancing of positive and negative spiritual forces.

Kopuwai is king of the demon dogs—those two-headed monstrosities that grovel at his feet waiting to do his evil bidding. Kopuwai and his court are symbols of nature gone mad to the ancient Maori. Even to this day, the sound of unknown dogs howling in the distance, particularly at night, raises goose bumps on the arms of the traditional Maori.

Patupaiarehe

FROM THE MAORI OF NEW ZEALAND

Monica and Arlen Benton taught archaeology at a small college in eastern Georgia. Although they dutifully worked the numerous local archaeological sites, cranking out reports and scholarly papers, their first love remained the prehistory of New Zealand and, particularly, the culture of the indigenous people called the Maori. When the Bentons had put in enough time to warrant a six-month sabbatical from the college, they rented out their house to a couple of graduate students and set out for New Zealand. They were especially excited about the bicycle tour of the classic Maori archaeological sites that they had planned.

After renting bicycles and light camping gear in Hillston, Monica and Arlen mapped out a two-week camping tour of the North Island, where most of the contemporary Maori live. To acquire a better feel for the people of New Zealand, they bought food at small shops along their route, sampling local fare as well as dialects and customs. Each day proved a marvel of emerald green hills, sparkling streams and lakes, friendly people, and snowcapped mountains looming in the distance. With perfect weather for cycling, the strain of the past decade of constant research and publishing melted away beneath the wheels of their bicycles.

One morning, the couple stopped at a little roadside market for bottled water and fruit. An old man with thick white hair greeted them from behind the counter and, in a short time, had charmed them completely. When they explained that they had come to New Zealand expressly to study the Maori culture, the old man grew serious.

"Ah, yes, a worthwhile endeavor to be sure," he said. "Do you know that there is an ancient hill fort of a local Iwi—that's what they call a tribe of Maori—up there in the clouds on Turners Ridge?" He indicated the direction with a tilt of his chin.

Monica stepped out from under the awning and, shading her eyes against the brilliant sun, looked toward the cloud-draped mountains to the northwest. "Up there?" she asked.

"Yes," the old man replied. "You'll find that it has a wonderful view and a number of nicely kept campsites."

"I wonder why the travel agent didn't include it on our itinerary," mused Arlen.

"Oh, very secret. Only the locals know about it, and I only tell people I think would truly appreciate its significance—people like you," the man said.

Flattered, the Bentons, after receiving detailed directions from the shopkeeper, were on their way to the ancient Maori fort. The old man watched them go until they left the main road for a dirt track leading into the hills. As he gazed in the direction they had gone, intricate dark blue patterns—the famous Maori tattoos called *Ta Moko*—slowly emerged on his weathered face.

"Yes, sweet couple, go to your fate," he whispered. "It will surely come when the Patupaiarehe welcome you to their fortress."

Within minutes, the old man and his small market had disappeared.

Late in the afternoon, Monica and Arlen found themselves in the clouds that hung along Turners Ridge. With limited visibility, they had to walk their bikes up the hill.

"There it is. Look!" shouted Arlen

As the mist wafted over the hilltop, stone walls and towers appeared and disappeared. The couple hurried toward the ancient structure. In his fascination, Arlen didn't see the archaeologist's trench that had been dug around the walls many, many years before by some local amateurs. He tumbled into the deep depression, and his bicycle landed on top of him.

"Honey, are you okay?" Monica cried.

"Yeah, I guess. My knee feels kind of funny, but I don't think I broke anything," he said.

Monica let out a heavy sigh of relief, but when Arlen tried to stand, he winced and sat back down. "I'm not going anywhere soon," he told her. "I guess we should camp here tonight, and tomorrow we'll see how my knee is doing. You might have to peddle on back to that old man's shop and get some help for me."

As Monica helped Arlen out of the trench, she was concerned but confident that he'd be okay. Once he was settled, she gathered wood and rolled out their sleeping bags. She dumped a pile of wood by Arlen, who managed to build a fire and put on a small pail of water for tea. A full moon rose shortly and created a soft light that struggled to penetrate the mist that rolled continuously over the hill, casting the ancient fort in eerie light.

To take their minds off Arlen's leg, the couple chatted about the adventures they had had so far when a shrieking, cackling laugh echoed from the fort. Arlen raised himself on one arm. "What in the hell was that?"

"Shhh," Monica whispered.

The weird laugh came again, this time closer. Monica aimed her flashlight into the trees, and about halfway up a twisted black pine, they saw what looked like a round face with slits for eyes. It appeared to be engorged with blood, like a balloon about ready to burst. It opened its mouth, and the bizarre maniacal laughter again tore at the night. It moved, by what means they couldn't see, to another branch, and when Monica shone her flashlight on it, it moved again.

"It doesn't like the light," said Arlen, "whatever the hell it is."

"I'm going to take a closer look," Monica said.

"No, don't go near it," Arlen warned. "We don't know what . . ."

"It can't be too dangerous if it's afraid of the flashlight beam," replied Monica reasonably.

She walked toward the tree, but the strange floating face vanished. Suddenly, a rock flew out of the darkness and struck her. She fell to one knee, pressing her hand to her head. Arlen stared at the trickle of blood between her fingers.

"Monica, get back here, quick," he called to her.

She tried to stand but to her horror found that she was stuck to the ground and, in fact, had sunk a few inches into it. "Arlen, I can't move. I'm stuck somehow."

The crazed laughter came again.

"I'll try to get to you, honey. Hang on," Arlen said in a panic.

Arlen's knee was now badly swollen. He crawled toward his wife, but he had not made it very far when a figure appeared out of the mist. He strained to focus on it but could only distinguish an outline of what appeared to be a boy or small adult.

"Over here," he called out. "Please help us."

Then, another figure materialized and another. Arlen called to them, but they ignored his desperate pleas and moved toward Monica, who struggled to free herself from the unearthly force that held her to the ground. When one of the creatures moved into the light of the campfire, Monica let out a blood-curdling scream. It was as white as a sheet and glistened in the fog as if it were covered with mucus. Its luminous eyes had no pupils. Garish red hair hung lank upon its head, and its fingertips were armed with long talon-tipped claws. There were at least a half a dozen of the creatures moving toward her.

"Oh, God, Arlen. Help me!" Monica shrieked.

"Hang on, sweetheart!" Arlen cried.

Monica struggled, and a flood of tears flowed down her cheeks. One of the things reached out and raked its claws across her back. Monica howled in pain and became sickened as the creature licked her blood from the tips of its claws. Then, the creatures converged around her and leisurely picked her to pieces.

Arlen, too terrified now to consider anyone but himself, crawled to the fire and, cringing like a terrified animal, yelled in an attempt to drown out his wife's piercing screams. Mercifully, her cries died fairly quickly, but after a moment of silence, Arlen heard footsteps moving toward him. He threw more sticks on the fire, and when the flames rose, he could see the creatures gathering around him. The flickering light, however, seemed to keep them at bay, and they groaned and muttered among themselves.

When the fire died down, they moved closer. Already having burned every twig within reach, Arlen pulled off his shirt and held it in the flames. It ignited and the creatures backed away again. Arlen fed the flames his shoes and then his knapsack, while the creatures waited anxiously to feast upon him. Finally, nothing remained to burn. Arlen lay naked and stared up at the ancient fort, and over at the bones and gristle that had once been his wife. The fire faded to nothing, and the fog shrouded the illumination of the moon. The faint light was not enough. Not nearly enough.

Information about the culture and spiritual beliefs of the Maori can be found on page 192 under Kopuwai. Please refer to that section for some insight into their ways.

The *Patupaiarehe*, demons of graveyards and deserted places, hunger for human flesh, but since they were consigned by Io to the less traveled areas, these cursed souls are constantly famished. When humans do appear, the Patupaiarehe go on a feeding frenzy. Rarely do their victims escape them.

Ruruhi-kerepo

FROM THE MAORI OF NEW ZEALAND

I n late January, people noticed a light burning in the old cottage on the path that led along Highsmith Gorge, where the Tumbalee River roars out of the Black Iron Mountains. Mist curling up from the gorge often hid the feeble light in its gray, wispy shroud, lending a mysterious aura to the place. The townspeople wondered who had taken up residence in the old, rundown house, but nobody cared enough to check it out—it was an eight-mile hike on a narrow, slippery trail.

Around the middle of February, two woodcutters who had been working a stand of maples in the gorge failed to return home. Constable Fitzhugh led a search party into the wild place, but found no signs of the lost men. Then, six months later, four young people who had hiked the Tumbalee River trail for a picnic never returned. Again a search ensued but nothing turned up. A year later, a photographer stopped at the Farther Inn and asked for directions to the waterfall in the Highsmith Gorge. He, too, was never seen again.

Rumors circulated that a maniac lived in the Highsmith Gorge cottage and was responsible for the missing people. In an attempt to settle the nerves of the townspeople, Constable Fitzhugh gathered several volunteers for a search of the area. The day they set out proved inauspicious. Cold rain dropped from the sky like a shroud, and lightning tore at the landscape. The trail grew increasingly treacherous as they advanced: slick mud underfoot, a cliff to their left, and the raging Tumbalee River below. Still, they pressed on through the downpour and had almost reached the rim of the gorge when they heard the sound of two hard things being tapped together. *Click, click, click.* The sound came muffled through the storm. *Click, click.*

The sound moved closer as the men huddled on the trail and looked ahead of them trying to discern its sources. They strained to see, and finally, faintly through the driving rain, the constable recognized the silhouette of someone approaching, someone with a long cape who tapped at the rocks along the path with a long white cane. It was the Ruruhi-kerepo, the "Old Woman Monster."

The figure came within a few meters of the constable when a lightning bolt crashed into the gorge below. In that moment of illumination, the men found themselves confronted by an old blind woman. She faced them, her head slightly tilted, as if she was listening attentively for something.

"Are you lost, Ma'am?" Fitzhugh asked.

"Never in my life," replied the old woman.

"Perhaps you can help us out. We are investigating the disappearance of a number of people in this area," Fitzhugh told her.

"I know, I know," she said, "those poor innocent children. Those poor, poor woodcutters. How very, very sad."

Lightning ripped a rocky outcrop on the far side of the gorge, and the resulting brightness revealed that the old woman was crying . . . tears of blood.

"I say, are you ill?" Fitzhugh asked.

"No, lad, only hungry," said the blind woman. "So very, very hungry. So endlessly hungry." She rocked her head back and stared into the sky, and her mouth opened so wide that her jaws appeared unhinged. As the men stared at her, a keening wail issued from her throat, building in volume. They tried to muffle the grating sound by pressing their palms against their ears. Still it rose in intensity. They felt a searing fire burn through their bones, and one by one they fell to their knees before the screeching woman.

Constable Fitzhugh, gathering his strength, struck the woman with his walking stick, but instead of the sound expected when a body is struck by a thick staff, the men heard the sound of something hard clashing with something hard. The old woman stood unaffected by the blow, red tears rolling down her face, and all did their best to aid Fitzhugh in his attack. Suddenly, she threw off her cape. The men recoiled at the sight. Bones protruded from every inch of her body as if they were sticking through her skin but not penetrating it. In a flurry of motion, the old woman swung her cane and knocked Fitzhugh into the gorge. The others tried to flee, but she leapt through the air, almost flying, and dragged them to the ground. Their screams mingled with the thunder and roar of the waterfall crashing out of the gorge, but only briefly. The creature sat in the mud and swallowed them, limb by limb.

When she finished her feast, she picked up her cape and refastened it.

Tapping in front of her, she turned back up the trail toward the cottage, mumbling as she went, "Why would anybody want to hurt a poor old blind woman? What is this world coming to?"

Information about the culture and spiritual beliefs of the Maori can be found on page 192 under Kopuwai. Please refer to that section for some insight into their ways.

The Ruruhi-kerepo appears to travelers in lonely places as a lost or helpless old woman. Its pitiful and harmless-looking guise relaxes its victims until it draws close enough to pounce. The Ruruhi-kerepo swallows its victims whole by hideously distending its jaws. The murdered people's bones protrude from its stomach, a fact it usually hides under a long dark cape. It is also believed that it cries tears of blood and is capable of uttering a paralyzing shriek to immobilize its victims if they appear to be on the verge of escaping.

Tavogivogi

A no-gong was a successful trader and businessman, a *Tonowi*, meaning "Big Man"—the common term for such men in the islands of the southwest Pacific. He skillfully entangled his business rivals in various deals that left him in control of many gardens and dozens of prize pigs. This was as it should be. This was the life of the Tonowi. His only fault seemed to be his wandering eye for women. In his time he had fought, run from, or paid off a number of husbands, brothers, and fathers because of his dalliance with the women of their households. When confronted by his wife or his wife's people, Ano-gong proclaimed his innocence; in this respect, he was also an accomplished liar.

One evening when returning home from a session of pig trading with men from a nearby village, Ano-gong spotted a beautiful young girl on a ridge about a hundred feet from the trail. She reminded him of a girl he had once met from a village to the south. Her hair floated in the balmy breeze that blew off the ocean, and she wore a garland of flowers looped around her neck and over her shoulders. Even at a distance her eyes seemed to sparkle. She smiled and beckoned to him. Seeing no one nearby, Ano-gong stepped off the trail in her direction. She laughed lightly and held out her arms to him, urging him closer as he clambered up the ridge after her.

"I'm on my way, pretty bird," he whispered. "Wait for me, and you won't be sorry."

He pushed his way through the thicket that lay between them, but she retreated while still beckoning him onward. Ano-gong burned with desire for the girl, and as she withdrew, he followed. Finally, he stood before her. She was even more tantalizing up close. She licked her lips seductively, and he hungrily reached for her. She easily slid out of his grasp, still smiling.

Ano-gong grew tired of the game. "Stand still, girl," he ordered as he reached for her again. Once more, she stepped back, this time swaying before him, her body writhing slowly, reminding him of a snake. Ano-gong's mind grew cloudy, but he was still mad with desire.

"Oh, yessssss," she hissed as Ano-gong fell under her dancing spell.

He pulled her to him and pressed his lips hard against hers, but pain stung his mouth as if someone had slapped him hard. "What the . . ." he muttered, staring at the girl. His lips burned, and he could feel them beginning to swell. He grabbed her breast roughly, but his hand went numb when he touched it. "What are you?" he stammered.

Then he noticed a patch of reptile skin glittering on her neck. He froze. The girl began her dance once again, and this time Ano-gong realized why her motions looked so snakelike: her knees and elbows bent the wrong way, or rather, they could bend in any direction. Before he could move, the girl struck his body with her fingertips. Each touch produced a ghastly inflamed boil.

"I wonder what kind of lie you will use to explain this," she said, and tapped his eyelids with her index finger. Large boils erupted on the tender skin, almost blinding him. He tried to speak, but his lips had become so swollen that he could barely open his mouth. His clothing stuck to his body from the puss of oozing boils dribbling down his skin.

Before his eyes, the girl slowly transformed into a *Mae*, a changeling snake, while the horrified Ano-gong stood transfixed under the giant serpent's gaze.

"You think you are Tonowi, little man," the snake spat out, "but you are nothing to me but my pig. I collect the souls of men like you. I herd them. I eat them. I trade them for profit. I am Tonowi of the spirits, and you are nothing to me but meat to use as I wish."

Ano-gong's last awareness was the hissing in his ears and the excruciating pain he felt as he was raped to death by the hideous serpent.

The people of the New Hebrides live in small villages and combine gardening, pig husbandry, fishing, and trading as the basis of their economy. All boys want to grow up to be Tonowi, men who control others through skillful economic manipulations such as judicially allocated loans and investments. The women of the villages specialize in gardening and pig rearing, and their production efforts often provide the surplus that their husbands use in their business dealings.

The religious life of the islands is complex and centers on trade, gardening, and fishing rituals and beliefs. Major categories of religious practitioners include the healing shaman; the priest or ritual specialists; and the witch, inveterate doer of evil. One of the most powerful beings in the religious system is called *Tavogivogi*, an evil spirit, which corresponds to a type of mysterious snake called a *Mae*. The Tavogivogi can manifest as a bird, as well as other creatures, but its most infamous form is that of a beautiful, seductive young snake woman. In fact, the shape-changing powers of the Tavogivogi are noted in the root of the name, which means "to change the form."

In its snake form, the Tavogivogi can be recognized by various unsnakelike behaviors. It may be seen, for example, bathing its young and singing native children's songs, or it may bark like a dog if approached. In its human form, it can be recognized by a patch of reptilian skin low on its neck. Swelling and oozing sores erupt on the body of anyone who is unfortunate enough to be touched by the Tavogivogi.

R.H. Codrington, who studied various Melanesian groups in the late 1800s, wrote with regard to the Mae, "Nothing seems to be more fixed in the minds of natives, even those who have some education, than the persuasion that all this is true."

Mulukwausi

FROM THE TROBRIAND ISLANDS OF MELANESIA

"**H**ot damn!"

Bob Doolittle, a graduate student in anthropology at the University of Washington, was ecstatic as he stood before his mailbox waving a letter in the air. He had applied for the Melanesian Ethnographic Research Grant, and the notice informed him that he would receive full funding for a year of field research in the Trobriand Islands of Melanesia. He glanced again at the starting date for the grant and frowned.

"Gotta hustle," he mused. "Got a lot to do before the end of the month."

In the following weeks, Doolittle finalized his research plans with his academic advisor. He would perform a study of contemporary religious beliefs of the Trobriand villagers on the small, relatively unknown island of Minau. It would fulfill his research requirements for a Master's Degree in Anthropology. He arranged transportation from an airport in New Guinea to Minau, and before he knew it, he was over the Pacific in a two-seater pontoon-equipped airplane headed for the primitive landing field on Minau. Several of the villagers stood on the edge of the runway and offered, for a small fee, to carry his luggage into the village.

First stop was the house of the village Headman, where he was told to show the official forms that permitted him to be on the island and authorized his scientific research.

Ginka-ram, the Headman, glanced at the papers and leered at Bob.

"So, you have come here to study our primitive religion, have you?"

"Yes, sir, I am . . . I mean . . . no, sir." Bob felt confused as he stared into Mr. Ginka-ram's unblinking black eyes. "I wouldn't say *primitive*," he stuttered.

"Well then, why are you here? Why don't you study religion where you come from?"

"Mr. Ginka-ram, I don't mean to cause trouble. I thought these forms were supposed to let me . . ."

"The forms," the Headman replied contemptuously, "are signed by men who have never even been to our village. How can they give you permission to do anything in our village?"

Bob shifted his feet uneasily. "Maybe there has been a misunderstanding. You see, I received this research grant . . ."

"From our village elders?"

"No . . . I . . ."

"Of course not, because we wouldn't give you such permission," Ginka-ram interjected. "We native peoples are sick and tired of—" Ginka-ram stopped and looked off in the distance. A smile formed on his lips. "Maybe there is a way, Mr. Doolittle. I don't want you wandering around our village bothering people, but there is a woman who lives outside town who knows quite a lot about old-time religious beliefs and such, and there is an abandoned house that is near her place. She's out there with her daughter by herself. She might talk with you about your interests."

Bob was thrilled and hired a young man to carry his luggage. With the map that Ginka-ram had drawn in hand, he set out for the abandoned house on the edge of town.

Ginka-ram watched him leave and whispered, "Oh, yes, Mr. Doolittle, I forgot to mention that the woman is a Yoyova. She is also my mother. Details, details." He laughed softly.

Bob found the abandoned house without a problem, paid the young man, and decided to take a look around before moving his things into the one-room thatched hut. He was, he guessed, about a mile from the village. The trail to the hut looked like it hadn't been used for weeks, maybe months. Up the path on the right, another hut huddled in the deep shade of a banana grove. The thatch looked rotten, and mold and mildew covered the flimsy walls.

Bob realized he was tired. "It's been a long day," he thought. As the shadows deepened, he dragged his luggage into the hut and lit a small lantern. By its feeble light, he pumped up his kerosene camp stove and boiled some water for tea. That and a few handfuls of dried trail mix would be his supper. After his meal, he turned the lantern down, lay back on his sleeping bag, and was asleep in minutes.

Somewhere deep in the night, the sound of a little girl squealing with delight brought him awake. He peeked outside through a crack in the wall. He couldn't believe his eyes. Over by the banana grove, a woman picked up the small child and threw her over the hut. The child giggled as she flew through the air. The woman moved with uncanny speed to the other side of the hut and caught the little girl as she fell. As Bob watched, they repeated this "game" several times.

Bob leaned back on his pallet. "Gotta be a dream," he thought. "Just has to be a dream. I've had a long day. A real long day."

Bob awoke to a beautiful, bright day. The trade winds ruffled the palms and banana trees with a fresh balmy breeze. He picked some bananas and sat in the early morning sunlight to eat his breakfast. A sound caught his attention. Up the path, the woman next door left her hut with a bowl of liquid. She tossed the liquid into the bushes.

"Good morning," Bob called out.

The woman looked over at him. It appeared that she hadn't noticed him previously. Bob waved, and she nodded politely before returning to her hut.

"Well, she didn't start screaming," Bob thought. "That's a good sign."

An hour later, notebook in hand, Bob approached the woman's hut.

"Good morning. Is anyone there?"

A middle-aged woman appeared from the shadows. "What do you want?" she asked abruptly.

"My name is Bob Doolittle . . . from the states. I'm a student, and I'm interested in learning about old-time religious beliefs and such in this area. Mr. Ginka-ram said . . ." The sudden smile on the woman's face startled him, and his words trailed off.

"Oh, he sent you to me, did he? How kind of him."

Bob wasn't sure what to make of the woman's statement.

"Come, sit down and we will talk," she said.

Bob sat in the shade next to the woman. He would have been more comfortable inside, at a table, perhaps, but he didn't want to push his welcome. "May I take notes, Mrs. . . . Mrs.?"

"I am Neeta-sangh, and yes, you may take notes."

As Bob pulled his pen from his shirt pocket and opened his notebook, a movement caught his attention. A little girl squatted by the door watching him. He remembered the dream he had had the night before.

"Come out here and meet Mr. Doolittle from the states. He is a student like you, my daughter."

The child stepped into the mottled light, and Bob barely suppressed a gasp. She was filthy. Her skin was dank and pale, her hair was matted, and her eyes glistened with a feverish glow.

"Yes, here is my little student," gushed her mother. "Now, what do you want of me?" she asked Bob.

"Well, like I said, ma'am, I am interested in religion and . . ."

"Do you know of the Yoyova, young man?"

"No, I . . ."

"Do you know of the witch's organ?"

"No . . . how do you spell Yoyova?"

"Spell! Spell!" she laughed. Bob didn't like the edge he heard in her laughter. "I make a spell like this," she said and waved her hands in front of Bob's face.

Bob was ready to tell her that he didn't mean a magic spell, but he found that he couldn't make a sound. He sat in the shade before the woman's hut, his feet stretched out before him, fully conscious, but he could not move a muscle.

The woman pinched his cheek—hard. "A student of old religion, how fascinating." The woman laughed. "Don't you think that is fascinating, child?" she asked the little girl.

"I want to eat him for breakfast," the child responded.

"Well then, go right ahead."

Bob struggled to move, to make a sound, to scream for help, but he was frozen. He watched in growing horror as the strange child sat down beside his feet and unlaced his shoes. She slipped off his socks, folded them neatly, and set them beside her.

"Oh, Mother! Look how white his little toes are." Without another word, she bent over and bit Bob's little toe off. Blood gushed from his foot as she lapped at it.

Pain vibrated through Bob's body, and sweat beads popped out all over his face. Next, she bit off the big toe on his right foot. Bob heard the snap and crackle of his gristle and bone as she chewed.

"Now, my daughter, enter him and feast as the Mulukwausi."

Bob watched as the child closed her eyes, clasped her hands in an odd configuration, and hummed to herself. There was a flash of light, and the little girl turned into a needle, which, in the next instant, shot into Bob's eye. He could not believe that the pain could become more intense, but it did as the bewitched needle forged into his brain and stitched through his liver and tongue. His world went black as the needle tore through his other eye. For an eternity, he was wracked with pain so deep and so profoundly horrible that he struggled to die, with no success. Meanwhile, the little girl and her mother danced around him in the bright late morning light. The last sound he heard was the delighted squeal of a small child.

The Trobriand Islanders of the southwestern Pacific subsist by lagoon and deep-sea fishing; gardening, in which the yam plays a conspicuous role; and the *Kula Ring*, a long-distance inter-island trade network. They reside on the beach and in select inland locations in large well-planned villages and enjoy a generally harmonious and cohesive society. Living in a benign climate with year-round gardens and bountiful seas, the Islanders revolve their image of evil around disease—a rare event that is greatly feared and over which they have no control. They explain the nature and cause of illness through the belief in the *Mulukwausi*, the shape-shifting cannibal ghoul.

The Mulukwausi sometimes descend on lone travelers from perches in trees or on the roofs of houses, or they may assail small groups of humans in packs. They seek out dying humans or attend funerals, where they attack mourners and afterward feed on the newly dead. They roam the seas of the Trobriand Islander's world, preying upon victims of shipwreck and storm.

A village may have one or more female witches known as *Yoyova*. These women are believed to have an extra organ in their bodies called the *Kapuwana*. Such a Yoyova can direct her consciousness to blend with the Kapuwana to form a Mulukwausi. The Yoyova, in this form, can transform herself into any shape required to kill her prey.

Only the child of a Yoyova who can project a Mulukwausi can become a Yoyova with the powers to become a Mulukwausi. Before the Yoyova's daughter is an hour old, her mother begins the rituals that will draw forth the child's hidden powers. She cuts the umbilical cord and buries it, not in the garden, which is the traditional place, but in the floor of the house. And whereas most mothers sleep with their newborns near the light and warmth of the fire, the Yoyova takes hers to the dark and cold. Within the first year of life, the mother presents her daughter at secret meetings of the Mulukwausi, where the baby is ritually acknowledged by the ghoulish coven. Later, she is taught to eat human flesh. A witch's child can project her Mulukwausi powers by the age of five. Her mother polishes her powers of flight during nighttime practice sessions, where the mother throws the child over the roof and employs her supernatural speed to race to the other side and catch her before she hits the ground.

Rawa Tukump

FROM THE TSEMBAGA OF NEW GUINEA

The warriors cautiously approached the fighting grounds where they would meet the Dugumkuli, their enemies from the other side of the valley. They carried spears and bows and arrows, and they had come, not for a day of dangerous sport as most of their battles could be characterized, but for killing.

A raiding party had surprised some of their women as they tended their gardens and had killed three of them. The remaining women were sent back to the village to report what had happened. The Dugumkuli wanted to fight, and this horrendous act was sure to bring the kinsmen of the dead onto the battleground to seek vengeance. They were right.

At dawn, two packs of hundreds of howling men stood several hundred feet apart on the fighting grounds and hurled verbal insults and spears across the no man's land.

Kuluai stood just out of range and scanned the enemy, focusing about a yard above the warriors' heads. He was looking for signs of *Kun Kaze Ambra*—the white smoke woman who marked warriors for death. As the dust rose from the skirmishes along the front lines, Kuluai saw what he was looking for. The figure of a young woman floated above the fighters' heads as if being wafted on an errant breeze, easily, almost casually. From time to time, she dipped down and touched a warrior on the head, and within seconds an arrow found the cursed warrior's body.

The Kun Kaze Ambra spotted Kuluai and drifted in his direction. He backed away quickly, not daring to run for fear of being labeled a coward by his cohorts. The Kun Kaze Ambra pressed on toward him, and as she was about to make contact, Kuluai stepped behind Madang, a fellow villager, and her deadly touch found him instead. The enemy arrow struck Kuluai's neighbor seconds later, and though the Kun Kaze Ambra frowned and reached for Kuluai, the spectral wind that she rode carried her back toward the front lines.

Kuluai's relief was brief. His wife's brother, Tultul, stared at him, shock covering his face. That evening, after the battle lines had drawn apart for the night, Tultul confronted Kuluai in a banana grove outside the village gates.

"I saw you cheat your fate and draw death upon Madang," he said angrily. "You might as well have killed him with your own hand. When the warriors find out . . . well, I wouldn't want to be you," his brother-in-law said.

"They won't find out unless you tell them, my friend," muttered Kuluai.

Tultul recognized the threat and reached for his bush knife, but Kuluai proved faster and buried his own knife in Tultul's chest before the accuser had completed his draw. As Kuluai considered how to dispose of Tultul's body, he heard a faint whispering, and the air in the banana grove grew heavy. With his knife poised, he crouched in a defensive posture.

"Who's there?" he whispered.

The banana leaves rustled, and a shadowy figure appeared about ten feet away. It appeared to be covered in some kind of black dirt or mold. It was the *Rawa Tukump*—the spirit of rot and decay. "You have defiled my house," the black shape moaned. "You have shed blood in my place of rest."

Kuluai swiped at the figure with his knife, but the blade found only air.

"Your foul presence will be expunged immediately," the voice said.

Kuluai threatened with his knife again and said, "Go ahead and try it."

Kuluai's feet felt the attack first. They began to sting and burn. He chanced a quick glance down, trying at the same time to keep his awareness on the shape that hovered just out of his knife range. Black dirt covered his feet and was moving up to his ankles. He scratched at it, but the dark, sticky substance adhered to his hand. Soon it was up to his knees, and the patch on his hand was growing quickly toward his elbow. Kuluai dropped his knife and frantically brushed at the black goo, which burned his skin like fire. It spread until Kuluai was completely covered. The burning mold edged into his mouth and down his throat, then flowed into his eyes, his ears, and his nose. He was mad with pain and terror when death came.

The Kun Kaze Ambra watched from the edge of the banana grove, satisfied with Kuluai's end. The man who had escaped death once today hadn't felt her touch him as he brushed past her on his way into the grove.

The Tsembaga are comprised of about 200 Maring-speakers who live in the Simbai Valley in east-central New Guinea. The Australian government brought the area under control in 1962, but some small-scale battles were still being reported a year later. Gardening, hunting, and warfare are the major occupations of men in this part of the world. Their military technology includes only the bow and arrow, spear, axe, and wooden shield. They hunt with bows and arrows and set snare traps for small game—the most common being members of the marsupial family. Otherwise, like most highland New Guinea peoples, their lives center on yam gardening and pig husbandry.

The Tsembaga live in a world of spirits of nature and of the living and the dead. Getting along with the spirits that inhabit their territory is a major religious preoccupation. *Rawa*, spirits, come in several forms. The *Rawa Mai* live in the lower part of their territory and are responsible for all things lower. For example, sicknesses of the lower part of the body are thought to be caused by their anger, and low-lying areas are attractive to them. There are two basic categories of these Rawa, the most important being the *Koipa Mangian*. These dangerous spirits often coordinate their evil activities with their allies, the *Rawa Tukump*, the spirits of rot and decay. The Rawa Tukump is also conceived of as conscious, supernatural corruption that is experienced spiritually and physically as creeping black rot.

The upper territory is the realm of the *Rawa Mugi*, red spirits, spirits of those who have been killed in battle. Their lairs lie in the high mountain forests. *Kun Kaze Ambra*, the white smoke woman, also dwells in the upper territory. The Tsembaga connect her to the tobacco smoke that the Tsembaga shamans use to enter trance states for communicating with spirits of the dead. She enters through the nose when she seeks to possess another's body. But she doesn't seem to have a special place in which she dwells, nor is she connected to special animals or plants as are the other types of Rawa. Her main occupation is marking those who are about to die.

Ialus

FROM THE ULITHI OF MICRONESIA

Renna screamed and dropped her hoe when she saw her sister Migo fall.

The women in the nearby gardens ran toward the fallen woman, asking "What is it? What's happened?"

"She just fell," Renna explained, obviously shaken.

Migo twitched on the ground, and sweat poured from her body. A village doctor happened to be passing by, and the women called for him to come quickly.

"You know the rules," he shouted.

"Forget all that foolishness and help us," one of the younger women yelled.

"Be careful how you speak, sister," an older woman warned. "Ialus are in this place."

"Yes, I'm sorry. No offense to the spirits," the offender replied humbly.

The doctor excused himself again. "You know that I can't come into the garden while I'm involved in doctoring. It is the rule of the Ialus of the swamp gardens. You all know that is true."

"But Migo looks real bad. You must help," Renna pleaded.

"What's going on here?" asked a large, middle-aged man as he pushed to the front of the small group that had gathered outside the garden. Everyone recognized Waruan, a widower from the next village.

"Migo can't get up. She's too heavy for us to lift. We need somebody to pick her up and carry her back to the village," one of the women told him.

Waruan stepped forward, but a voice in the crowd warned, "You can't go into that garden. You were down by the river helping the priest dig a grave just a few hours ago. You know the rules."

"I'm not afraid of spooks," Waruan replied. "This woman needs my help, and I'm going to give it to her. To hell with any spooks hanging around."

At the edge of the crowd, an ancient woman, layers of long black nets covering her entire body, clutched a lidded basket to her chest. "He dares to mock me?" she said quietly to herself. As the crowd made way for the man to carry Migo up the hill to her family's house, her astonishment at his audacity turned to rage and an escalating desire for bloody revenge against the impudent human. The crowd broke up and the entity in the long nets melted into the forest.

Migo bounced back quickly with water and some rest in the shade. The women concluded that she had had too much sun, and told her to remember to drink water often while she was working in the garden. Migo expressed her appreciation to everyone for caring for her and smiled demurely at Waruan when she thanked him for carrying her from the garden to her home.

"Well, I'm happy that you are feeling better," he said. "If it's all right with you and your family, I'll stop by and say hello the next time my travels bring me into your valley."

Migo's smile widened. "Oh, yes, please do."

Migo's parents offered the traveler their hospitality for the night, and he quietly accepted. Waruan was grateful for a place on the veranda to lay his sleeping mat. But as the moon rose, sleep would not come. He thought about Migo and how light she was to carry, despite her size, and he thought about the rules of the Ialus of the swamp garden. "Stupid superstition," he muttered.

After tossing and turning for an hour, he went for a walk. He wandered past the men's and women's houses and quietly slipped the latch of the communal farm gate. He soon found himself at the garden where Migo had fallen. In their haste to care for her, they had left behind her work hat and knife.

As Waruan stepped into the garden to retrieve the objects, a sharp female voice startled him. "Are you never going to stop your vile affronts against me?"

He looked up, and there before him stood a strange-looking old woman with nets draped over her face and body; what hair and skin he could see was gray. She carried a crude wicker basket at her side.

"You have mocked me. You have violated my rules. You have had the impudence to come here again and repeat your offenses against me," she shrieked.

Waruan didn't for a moment suspect that the old woman was the

Ialus, and asked, "Who are you, old woman? Shouldn't you be home in bed? A spook might jump you here in the garden."

Tapping the lid of the basket, the Ialus asked, "Do you know what I have in here?"

Waruan shrugged; he didn't care.

The apparition shook the basket, provoking a loud buzz and a fragile rattle that sounded like the clattering of insect carapaces. Deftly the creature poked her hand under the lid and removed something from the basket—something small.

"We are going to say 'hello' now," the Ialus said opening her palm, and a yellow jacket flew toward Waruan's face and stung him in the eye. He screamed out in excruciating pain.

"Hello, hello," the Ialus mocked and reached into her basket once again, this time for a handful of wasps, and then threw them at Waruan. Swatting at them proved futile, and soon their stings covered his body in a blanket of fire. As he convulsed on the ground, he felt something moving in his mouth. He gagged, and to his horror he vomited cockroaches. His muscles spasmed, and he rolled helplessly in the dirt of the Ialus's garden.

"Now are you sorry for breaking my rules?" the demon screeched.

"Yes, yes, yes! Please don't kill me," Waruan begged, now fully believing in the Ialus's power.

"Kill you? What an interesting thought: Killing." The Ialus seemed to consider that possibility for a moment. Then, she pointed to the ground and said with a sarcastic lilt, "Oh, my goodness. What is that?"

The ground beneath Waruan became an undulating carpet of poisonous ants several inches deep. The Ialus again reached into her basket and this time let loose a handful of fireflies. "To brighten the scene for my little warriors," she cooed.

Waruan was soon completely covered with ants. He thrashed in the ghostly green light of the fireflies as the insects stripped the skin off his body. His insane howls of pain slowly subsided when the thickening blanket of ants stripped away his muscles, then his tendons, and finally his veins.

The Ialus smiled wickedly at Waruan's skeleton glistening in the moonlight, and said, "Come, my warriors. It's time to go."

As she carried her open basket from the garden, the wasps, bees, cockroaches, ants, and fireflies flowed back inside. The Ialus closed the lid and tapped on it, whispering, "Time to find a tiny tender child to finish off a perfect night."

Ulithi Atoll, which is composed of thirty small islands, sits near the equator in the western Pacific. It is the northernmost of all the islands of the Carolinian Archipelago. The Ulithi live in small villages along ocean and lagoon beaches and work at gardening and fishing augmented by some gathering. They tend two types of gardens: those that are found in swamps and those that are not. The swamp garden is the larger of the two. Major crops include coconut palm, taro, elephant ear stalk, sweet potatoes, and breadfruit. Fishing is almost always productive in the variety of fishing grounds available to the Ulithi.

In their religious life, the Ulithi pay loving attention to the spirits of the dead, who through ritual play an active part in the lives of their families. They also pay heed to the existence of the *Ialus*, demons. The Ulithi say that the Ialus have the ability to be almost anything, which makes them very difficult to defend against—they can be large or small; tall or short; female or male; animal, plant, or human; diurnal or nocturnal; transparent or opaque; standing or reclining; and dark or light. They moan, whistle, cackle, sing, and speak a variety of languages. Sometimes they are seen hovering several inches off the ground.

All Ialus are sticklers for detail. Strict rules set down by the Ialus govern all behaviors, and the rules must be obeyed. This is the only psychological trait that these demons have which mortals can understand. A very powerful Ialus, like the spirit of the swamp gardens, may forbid humans to enter its garden if they are in mourning, menstruating, or barren. Men who have fished with a hook and line within the past four days or who have dug a grave within the previous five months are likewise prohibited by Ialus law from entering gardens. Medical practitioners in the process of caring for a patient are also forbidden entrance. The Ialus of the swamp gardens attacks those who violate the rules of her fertile realm by inflicting them with boils. She has the power to send insects to destroy the gardens of her enemies, and sometimes the enemies themselves.

Conclusion

E vil appears throughout our world in many different shapes and with many different faces. There are, however, some recurring themes from one culture to the next. The belief in the existence of a singular dominant evil being, such as Satan, tends to occur in societies with a centralized form of government. Alhough this incarnation of evil is familiar to us in the Western world, it is not the most common in terms of a worldwide cultural survey.

By far, the most typical evil being is the witch, or wizard/sorcerer, who must not be confused with those mortals who merely dabble with spells and potions. Witches possess supernatural powers. They are shapeshifters, capable of appearing in a mortal human guise, but also entirely capable of transforming into other forms, most commonly animals—favored ones being owls, snakes, wolves, and large cats. Sometimes it is difficult to determine whether the witch is a human with the powers to change shapes or an entity that possesses the ability to appear human. Whatever the case, witches always lie to achieve their evil ends, and their ability to shape-shift dramatically exemplifies that they cannot be trusted in word, deed, or appearance. Their deception always involves placing an unsuspecting mortal in a position to become prey. Witches see a predator-prey relationship in all their interactions with humans. They are ghouls and insatiable cannibals. They feed off human flesh, which offers them the power of immortality. Witches also often hunt and destroy humans simply for pure enjoyment.

Another common incarnation of evil is the demon snake-woman. Most typically this demon appears in the form of a large snake with a woman's head or upper body. Other demons are likely to be described as having a rank pelt of black hair, menacing claws, large sharp teeth, and piercing bloodshot eyes. They often reek of decaying flesh and behave in a psychotic or insane manner, to say the least.

It is tempting to view demons as having the reverse of essentially positive human qualities. They may be said to exist as living, breathing examples of how not to behave. These immoral, unethical evil beings can change their shapes at will, and so are never what they appear to be. They seek the destruction of their neighbors, dine on human flesh, and delight in causing pain and suffering. They love to attack children, possess young women, and harass the elderly and those with religious or educational pretensions. They mock us, belittle us, and impede our attempts at personal, spiritual, and social growth. No matter their form, they have always been with us. To a great degree they *are* us, or are a facet of who we are. The true horror is that they show no signs of disappearing. It seems that one of the prices we pay for living in this world is that we must forever share it with our demons.

Bibliography

1. DEMONS OF NORTH AMERICA

Kalona and Tsi Sgili

Kilpatrick, Alan. *The Night Has a Naked Soul.* Syracuse University Press: Syracuse, New York, 1997.

Budu

Jones, David E. *Sanapia: Comanche Medicine Woman.* Holt, Rinehart & Winston, Inc.: New York, 1972.

Ga-git

Harrison, Charles. *Ancient Warriors of the North Pacific.* H.F. & G. Witherby: London, 1925.

La Malogra

Paredes, Americo (ed. & trans.). *Folktales of Mexico.* The University of Chicago Press: Chicago, 1970.

Weigle, Marta and Peter White. *The Lore of New Mexico.* University of New Mexico Press: Albuquerque, New Mexico, 1988.

Kikituk

Giddings, James L. *Kobuk River People.* University of Alaska Studies of Northern Peoples, No. 1, Fairbanks, 1961.

Lantis, Margaret. "The social culture of the Nunivak Eskimo." *Transactions of the American Philosophical Society,* n.s., vol. 34, 1946.

Oswalt, Wendell H. *Alaskan Eskimos.* Chandler Publishing Company: San Francisco, 1967.

Wi-lu-gho-yuk

Forman, Werner (ed.). "Echoes of the Ancient World," in *The Eskimos.* Macdonald & Co. Publishers: London, 1988.

Hawkes, E.W. *The Labrador Eskimo.* Government Printing Bureau: Ottawa, Canada, 1916.

Malaurie, Jean. *The Last Kings of Thule.* E. P. Dutton, Inc.: New York, 1982.

La Llorona

Paredes, Americo. *Folktales of Mexico.* The University of Chicago Press: Chicago, 1970.

Weigle, Marta and Peter White. *The Lore of New Mexico.* University of New Mexico Press: Albuquerque, New Mexico, 1988.

Mai Tso

Kluckhohn, Clyde. "Navaho Witchcraft." *Papers of the Peabody Museum of Archaeology and Ethnology,* vol. 22. Cambridge, Massachusetts, 1944.

Kluckhohn, Clyde and Dorothea Leighton. *The Navaho.* The Natural History Library Edition: New York, 1962.

Windigo

Hallowell, A. Irving. "Some Psychological Characteristics of the Northeastern Indians," in *Man in Northeastern North American,* Johnson, F. (ed.). Papers of the Robert S. Peabody Foundation for Archaeology, 3, 1946.

Mack, Carol K. and Dinah Mack. *A Field Guide to Demons, Fairies, Fallen Angels, and Other Subversive Spirits.* Arcade Publishing: New York, 1998.

Teicher, Morton I. "Windigo Psychosis: A Study of the Relationship Between Belief and Behavior Among the Indians of Northeastern Canada," *Proceedings of the American Ethnological Society,* pp. 44, 107-9. Seattle, 1960.

Unkcegila

Kehoe, Alice B. *North American Indians: A Comprehensive Account.* Prentice Hall: Upper Saddle River, New Jersey, 1992.

Powers, William K. *Oglala Religion.* University of Nebraska Press: Lincoln, Nebraska, 1975.

Win

Saler, Benson. "Nagual, Witch, and Sorcerer in a Quiche Village," *Ethnology* 3 (3), 1964.

Nia'gwai'he'gowa

Parker, Arthur C. *Seneca Myths and Folk Tales*. Buffalo Historical Society: Buffalo, New York, 1923.

Water Babies

Downs, James F. *The Two Worlds of the Washo*. Holt, Rinehart & Winston, Inc.: New York, 1966.

2. DEMONS OF SOUTH AMERICA

Kharisiri

Wachtel, Nathan. *Gods and Vampires*. Carol Volk (trans.). The University of Chicago Press: Chicago, 1994.

Kupe-dyeb

Nimuendaju, Curt. *The Apinaye*. Robert H. Lowie (trans.). Anthropological Publications: Oosterhout, Netherlands, 1967.

Wamu

Wright, Robin M. *Cosmos, Self, and History in Baniwa Religion*. University of Texas Press: Austin, Texas, 1998.

Maereboe

Crocker, Jon C. *Vital Souls: Bororo Cosmology, Natural Symbolism, and Shamanism*. The University of Arizona Press: Tucson, Arizona, 1985.

Yacuruna

De Rios, Marlene Dobkin. *Visionary Vine: Hallucinogenic Healing in the Peruvian Amazon*. Waveland Press, Inc.: Prospect Heights, Illinois, 1972.

Kwifi Oto

Basso, Ellen B. *The Kalapalo Indians of Central Brazil*. Holt, Rinehart & Winston, Inc.: New York, 1973.

Winti

Herskovit, Melville J. and Frances S. Herskovits. *Suriname Folk-Lore*. AMS Press: New York, 1969.

Kenaimas

Thurn, Everard F. *Among the Indians of Guiana*. Dover Publications, Inc.: New York, 1967.

Karaisaba
Wilbert, Johannes. "Folk Literature of The Warao Indians: Narrative Material and Motif Content," *Latin American Studies Center Publication.* University of California: Los Angeles, 1970.

Hekura
Chagnon, Napoleon. *Yanomamo: The Fierce People.* Holt, Rinehart & Winston, Inc.: New York, 1968.

Chochoi
Stearman, Allyn Maclean. *Forest Nomads in a Changing World.* Holt, Rinehart & Winston, Inc.: New York, 1988.

3. DEMONS OF THE WEST INDIES

Ghede
Denning, Melita. *Voudoun Fire.* Llewellyn: St. Paul, 1979.

Metraux, Alfred. *Voodoo in Haiti.* Schocken Books: New York, 1972.

Ligahoo, La Diablesse, Mama Dlo, and Soucouyant
Besson, Gerard. *Folklore of Trinidad and Tobago.* Paria Publishing Co.: Port of Spain, Trinidad, 1989.

4. DEMONS OF AFRICA

Kalengu
Van Beek, Walter E. A. "The Innocent Sorcerer: Coping With Evil in Two African Societies," in *Religion in Africa.* Thomas D. Blakely, et al. (eds.). Heinemann: Portsmouth, New Hampshire, 1994.

Yamo
Curley, Richard T. *Elders, Shades, and Women: Ceremonial Change in Lango, Uganda.* University of California Press: Berkeley, California, 1973.

Adro
Middleton, John, and Edward Winter (eds.). *Witchcraft and Sorcery in East Africa.* Routledge: London, 1963.

Genie
Parrinder, Geoffrey. *African Traditional Religion.* Greenwood Press: Westport, Connecticut, 1962.

5. DEMONS OF ASIA

Oyasi

Ohnuki-Tierney, Emiko. *The Ainu of the Northwest Coast of Southern Sakhalin.* Holt, Rinehart & Winston, Inc.: New York, 1974.

Huli Jing

Dore, Henry. *Research Into Chinese Superstitions,* 12 volumes. L.F. McGreal (trans.). Tusewe Printing Press: Shanghai, 1920-1938.

Roberts, Moss (ed.). *Chinese Fairytales and Fantasies.* Pantheon Books: New York, 1979.

Tamboree

Williams, Thomas Rhys. *The Dusun: A North Borneo Society.* Holt, Rinehart & Winston, Inc.: New York, 1965.

Oni

Mack, Carol K. & Dinah Mack. *A Field Guide to Demons.* Arcade Publishing: New York, 1998.

Piggott, Julie. *Japanese Mythology.* Hamlyn: London, 1969.

Sansom, George B. *Japan: A Short Cultural History.* Stanford University Press: Stanford, California, 1978.

Pisatji

Geertz, Clifford. *The Religion of Java.* Collier-Macmillan Limited: London, 1960.

Rai Na'in

Hicks, David. *Tetum Ghosts and Kin: Fieldwork in An Indonesian Community.* Mayfield Publishing Company: Palo Alto, California, 1976.

6. DEMONS OF THE PACIFIC

Nokondisi

Newman, Philip L. *Knowing the Gururumba.* Holt, Rinehart & Winston, Inc.: New York, 1965.

Tege

Pospisil, Leopold. *The Kapauku Papuans of West New Guinea.* Holt, Rinehart & Winston, Inc.: New York, 1963.

Bolrizohol

Hiatt, L.R. and C. Fayawardena (eds.). *Anthropology in Oceania: Essays Presented to Ian Hogbin*. Chandler Publishing Company: San Francisco, 1971.

Kopuwai, Patupaiarehe, and Ruruhi-kerepo

Reed, A.W. *Treasury of Maori Folklore*. A.H. & A. W. Reed: Wellington, New Zealand, 1967.

Tavogivogi

Codrington, R.H. *The Melanesians: Studies in Their Anthropology and Folk-lore*. Clarnedon Press: Oxford, 1891.

Mulukwausi

Malinowski, Bronislaw. *Argonauts of the Western Pacific*. Waveland Press, Inc.: Prospect Heights, Illinois, 1984.

Rawa Tukump

Rappaport, Roy A. *Pigs for the Ancestors: Ritual in the Ecology of a New Guinea People*, 2nd edition. Waveland Press, Inc.: Prospect Heights, Illinois, 1984.

Ialus

Lessa, William A. *Ulithi: A Micronesian Design for Living*. Holt, Rinehart & Winston, Inc.: New York, 1966.

Index